Take Heart

Take Heart

From Despair to Hope in Turbulent Times
—A Theopolitical Commentary

Hemchand Gossai

PICKWICK *Publications* · Eugene, Oregon

TAKE HEART
From Despair to Hope in Turbulent Times—A Theopolitical Commentary

Copyright © 2022 Hemchand Gossai. All rights reserved. Except for brief quotations in critical publications or reviews, no part of this book may be reproduced in any manner without prior written permission from the publisher. Write: Permissions, Wipf and Stock Publishers, 199 W. 8th Ave., Suite 3, Eugene, OR 97401.

Pickwick Publications
An Imprint of Wipf and Stock Publishers
199 W. 8th Ave., Suite 3
Eugene, OR 97401

www.wipfandstock.com

PAPERBACK ISBN: 978-1-6667-1994-9
HARDCOVER ISBN: 978-1-6667-1995-6
EBOOK ISBN: 978-1-6667-1996-3

Cataloguing-in-Publication data:

Names: Gossai, Hemchand, author.

Title: Take heart : from despair to hope in turbulent times—a theopolitical commentary / by Hemchand Gossai.

Description: Eugene, OR: Pickwick Publications, 2022. | Includes bibliographical references and index.

Identifiers: ISBN 978-1-6667-1994-9 (paperback). | ISBN 978-1-6667-1995-6 (hardcover). | ISBN 978-1-6667-1996-3 (ebook).

Subjects: LCSH: Bible. Old Testament—Criticism, interpretation, etc. | Bible. New Testament—Criticism, interpretation, etc. | Hope—Religious aspects—Christianity.

Classification: BS1192.5 G67 2022 (print). | BS1192.5 (ebook).

02/28/22

For Viera

Contents

Acknowledgments

Rarely it is the case that one writes a book entirely in the solitary spaces of one's existence. As always there are influences of family or community or the circumstances of nation or world that come to bear, bidden or unbidden, known or unknown. *Take Heart* is such a book. When I first imagined writing a book entitled *Take Heart*, I had in mind a scholarly exploration of the Hebrew biblical texts that would generate hope in times of despair, a theme that is universally present. While this book certainly does some of this, the last five years have prompted me to reshape the manner in which this theme might be construed more broadly particularly in light of the political and pandemic realities that have entered our lives, and over a period mired us in despair.

I bring to this writing the abiding imprint of family from my boyhood years, together with the collective wisdom of many others who have left their mark through the journey to the present. Between then and now lies numerous other moments that have been defining, and which have left ingrained marks on my thinking and worldview. I believe that *Take Heart* is a particular example of how the beginning of a journey may take an unexpected shape as circumstances in the life of a community and nation emerge and recast the very landscape of our lives. Given the trajectory of this journey one cannot continue in an unaffected manner, and not coincidentally these turns of events have shaped this book into becoming what it currently is.

I am grateful to K. C. Hanson, editor in chief at Wipf & Stock publishers for his ongoing support and encouragement, and for his acceptance of this volume under the Pickwick imprint. My heartfelt gratitude and love to the circle of my immediate family. For Nathan, Krista, Chandra, Dave, Josh, Caitlin, Rachel, and Chung who will carry on the journey of taking heart in the midst of the vicissitudes of life and who will continue to believe in a world where hope displaces despair, and light pierces darkness. Most of all, for Viera whose unwavering belief in the efficacy of *Take Heart* and her abiding and constant love are beyond measure. And it is to her that I dedicate this book.

Introduction

The soul is the piece of your consciousness that has moral worth and bears moral responsibility. A river is not morally responsible for how it flows, and a tiger is not morally responsible for what it eats. But because you have a soul, you are morally responsible for what you do and don't do. —David Brooks, *The Second Mountain*

Humans are caught—in their lives, in their thoughts, in their hungers and ambitions, in their avarice and cruelty, and in their kindness and generosity too—in a net of good and evil. I think this is the only story we have and that it occurs on all levels of feeling and intelligence. Virtue and vice were warp and woof of our first consciousness, and they will be the fabric of our last . . . A man, after he has brushed off the dust and chips of his life, will have left only the hard, clean questions: was it good or was it evil? Have I done well—or ill. —John Steinbeck, *East of Eden*

But immediately Jesus spoke to them and said, "*Take heart*, it is I; do not be afraid." (Matt 14:27)

Guyana sits on the northeastern tip of South America. It is the land of my birth and the landscape of my boyhood years. In those boyhood years, a young life suffused with a range of joyous experiences, there was a regular dose of brief aphorisms that were routinely dispensed, most often by elders in the family. It is perhaps only in retrospect that I have come to recognize the importance and depth of these statements. Two in particular have become principal for me over the years: *Walk Good*; *Take Heart*.

These phrases, in themselves, taken out of context, might not appear to make much sense. First, when one hears *walk good*, there is a quality of grammatical discord that immediately propels us to change the verbal construction. But these two words side by side are exactly right as they were used in that context. I think of the idea of walking as having to do with living. And in this regard, *walk good* is to live life that is full of virtue and goodness, a journey that is noble and just; a path of mercy and compassion; the capacity for empathy. These words are of course not to be housed in protected cases for decorative adjectival purposes but must be active in order to be meaningful. One cannot do or be any of these in the abstract.

The Hebrew *halakhah* means "walk." The particular importance of having laws is not for them to be stagnant and rigid, but rather for persons to walk in them, live them, do them. *Halakhah* is a term that has a universal claim in that while it has a particular alignment to Judaism, it is also a reminder of that which binds one to tradition, beliefs, etc. It is also that which must be *walked* and *lived out* in all contexts and circumstances of life. *Halakhah* is a way of life.

I am confident that while this phrase was repeatedly gifted to me by my mother, as a benedictory word of care and blessing, she was not thinking about *halakhah*. It is, however, the literal, and arguably the most meaningful translation of *halakhah* that for me, brings fullness to the phrase, *walk good*. So, while *halakhah* is typically understood as a codification of a multitude of practices in Judaism, ranging from the extraordinary and significant, to the ordinary and mundane, it is exactly this that should lead us to the root of the term as the basis for an understanding and application. That is to say, every step taken, every moment journeyed, must be viewed as sacred. For every step in the journey constructs the whole. While *halakhah* is the path or journey, what one does on that journey, will give definition to the journey. This is what it means to *walk good*. Not only to walk and complete a journey that is of no consequence, but a journey of goodness and grace; justice and kindness; compassion and care. A code of law only has merit and significance when it is regarded, respected, and practiced. It is not enough only to cite such laws or have a framed version or bound collection for the world to see. When my mother said *walk good*, it was not reserved for long and faraway journeys, but more often for a journey to the city or the cinema or school. The very ordinariness of life takes on significance, and so, one does not wait for the grand and extraordinary moment to *walk good*.

The second phase of memorial quality is *Take Heart*, the title of this volume. *Take Heart* reflects a phrase with universal resonance. It might not be self-explanatory with a self-evident meaning, but I would propose that it gets to the very core of what it means to have hope in the midst of despair, hopelessness, and turbulent times. Despair need not be on a grand scale such as war and genocide, which are often unfathomable and beyond the typical human scope, but despair is often in the ordinariness of everyday life, where for a moment one with a broken heart might need to be assured to *take heart*. Or one who has wondered about vocation or one whose marriage unravels to be granted a word of assurance to *take heart*. The particular realities in which *take heart* has the potential to bring hope, are inexhaustible. To *take heart* is to believe beyond the immediate; believe that the horizon beckons and is forever beckoning; to believe that life is more than the extremes; to believe and know that there is grace beyond despair.

Never be afraid of pruning bushes and plants. This is the definition of hope; it is the expectation of new and renewed life. In doing so one imagines and believes that there is life beyond what might be seen. Allowing the present to define all that is, and what will be, is to have a narrow vision, and what potentially may lead to despair or arrogance being rooted in the status quo as permanent. Pruning not only believes in that which is not immediately apparent, but it allows us to shape and direct and believe. This is the essence of *take heart*.

In crafting this study, I begin with a reading of texts and narratives from the perspective of one who is a first-generation immigrant to the United States, whose parents were indentured servants taken from India to then British Guiana, and who has lived and studied on three continents. Thus, in part, what I bring is a life that is shaped by my ancestral journey and socio-economic status, and my choice to emigrate and pursue both education and life more broadly in a very different land. The United States has afforded me new pathways, and it has also afforded me the somewhat rare opportunity to view texts and life through a variety of lenses. Over the years as a scholar, interpreter of biblical texts, and observer of cultural and societal mores, I have come to the conclusion that I cannot allow my lenses to be so clouded as to conform readily to the established tradition, or for that matter uncritically embrace the status quo. For example, in biblical studies while I certainly have regard for historical criticism, I cannot only seek what lies behind the text and overlook the text itself with all of the layers and complexities. While undoubtedly the historical and structural qualities of a text are important, they are not the last word. So, in my exploration, I seek to understand the possibility of new beginnings, and where text and ever changing and new contexts intersect and shape each other. The possibility for interpreters such as myself who bring a variety of contextual experiences, the move beyond narrowly defined lenses through which texts may be read and interpreted, will further enrich the manner in which biblical texts continue to speak to a range of societies and peoples. It is clear that there is no universal and self-evident truth in every text. Rather, the reader and the audience will inevitably bring who she or he is to the text, and in this way the newness and the breadth of the lenses allow and invite a richness and creativity to the spectrum of implications. One reads and interprets in the context of community and therefore there are inherent freedoms and constraints.

Everyone who reads, interprets and explores biblical texts do so from particular contextual considerations and a variety of theological, social, cultural and ideological circumstances. We are all shaped by what have defined us, particularly through inheritance of ideas, beliefs, experiences, station in life. For many of us, such inheritance, scholarly or otherwise are examined and challenged as we seek to forge new directions, new perspectives, new visions of how interpretation of texts are shaped by societies and groups that are on the margin.

It is the case that in some long established scholarly circles, there is the unspoken and sometimes spoken assumption that there are technically correct ways of reading a text. One of the principal purposes veiled in this assertion is to ensure an *historical purity* in the interpretive enterprise. Ricoeur has argued that there is no inherent dynamic within the text that dictates qualities of significance or marginality in terms of importance. He has suggested: "there is no necessity, no evidence, concerning what is important and what is unimportant."[1] Simply to restrain any new voices, or interpretation only finally leads to a maintaining of the status quo and thus effectively silences the voices from those contexts that have been voiceless for a while. More troubling is a silencing of the voice of the text as if to suggest that the text is static and not dynamic.

This is precisely one of those moments where perhaps education, broadly construed, as all civilized persons should have, becomes principal. To be educated is to make the world better, to use it, to share it, to cause the circles to expand. That is the virtue of being educated. To die with an unused education is to die in a state of depravity. Or as Leonardo Da Vinci, *The Notebooks*, observes, "Shun those studies in which the work that results die with the worker."

---

1. Ricoeur, *Interpretation Theory*, 77.

1

The Power of Words

Our world is dangerously polarized at a time when humanity is more closely interconnected—politically, economically and electronically—than ever before. If we are to meet the challenge of our time and create a global society where all people can live together in peace and mutual respect, we need to assess our situation accurately. We cannot afford oversimplified assumptions about the nature of religion and its role in the world. —Armstrong, *Fields*, 15

Always egalitarian, the moral mind extends compassion and protection to all other human beings, not only to its own family or group . . . To the moral mind, there are no strangers, no outsiders, and human beings are entitled to moral respect just because of their human vulnerabilities and capacities. In this way, the moral mentality creates a community, a warming sense of *us* and comfort in our shared life, our mutual care and respect. —Mendelson, *The Good Life*, 55

We witness the specifics of such a polarization being manifested in different parts of the world. In particular, within the United States, the polarization is accentuated and galvanized by sustained vitriolic and corrosive rhetoric from President Donald Trump. President Trump's rhetoric and actions have sharpened the divide in the nation between *us* and *them* based on a variety of qualities, including race and ethnicity, religion and ideology. Such divisiveness continues and not only leads inexorably to increased expressions of hatred and violence but leaves scars that will be inherited by generations. At any given point, vile and hateful speech by any individual at any time is harmful and potentially destructive. However, when such speech is generated by a person in a position of exalted power and influence, the danger and potential for further division is escalated. We have witnessed both words and actions in this regard from President Trump. For the sake of space and focus one can identify a few from among many, and these represent the quality of despair and pain, and the inevitable proliferation and amplified effects. For example, there have been devastating bloody domestic terrorist attacks on two mosques, killing fifty worshipping Muslims. The killer's manifesto indicated that he was inspired to do so by the earlier actions and words of President Donald Trump. On August 12, 2017, in Charlottesville, Virginia, a rally titled, "Unite the Right" generated an intense and violent clash with counter protesters. In that volatile clash, a man from Ohio who identified with the white supremacists drove his car into a group of counter protesters killing a woman, Heather Heyer and injuring a dozen others. President Trump spoke about the demonstration and violence and the simmering dis-ease in Charlottesville and the racial divisiveness that crept across the country. In a televised press conference, the President remarked that there were "fine people on both sides," without any condemnation of the white supremacists and their vitriolic rhetoric that appealed to Nazism and abject repulsive antisemitism. The President's moral incapacity to unequivocally denounce the physical and verbal violence spawned a type of unearthing of deeply rooted racial, religious and nationalistic violence. What the New Zealand terrorist who massacred Muslims at worship said in his manifesto may not be construed as causal, but arguably correlative. These examples in part illustrate and verify the real and distinct reality of the widespread and ongoing effect the words and actions of a leader may have.

Moreover, the violence was perpetuated in places of worship; Jews in a Pittsburgh synagogue; African American Christians in a church in Charleston, SC; Muslims in two New Zealand mosques. In moments when God and humans come together at a place and time set apart for that union is particularly heinous and nefarious. "[W]e respond to God's love with our own love of God in the form of an ultimate commitment. Yet, God, the ultimate giver always turns our love toward our human neighbor."[1] And yet, at its very core, it is the wanton disregard for neighborly love that was central to the largely evangelical alignment with Donald Trump. The fear that is spread is palpable. The fear that finds itself spreading globally might be seen in President Trump's decision to announce that the Golan Heights, a long-disputed territory should be governed by Israel, thereby sowing discord and stoking an already tumultuous Middle East environment to a precipice of violence. Further, the Trump administration have withdrawn from the Paris Agreement, known more widely as the Paris Accord on climate change. The agreement that was drafted and agreed upon in December 2015, was put into effect in November 2016. There were one

---

1. Marandiuc, *The Goodness of Home*, 103.

hundred and ninety-five signatories. On June 1st, 2017, President Trump declared that the United States was withdrawing from the Accord. Other nations that had signed the accord, did not follow suit, but in withdrawing, Mr. Trump has placed the future of generations and the very planet at risk. These representative examples illuminate the despair of the present and the inherent fear that comes with tomorrow. As the world becomes more connected, particularly through social media, there is the breadth of substantial evidence to demonstrate that with this connection comes a dangerous quality of divisiveness and separation.

Perhaps one can make the following assertion at any period in human history, and yet, I cannot think of a more pointed time than the current period in US history, when the invitation and admonition to *take heart* is more à propos and urgently relevant. For some who may be directly and pointedly affected by many of President Trump's executive actions, policies and legislations, both domestic and global, this is a time of anxiety, fear and despair. Times of despair and disillusionment are exactly the times when hope and its deep rootedness will surface. But such hope cannot be exclusionary and cannot be rooted in *us* and *them*. Hope, thus, cannot and must not be partisan. In the invitation to *take heart* the prospects also include practical realities of all of life. The language of *take heart* cannot become a platitude; there must be a concreteness to ensure that there is no sense of emptiness to the vision of *taking heart*.

We are constantly reminded of the henotheistic nature of our society where many claim a particular and privileged place for freedom for all, and indeed allegiance and belief in God. However, most of the henotheistic choices focus on wealth and power; privilege and entitlement. Thus, the mandate to use one's voice and challenge such wanton disregard for humane ideals of equality, care, belonging, mercy, justice among others. Moreover, one must be courageous in pointing to the glaring disconnect between what one confesses and how one lives, where far too frequently actions betray words, and words are used unabashedly and deceptively to veil one's actions. The idea of having a mind that is sharp, as Descartes notes is to use it, and not simply set out to accumulate knowledge and keep it to oneself.

In Rainer Maria Rilke's book, *Love and Other Difficulties*, the author captures one aspect of life that is frequently overlooked, or around which we navigate. There is certainly a sense in which love is difficult if only like most things of note and which are worthy of our energy and our hearts. In large part this is true of friendship, love, marriage, vocational passion, public service, civic engagement, etc., all of which take work, commitment, patience, habit, believing and knowing that there will be a tomorrow. There is rarely a life that can be said to be without any challenges or difficulties, and certainly some lives for a variety of reasons are replete with difficulties. Let us acknowledge this and know that it is true, and in this very acknowledgement will come a freedom to begin with this as a basic recognition. There is a universal claim here.

Anything of note in life takes work. Relationships with each other, and a relationship with God both take work, and both have remarkable life giving and life transforming qualities. So, we work; we are committed because we know that in doing so, we build and strengthen each other and are drawn closer.

In friendship, as in love, a defining feature and guiding principle is the fact that one's presence in the other's life must somehow enhance and bring even greater goodness, grace and gratitude to that person's life. The wonder of such cannot be equated with ease and ordinariness. If one poses to a group the question as to what is better reflective of who one is or what is preferable to a person, security or risk, I would venture to say that for the majority this might seem to be an unreasonable choice, maybe even a false binary. But I propose a scenario for those who are more inclined to be tightly secure, where security is seen as safe, and plainly preferable. Is security plainly preferable? Of course. As always though, one has to wonder if it is the whole truth. So, an example of security vis à vis risk.

It is entirely possible that simply as a rite of passage, many, perhaps most of us in our youth who have lived in open areas away from urban settings, have climbed a large tree with sturdy branches, and a formidable trunk. Some of us have had treehouses built in such trees precisely because of the sturdy branches and the seemingly indestructible trunk. One needs these qualities to ensure that there is security and protection. But let me alter the scenario. Imagine the scenario where one is climbing a large fruit tree; I would suggest that typically there are two options in such a venture. First, one could climb such a tree and hold on very closely and cling tightly to the trunk for security and protection; by any measure that would seem to be a wise thing. One could perch on a branch or on the fork between the trunk and limb, and sit there, comfortably and securely. And for all practical purposes the adventure would end there, comfortably, and with a level of security. Security certainly has its place, and in some cases an essential place.

There is also another perspective and aspect to the adventure. One could indeed venture out on the branches, and the limbs and in every measure that is likely to be more precarious. When one goes *out on a limb* an axiom in our everyday lexicon, it implies an element of risk beyond the norm. There is a good reason for this. Going *out on a limb* is indeed risky and there is no universal guide in terms of who should go, and how far one should go. But there is something universal about what one is likely to discover. If the quest is for the sake of solitude and retreating, then certainly there is a perfectly legitimate reason to perch comfortably and securely and hold onto a trunk. However, if the quest is to discover what lies beyond, then one must take the risk and venture out on the limb. How far one goes can only be determined by who one is, and one's capacity, together with the strength of the limb on which one climbs. Indeed, one might not be even sure until one tries. But here is the universal truth that must be reckoned with. Security might be on a trunk, but one finds the fruit only on the limbs, and therein lies the challenge. *The fruit comes with risk.* Knowing that one might be secure on a trunk might be the impetus to take the risk to venture out on a limb. Or one could rest or hold tightly to the trunk and gaze at the possibility from afar, but never venture. Yet, in this latter case there is little chance to reach the fruit unless one has the capacity and willingness to loosen one's grip on that which one holds too tightly.

Second, I have found the metaphor of fishing to be instructive. I know little about fishing except the very rudimentary idea of rod and hook, and the essential importance of patience. I know for those men and women who fish avidly, it is both art and science, and I certainly make no claim to having such general knowledge, let alone being able to make nuanced distinctions. However, I explore fishing as a metaphor. Like so many aspects of our lives, we do also have a choice about where and how we fish. Certainly, there are some of us who might wish to stand at the end of the shore or on a dock and fish from there. Perhaps one of the advantages of such fishing is that one might be in close proximity to the shore, to safety, *terra firma*. Beyond this, there is also the reality that the water may be transparent enough, perhaps shallow enough to actually see what lies beneath; to see what swims beneath the surface. There is certainly a place for knowing what lies beneath, that is, what can be seen and what is known. Moreover, one might be able to catch fish from the shore, though invariably these would be the small fish, perhaps not fully developed, perhaps unable to swim into the deep, and thus can only be close to the shore. If fishing for the immediate, where instant fulfillment is what is being sought, then there might be gratification in fishing from shore or dock.

Yet, there are alternatives. One might prefer to fish in the wider expanse of water, where one must leave the shore, where the water is deep and perhaps opaque, and seemingly impenetrable. Inescapably, such a venture brings with it peculiar challenges. One cannot see what lies beneath; one is distant from the shore of security; one cannot be sure that anything of note lies beneath. But, then to go beyond the shore, beyond what one is able to see may bring about new and exceptional possibilities. There is always the possibility of at least two things happening. One might very well explore the depths all day and return to the shore empty handed; convention might suggest that this was a failed journey. I would suggest otherwise. The journey into the deep might itself be the reward, simply to have the courage to travel into the unknown with uncertainty, but with a sense of the mystery and hope. This is precisely the larger and more important idea in exploration. Yes, while there is a place for security and certainty, there surely must be a privileged place given to that which we may not see, but where there is hope. And is it not the case that hope reveals itself in the darkest moments? One reflects on the first stanza of Seamus Heaney's poem.

> History says don't hope
> On this side of the grave,
> But then once in a lifetime
> The longed-for tidal wave
> Of justice can rise up,
> And hope and history rhyme.[2]

It is an invitation to imagination; an invitation to believe in the unknown and dare to journey there. Further, this is not about being reckless, but taking a risk, and be daring for the distinct possibility that everything may not be achieved and fulfilled into the time we have determined, and with the view that the present is primarily by what we see and the immediate. So, part of the challenge is that we cannot see beneath the surface of the water, and so we cast and wait, and wait; we hope and hope for things unseen. It is entirely possible that one might cast and cast and at the end of the day, simply return without a catch. At this point one has to determine what next to do; a choice has to be made. If what one seeks is more than what lies on the surface and what is immediately apparent, then there must be a vision for tomorrow, for the depth. Tomorrow brings possibility, newness, new hope, a sense that this might be the day where the deep bring forth a new and perhaps unimagined reality. Perhaps it will take days and weeks, and who knows, perhaps years. Thus, the question becomes our resilient hope. Hope beyond what is seen to what is believed, and what is envisioned. Truth sometimes lies in the deep and one might be able to immediately discover such. This might be the case in friendship, love, vocation, among others. What lies in shallow waters, and what is quickly encountered and discovered, need not be the last word.

I grew up in walking distance from the Atlantic Ocean. As a young boy I never quite appreciated the wonder of being able to walk to the ocean, play on the beach, and simply having this accessible at our everyday disposal.

2. Heaney, *The Cure of Troy*, 77–78.

Years after I left Guyana, I returned for a visit, and with such boyhood memories as part of the landscape of my life, I again went to the ocean. I stood on the seawall and gazed upon the high tide at its zenith best as it lashed fiercely against the wall. What struck me then, but what I took for granted in my boyhood days, was the expanse of the water and the golden sunset that glistened on it. I stared at the immense breadth of the water, for as far as my eyes would take me. I knew then that there was much more beyond what I could see; there was a world beyond the eyes' horizon. I had known that there was of course something about one's personal experience that causes one to see things differently. Yet, there is a point at which we learn from others, listen to the experiences of others and embrace their experiences and remembrances into shaping one's view of life. So, I would seek to resist the temptation to *fish* in shallow waters; I believe that there is more one might discover in exploring the depth of the unknown; return again and again if need be. Often our society leads us to believe that what matters might be achieved in an instance or by taking abbreviated journeys. Perhaps for a fleeting moment there might some satisfaction in such a perspective, but finally there is no *ultimate* fulfillment in shallow waters.

In the remarkable memoir of Ishmael Beah, *A Long Way Gone*, a story of violence and loss of innocence; despair and hopelessness; pain and redemption; darkness and light; I was moved by the narrative and staggered by the unimaginable journey of Beah. It is impossible to begin to imagine such a journey if one has not travelled it. His was an extraordinary chance for a "second life" when it seems for a while that his life as a "boy soldier" that began with the loss of innocence, would move inexorably to a tragic end. Such is the typical narrative, and death at a young, but worn life, is often the last word. There is invariably a quality of ultimacy and fatalism associated with such a life. Yet, with Beah's story, there was a *take heart* moment that reminds us that despite the commonly accepted unnatural destruction of life at a very young age, it does not have to be the universal definition of life. Beah's experience reminds us that there can be hope in a foreign land; there can be newness and life beyond the margins of one's imagination; there can be a distant place to call home, both literally and figuratively. Yet, as Beah describes in *A Long Way Gone*, the journey to such newness may invariably traverse through treacherous terrain and navigate the steep and often perilous climb through violence, killing and death.

Perhaps for a while unimaginable, as indeed the climb out of such chasm seems unfathomable. And while these aspects in many respects make Beah's memoir unforgettable and indelibly stamped on the heart of the reader, it is not necessarily the principal idea that remains with me. I leave the reading of this memoir with a profound sense of the indomitable nature of the human spirit, the unwavering belief that there is life and possibility of that which lies beyond what is, the possibility of finding grace in unexpected places, and kindness in a manner both unexpected and unknown. So, in the depth of despair, Beah chose to *take heart*. We can expand this idea of the possibility of transformation in the face of that which appears insurmountable for a person, a family, a community, a nation, a world.

2

Leaving the Shore and Resouling

"Man cannot discover new oceans unless he has the courage to lose sight of the shore." —Andre Gide

"When a man is singing and cannot lift his voice and another comes and sings with him, another who can lift his voice, the first will be able to lift his voice too. That is the secret of the bonds between spirits." —Martin Buber

"Whoever destroys a single life is as guilty as though he has destroyed the whole world; and whoever rescues a single life earns as much merit as though he has rescued the whole world." —Talmud

Despite the popularity and default use by some scholars, it is very difficult to maintain the notion of objective reading and interpretation of a biblical text. No reader is able to step outside of herself/himself in terms of the various experiences and contextual considerations that are brought to a text. One should indeed be very skeptical of any interpreter who claims an objective interpretation or one that is universally accepted. The fact is, the text itself with its numerous iterations of particular events, laws, history invites and reminds us that there will be variations, differences, contradictions in the manner in which we read and interpret them. Part of the challenge and mandate that readers have is to read and interpret the text with a quality of openness. If this is possible with its inherent challenges, it does allow for the distinct possibility of change, and for one's perspective to be transformed, bringing about a new self-understanding. The point is one should not elevate oneself as the ultimate arbiter of the text in terms of truth.[1]

Howsoever we construe or define our reality, as individuals we live in relationships; we live in community; by definition therefore a relationship must embody dialogue, and with dialogue, listening is essential. We speak

1. See, Ricoeur, *Freud and Philosophy*, 1970.

and we listen, and importantly we must be heard. In dialogue, the possibility always exists for change. The dialogue focuses on the power of words, the power of *logos* between parties.

It is not possible to speak to community without realizing that in doing so we are speaking to persons, individuals. When there are serious, life transforming and sometimes existential questions, it cannot be the case that only a facile "spiritual" solution is given. There is a privileged place for spiritual solutions, but not at the expense of, or to be used as an excuse to maintain a status quo, or for that matter to barricade that which potentially may transform an ideology. It is incumbent upon us, upon everyone who seeks to be fully human, not perfect, but humane and just, to enter into the suffering of others as compassion literally dictates—and then act. Not to act is finally a betrayal of one's humanity. As one wonders what it means to be human, we are struck by the fact that *being human* is defined and determined in the first instance by being in a relationship with God, and then with each other. In other words, the quintessential paradigm for being human is that of being in relationship. And an essential platform for any such human relationship is to listen and to attend to the narrative of the other in a way that is thoughtful and discerning of all that is noble. "In the doing of justice, the rule of humanness is not simply the keeping rules, but consists in the venturesome enactment of positive good, whereby human solidarity is maintained and enhanced."[2] Thus, the point of being human is in part to be vulnerable, for in so doing we will undoubtedly feel pain, and be hurt. But vulnerability is relational in nature, and one can only be vulnerable as one enters the life of another.

The whole point of being just is certainly not a matter of doing the minimum or for that matter simply "obeying" the rules. The Hebrew notion of *shema* captures the rich relational idea of listening, understanding and obeying. All of this can only be done in the context of relationship. To be neighborly is not a matter of doing the minimum, but rather, it is to go beyond the expected or prescribed; to do that which moves beyond the fulfillment of rules and convention, and instead fulfills a relational role. But there is yet another aspect to human rule.

"The Lord God took the man and put him in the garden of Eden to till it and keep it." (Gen 2:15) The text is often interpreted as suggesting dominance over creation, yet in looking at the Hebrew text, the two definitive verbs are *'bd* and *smr*, that is, *to serve* and *to keep*. These are the verbs that govern all of creation. We are reminded here too that *serving* and *keeping* are relational terms, not terms of domination or self-focus or

2. Brueggemann, *Money*, 68.

self-indulgence or self-aggrandizement. We see such care in a most sustained way in Psalm 121.

It is not uncommon in certain evangelical segments of the Christian
community to hear derisions cast against a government or judicial or political system if a particular position or policy is perceived to run contrary
to what *they* deem *godly* or *biblical*. Here too, we are reminded that those
who ideologically and theologically are in such a group, bring who they
are to the text.

Always of concern here, regardless, where one is on the spectrum of
biblical interpretation, the voice of the text cannot be silenced by the voice of
the interpreter. While one might argue the merits of such a position, it is instructive to examine for example the reign of Solomon whose rule has been
criticized by some for allowing widespread idolatry through his openness
and the effect of trade with nations that brought their religions and gods as
integral parts of their trade policy. Yet, a closer and more detailed exploration of the Solomonic reign indicates an internal unraveling of the society
due to institutional policies that were predicated on Solomon's propensity
for ongoing urbanization, and the abuse of the citizens who were powerless
and without recourse. No doubt, for a while, it seemed that the Solomonic
abuse would be endless, and when Rehoboam with a particularly strident
and arrogant sense of self-importance, refused to reverse his father's violent
policies, the Kingdom was divided. Solomon's violent and rampant injustice
for the sake of infrastructure generated for the elite, cannot be rewritten.
"Some biblical redactors tried to argue that Solomon's empire failed because
he had built shrines for the pagan gods of his foreign wives. But it is clear
that the real problem was its structural violence, which offended deep rooted principles.[3] In light of the United States and the global community with
the increased racially and religiously generated violence, the Solomonic era
might be instructive. As king, Solomon is a singular reminder that one may
seek gifts from God, sought after gifts reflecting all that is noble, and then
proceed on a journey that is an unmitigated betrayal of such gifts. In this
case, the betrayal of Solomon's gift of wisdom, took at least two forms. First,
he seeks a gift that would imply care for his people as he rules them wisely,
with all the qualities that a wise ruler would embody and execute. Second,
Solomon took this gift and did precisely the opposite, namely, enslaving
his own people for the purpose of Empire building. "What purports to be
'the glory of God' was in fact an exhibit of royal wealth that called attention
to Solomon as a winner in the great game of accumulation . . . Beyond

3. Armstrong, *Fields*, 114.

the success of temple accumulation, Solomon's confiscating effectiveness is evident in his trade policies."[4]

Solomon's policies and actions were variously replicated today by former President Donald Trump who perpetuate this notion of being a *winner*. Today, no less, the idea of *winner* is unfailingly an individualistic, accumulation of wealth. It is the idea of extreme consumption. Moreover, instead of Temple structure, today in the United States it is the construction of border walls under the guise of national security, and at the expense and vilifying of refugees and immigrants. "In being king, beggar, rich man, poor man, male, female, etc., we are not like each other—therein we are indeed different."[5] And this quality which is either inherent or societally designed has been exploited by the Trump administration and in so doing the further marginalization of the "outsider," anyone who might be considered different and then viewed as inferior. As the distinctions are made more pointed the communities become more splintered and the division become more pronounced between *us* and *them*. It seems the unkindness and indecency, as we see with Solomon, are hidden behind the claims of religion and security. As the story of Solomon drew to an end, the truth of his journey is manifested.

> King Solomon loved many foreign women along with the daughter of Pharaoh: Moabite, Ammonite, Edomite, Sidonian, and Hittite women, 2 from the nations concerning which the LORD had said to the Israelites, "You shall not enter into marriage with them, neither shall they with you; for they will surely incline your heart to follow their gods"; Solomon clung to these in love. 3 Among his wives were seven hundred princesses and three hundred concubines; and his wives turned away his heart.[6]

This text ends with the culminating phrase, *turned away his heart*. One might justifiably conclude that this phrase stands precisely as the platform from which one might *take heart*. After Solomon's self-consuming accumulation, those on, or beyond the margins, the invitation to *take heart* carries with it the potency of transformation beyond what is.

> It is well with those who deals generously and lend,
>
> Who conduct their affairs with justice . . .
>
> They have distributed freely,
>
> They have given to the poor;

---

4. Brueggemann, *Money*, 67.

5. Kierkegaard, *Love*, 81.

6. I Kgs 11:1–3.

> Their righteousness endures forever,
>
> their horn is exalted in honor.[7]

Among the many notable references in these verses is the idea that in the midst of business affairs, there must be generosity and justice.

> It is thus not only a matter of one's personal capacity or inclination or altruism, but in particular how one/a society conducts itself and their affairs of business, industry politics . . . to be human means to be willing and able to praise. We have seen that the drama of rehabilitation consists in completing, petition, and then thanks, as an act of shrill self-assertion."[8]

Human beings in whatever circumstances need hope to journey. Not a kind of airy hope or unrooted optimism, but hope rooted in the history of human goodness and the Divine who indeed promises. "Thus functionally, humanness is pervasively hope filled, not in the sense of a buoyant, unreflective optimism, but in the conviction that individual human destiny is powerfully presided over like this One who wills good and who works that good."[9]

It is commonplace in our society that hope is connected to something, a desired object or the fulfillment of some endeavor. To be sure we speak of hope in God, but here too it is frequently a last resort, when evidently all else has failed. But biblical hope is one that calls for hope in God as principal. Such hope is not predicated on stuff or things, but only God as one who creates and sustains all things. Moreover, biblical hope is not to be collapsed into a *spiritual* notion that is void of practical and social realities. The fact that humans cannot control, or in any existential way, predict and fully know the future, hope in all forms and expressions is essential.

Hope indeed may be manifested in seemingly unlikely or unexpected places. Thus, as counterintuitive as it might appear, the book of Job is one of hope as much as it is more conventionally known as one of despair, suffering and pain. At the most compelling level, hope is predicated on the belief that God is creator and sustainer for all of life. To be sure, restoration with all of its complexity, at the end of *Job,* is often highlighted to underline and emphasize the role of God, but throughout the book we are acutely aware of Job's unerring faith in God to the point where he held God accountable for the unexpected and unbidden devastating realities that he faced. A quality of hope here is the fact that he was confident that God would not abandon or reject him, and he is vindicated at the end, where the confidence expressed is

7. Ps 112:5, 9.

8. Brueggemann, *Money*, 84.

9. Brueggemann, *Money*, 85.

justified. Job complains and argues with God from a point of strength, while in a state of despair and pain. "Job is not trying to escape from his suffering: instead, he is confronting the one who he considers to be responsible for his suffering."[10] It is instructive to take note of Job's principal focus, God. Even in the midst of the intense discourse with his friends, his focus is on God. That which is noble, good or virtuous invariably finds itself as a footnote in society's consciousness. Yet, in *Job*, Job has no engagement with Satan; his suffering is not attributed to Satan; nor does he relegate God to a footnote in the process of seeking answers to his suffering.

Generosity, Abundance, and Restoration

One of the ever-present challenges that society has is the temptation to see and focus on the present and what is immediately before us, and neglect a vision for the future, particularly what we may not be able to see. In this regard, one thinks of climate change, the potential for the slow and in some instances even the imperceptible desecrating in the literal sense of the environment. Simply because one does not see the movement of the glacier; the deforestation of the rain forest; the extinction of species; does not mean that they are not ensuing. I believe that climate change and the devastating effects is one of the most potent moral issues of our time, and one unless attended to, will move beyond the human capacity to repair. It is a crisis of creation.

There is generosity in creation; not measured only as *enough* but in *abundance*. Thus, before the humans are created, brought into being, and given freedom and widespread responsibility, creation is brought about in plenty. Here, it is not only one area of light that is created; or one patch of land established for tilling; or one body of water. Indeed, the only boundary that is created is far apart, a world between heaven and earth. Thus, all humans live and wander as the circumstances dictate in East of Eden. It is a life without human generated boundaries. As we note in the Cain narrative (Gen 4), there is the possibility for goodness in East of Eden. There is *timshel*. The forces of chaos are still alive and active in the world, and there are moments in our lives when we might be led to believe that such forces of chaos so deeply embedded in our lives, would make it is impossible to imagine otherwise, and such a belief leads to despair. But the imagination that the world is mired in forever chaos or evil is to imagine that God is incapable, impotent, powerless or disinterested. Having said this, the very presence of God still does not destroy the presence of chaos/evil. In the face

---

10. Roxberg et al., *Consolation*, 119.

of chaos, hope is essential and indispensable. Hope finds its most notable, and perhaps most lasting expression in times and places of hopelessness, and darkness. But, equally significant, is the biblical reminder of where hope, newness, restoration and redemption might occur. A significant biblical example of such redemption might be seen in the book of Hosea. As difficult as the text of Hosea is, it does allow for a discernible instance of a movement from pain to wholeness; from divorce to restoration.

> Say to your brother, Ammi, and to your sister, Ruhamah.
>
> ² Plead with your mother, plead—
>> for she is not my wife,
>> and I am not her husband—
> that she put away her whoring from her face,
>> and her adultery from between her breasts,
> ³ or I will strip her naked
>> and expose her as in the day she was born,
> and make her like a wilderness,
>> and turn her into a parched land,
>> and kill her with thirst.
> ⁴ Upon her children also I will have no pity,
>> because they are children of whoredom.
> ⁵ For their mother has played the whore;
>> she who conceived them has acted shamefully.
> For she said, "I will go after my lovers;
>> they give me my bread and my water,
>> my wool and my flax, my oil and my drink."
> ⁶ Therefore I will hedge up her way with thorns;
>> and I will build a wall against her,
>> so that she cannot find her paths.
> ⁷ She shall pursue her lovers,
>> but not overtake them;
> and she shall seek them,
>> but shall not find them.
> Then she shall say, "I will go
>> and return to my first husband,
>> for it was better with me then than now."

⁸ She did not know
　　that it was I who gave her
　　the grain, the wine, and the oil,
and who lavished upon her silver
　　and gold that they used for Baal.
⁹ Therefore I will take back my grain in its time,
　　and my wine in its season;
and I will take away my wool and my flax,
　　which were to cover her nakedness.
¹⁰ Now I will uncover her shame in the sight of her lovers,
　　and no one shall rescue her out of my hand.
¹¹ I will put an end to all her mirth,
　　her festivals, her new moons, her sabbaths,
　　and all her appointed festivals.
¹² I will lay waste her vines and her fig trees,
　　of which she said,
"These are my pay,
　　which my lovers have given me."
I will make them a forest,
　　and the wild animals shall devour them.
¹³ I will punish her for the festival days of the Baals,
　　when she offered incense to them
and decked herself with her ring and jewelry,
　　and went after her lovers,
　　and forgot me, says the Lord.
¹⁴ Therefore, I will now allure her,
　　and bring her into the wilderness,
　　and speak tenderly to her.
¹⁵ From there I will give her her vineyards,
　　and make the Valley of Achor a door of hope.
There she shall respond as in the days of her youth,
　　as at the time when she came out of the land of Egypt.

¹⁶ On that day, says the Lord, you will call me, "My husband,"
and no longer will you call me, "My Baal." ¹⁷ For I will remove

the names of the Baals from her mouth, and they shall be mentioned by name no more. [18] I will make for you a covenant on that day with the wild animals, the birds of the air, and the creeping things of the ground; and I will abolish the bow, the sword, and war from the land; and I will make you lie down in safety. [19] And I will take you for my wife forever; I will take you for my wife in righteousness and in justice, in steadfast love, and in mercy. [20] I will take you for my wife in faithfulness; and you shall know the Lord.

[21] On that day I will answer, says the LORD,

I will answer the heavens

and they shall answer the earth;

[22] and the earth shall answer the grain, the wine, and the oil,

and they shall answer Jezreel;

[23] and I will sow him for myself in the land.

And I will have pity on Lo-ruhamah,

and I will say to Lo-ammi "You are my people";

and he shall say, "You are my God."[11]

In Hos 2:2–23, where on the heels of seeming lifelong brokenness and alienation, a new relationship is forged in the most unlikely places, the wilderness. This text should be explored for a number of reasons. Here we are reminded that no place or person is outside of the divine or for that matter human purview, as a possible source for renewal or redemption. No place should be discounted as a "right" or "wrong" place. The road to Damascus; the road to Jericho; the road to Mamre; the basket in the Nile, any place, even the seemingly inhospitable, might very well be the place for restoration.

In Hosea 2, the metaphor of divine divorce and divine renewal and reconciliation is precisely a predicate for *taking heart*. In the journey to restoration, it is the emphasis on the foundation that sets the framework for newness: justice, righteousness, mercy, faithfulness and steadfast love. The breadth of divorce and marriage encompasses the expansive sweep of all creation. Divorce to restoration will not be in fractions and will not be compartmentalized, but rather divorce is viewed as fracturing all aspects of life. Restoration will be brought about through the recognition that a relationship must again be established with a memory of what was. So, there is courtship that would lead to renewed trust and fidelity. Moreover, the quality of patience is in play, as YHWH understands the nature of covenant

---

11. Hos 2:2–23

relationship, which like creation, cannot be hastened into becoming. Rush to restoration is not the creative trajectory. What we witness in Hos 2:14, "Therefore, I will now allure her, and bring her into the wilderness, and speak tenderly to her" is a dramatic, perhaps textually, an unexpected turn of events. The initiative is by YHWH who had determined that the relationship must be restored in all its breadth.

From Hos 2:13, "I will punish her for the festival days of the Baals, when she offered incense to them and decked herself with her ring and jewelry, and went after her lovers, and forgot me, says the LORD" we know it is not divine fickleness, but the peculiar insistence that punishment and brokenness will not be the last word. Indeed, out of forgetfulness will come remembrance. That which is overtaken by the immediate, and the gilded present, including lovers, will ultimately drift away as they inevitably do. Gilded superficiality, (as all gilded elements and aspects are), might strike an immediate interest and enticement, but the allure of the divine as the prophet testifies will be permanent. The brokenness and human actions will affect all of creation, and as such the public shaming will not only be for humans, but for all elements of creation. Creation itself will be shamed. The prostituting of a people for greed and a collapsing of all the qualities of relationship is exactly the basis for the shaming. What will transpire is nothing short of a confinement and quarantine. There will be a quest for the lovers, but such a quest will simply lead to a wall. One of the more devastating indictments is the fact that the people forgot YHWH.

Precisely because the actions of the parents have an unavoidable impact on their children and the generations of communities, in restoration, the newness will be for all people. As we see in Hos 2:4, "Upon her children also I will have no pity, because they are children of whoredom" the punishment of the children, by all account, innocent, raises additional existential questions on the nature of divine punishment, which here, appears as a singular overreach and abuse. Yet arguably the principal focus here has to do with the extensive pain and suffering that the "parents" actions have wrought on their children, and generations to come. If for no other reason, this is most certainly a reminder of the consequences of actions or inactions on the family, community and world. What one does, particularly consequential acts, invariably have implications for those who inherit the effects of such actions. In this regard then, like the punishment, the actions of the people will not simply evaporate, but these too will not be the last word in terms of effects.

Before there will be *fullness* and *restoration*, there will be *emptiness*. *Emptiness* will come in a variety of expressions, from shame to rejection; from abandonment to barricading; from solitary existence to public punishment. It is from such *emptiness* and a state of powerlessness that a new relationship will be forged. For fullness and restoration to be, there will be an invitation at YHWH's behest to have the people return. Thus, in Hos 2:21–23: And I will have pity on Lo-ruhamah, and I will say to Lo-ammi "You are my people"; and he shall say, "You are my God." As the relationship is restored, renewal will come about as necessary sustenance will once again be available and accessible. While the relationship is initiated by YHWH, it will be a mutual relationship.

3

Voice for the Voiceless

"The bird that would soar above the level plain of tradition and prejudice must have strong wings." —Kate Chopin

"There exists an obligation towards every human being for the sole reason that he or she is a human being without any other condition required to be fulfilled, and even without any recognition or such obligation on the part of the individual concerned." —Simone Weil, *Need for Roots*, 4–5

"Our speaking is always time related; it is always incomplete and in search of the perspective of another . . . it is in search of tools for the critique and enrichment of its 'repertoire'–and quite often in full flight from such resources when they threaten to become excessively critical and unsettling." —Rowan Williams, *The Edge*, 84

"Man exists anthropologically not in isolation, but in the completeness of the relation between man and man; what humanity is can be properly grasped only in vital reciprocity." —Buber, *I & Thou*, 85

Beyond Quotes

It is almost ubiquitous during times of despair, violence, genocide, among other incomprehensible atrocities, that many reach into their memory or the historical lexicon to find experiences of courage, and the will to speak and live out truth to power. We appeal to those characters who have shaped the historical landscape of justice and a just world, and for hope in the current despair. We are guided to do this, to remind us, among other things that we are not alone. Let me point briefly to three examples from among many.

Martin Niemöller's widely acclaimed quote:

> First, they came for the Socialists, and I did not speak out
>> because I was not a Socialist.
>
> Then they came for the Trade Unionists and I did not speak out
>> because I was not a Trade Unionist.
>
> Then they came for the Jews, and I did not speak out
>> because I was not a Jew.
>
> Then they came for me—and there was no one left
>> to speak for me.[1]

It is not possible to hear these words and not be deeply affected by both their power and poignancy. We could add:

> First they came for the Muslims . . .
>
> Then they came for the homeless;
>
> Then they came for the migrant,
>
> Then they came for . . .

However, what must be reckoned with as essential is Niemöller's journey to this point. Niemöller journeyed through the dark and perilous period of having been a Hitler supporter. The issue here is not to point to his past, but rather to his human capacity for courageous transformation. His world was transformed into imprisonment, and as such, his transformation did not come about in a time of comfort where there were no consequences. It is not enough to simply pronounce platitudes without actions or for that matter wait for an opportune or self-promoting time.

Martin Luther King jr. may very well be one of the most quotable figures in American history. In part, this may be because of the era and the subject matter and who he was and what he represented. So, quotes such as "Injustice anywhere is a threat to justice everywhere" or his well-known reference to the words of the Hebrew Prophet Amos, "Let justice roll down like waters and righteousness like an ever-flowing strain," are ubiquitous. Like Niemöller it cannot only be the memorable quotable words of Martin Luther King jr. that become the final words. What are the actions that would follow such words? The journey to these moments must be reckoned with and embraced. King's journey was one that never wavered from a non-violent justice and in quoting the prophet Amos, he is aware that these prophetic words were a direct challenge to the religiosity of a people who did all of the right rituals but lacked righteousness and justice. That was the context. Moreover, after the pronouncement by the prophet, it was the priest, clearly in line with

1. Attributed to Martin Niemöller.

the monarch, serving as his deputy who demands that the prophet leave; the prophet is not welcome in the King's Temple. The prophet is banished and MLK is assassinated; the point of this is that their lives cannot be collapsed as a cliché. Theirs is a journey of courage.

Frequently cited also, and without the context of journey, is Dietrich Bonhoeffer. Bonhoeffer was keenly aware that Hitler ascended rapidly to that of an idol, generating fear and worship. This was the defining moment and many who saw him as their Savior fell in line. Bonhoeffer believed in non-violence, and yet in an extraordinary act acknowledged that not all systems and circumstances that are destructive, can be nullified non-violently. What in part this means is the reconfiguration of the various and peculiar circumstances that we face. Bonhoeffer knew that actions against Nazism and Adolf Hitler could not be merely incremental. Unequivocally, he knew that he could not remain silent, literally or figuratively. To do so out of some kind of misguided loyalty he believed to be a path to complicity. Every historical era where there has been such complicity, both intended well-unintended consequences have been devastating. It is not enough simply to say, "I am not a perpetrator." Washing one's hands à la Pontius Pilate is not an option. The Catholic Church 1933 Concordat with the German government is one of the most consequential institutional examples of seeking to wash one's hands of systemic evil under the guise of carrying on with its works. In so doing, it turned a *blind eye* to the systemic evil of the Nazis. Bonhoeffer believed that in the event that an automobile is about to crash into a group of people, it is not enough to bind the wounds of the wounded. Rather, if one is in the situation to prevent such a circumstance then one must seize the wheel. "If I sit next to a madman as he drives his car into a group of innocent bystanders, I can't as a Christian, simply wait for the catastrophe then comfort the wounded and bury the dead. I must try to wrestle the steering wheel out of the hands of the driver."[2] Certainly there is a notable and essential place for the binding of wounds, but only adding after the fact when prevention may be necessary and possible is a serious relinquishing of responsibility. The American Vice President Mike Pence has publicly proclaimed that it is his Christian faith, his belief in Jesus Christ that guides him; he is unequivocal in his pronouncement that this is the foundation of his political principles. Yet, fundamental biblical and theological principles such as the ones that Bonhoeffer embraced are discarded. As a nation, we have witnessed the devastating violence of the Rwanda genocide and many regrets are expressed later, and perhaps even more powerful, the total lack of interest by others, as well as genocide did not appear to have any personal

2. Bonhoeffer, "The Church and the Jewish Question."

adverse effects on them. Regret regarding Rwanda did not lead to any action or pro-action with the genocide in Darfur.

Arguably, the most intractable and fractious issue that continues to plague the United States has to do with the devastating stain of gun violence, from domestic family violence to street violence to domestic terrorism. Bonhoeffer's metaphor of "seizing the wheel" would be akin to having legislation on particular types of gun and handgun reform and have background checks and act urgently and immediately as New Zealand did in passing gun legislation after the horrific violence and murder of Muslims at worship in a Mosque. What instead continues to happen is the now vacuous cliché of "keeping in thoughts and prayers." Where once such a sentiment would have had an empathetic overtone, it has become meaningless and insulting to the suffering, as it is seen for what it is, a facile, empty veil of non-action. "To invoke God to justify violence against the innocent is not an act of sanctity but of sacrilege. It is a kind of blasphemy. It is to take God's name in vain."[3] The aim for anyone who professes a faith, arguably from any religion, is not to look heavenward to become like God, but rather to act and become better human beings. In so doing, humans may indeed become like God. The place to begin is to question and challenge the State and those responsible for the violence and injustice. Our faith should strengthen the human bonds that hold us together, not violently tear us apart. It is the weakly rooted faith that seeks to destroy and dominate. This is not to suggest that there will be instant transformation. Whatever we do will be transforming, though in the meantime there will be suffering. Yet, violence could be an option. Simultaneously, one must ensure that victims are attended to. To be sure, there will always be those who will seek to determine who deserves justice and who do not; who lives and who dies.

Our language, our ideas, our perspectives, our conclusions, regardless of the discipline, are penultimate and finite. Whether we embrace this notion or accept this reality, it does not change the truth. Some of us would like to imagine that some of what we say, believe, prove, etc., are ultimate and have infinite meaning. Instead, what penultimacy ensures is the fact we will continue to engage with the other; to listen and converse, all of which is to say, we continue to need community, and any insistence of ultimacy is inherently flawed.

3. Sacks, *Not in God's Name*, 5.

Patience and Silence

Patience like silence has at least two sides that stand seemingly in opposition to each other. I believe there is a conspicuously notable place for silence, sometimes even a privileged place.

When there are tragic and painful circumstances, there are no adequate, let alone definitive words to alleviate pain. Even though some have a natural impulse to explain, and worst yet justify suffering, silence in the form of "I am sorry" might very well be the only words available, and even the most appropriate at that point. Silence does have its place, for in the face of certain circumstances, one simply does not have the vocabulary, and as such one should not use one's voice to explain or justify. On the other hand, silence in the face of injustice in whatever form, not only when it seems to affect a person personally, in itself an injustice, but generally as a sustaining of the status quo.

What is evident is that silence in the latter sense carries with it a cost. And depending on the circumstances, the cost might very well be consequential and devastating, both personally and collectively. For a while the scars of silence may not immediately appear, but such hiddenness does not last forever. We know that out of shame or embarrassment or fear one may choose to be silent. Whatever the personal or collective circumstance, it is kept within and it ebbs away at one's spirit and psyche. One may break the silence with clichés or deceit or even involuntary sounds of despair, but this generates a cumulative ebbing away of one's constitution and moral grounding. To be sure there are also those who will notably use their voice in other egregious ways. First, they may use their voice to silence others. We certainly witness this in times of personal grief where some have been known to use their voice, perhaps even with the best of intentions to insist that the grieving person "move on." And this, perhaps, in an unintended consequence silences the grieving person. Second, there are those who seek to maintain the status quo, and who will not only use their voice, but will seek to do so to drown out the voice of those who seek just change.

Nobel Peace Laureate Elie Wiesel spoke eloquently on not being able to write about his experience in the Holocaust for ten years after he was liberated. He could not break that silence, not because he did not care or that it did not matter, but he wondered how one could begin to craft and memorialize the words for evil. But when he did break the silence as he knew he would, for he knew that silence was no longer an option. Thus, not only the Holocaust but all injustices, all genocide, became the principal landscape for his reflections. One such moment for publicly breaking his silence occurred on the occasion when he was the recipient of the Medal of Freedom from

President Ronald Reagan. It was this moment that he chose to speak publicly about his concern regarding a trip on which President Reagan was about to embark to Bitburg cemetery, in Germany. Wiesel on this public occasion, at the White House, spoke directly to President Reagan.

> Allow me Mr. President to touch on a matter which is sensitive. I belong to a traumatized generation; to us symbols are important. Following our ancient tradition which commands us to 'speak truth to power,' may I speak to you of the recent events that have caused so much pain and anguish?
>
> We have met four or five times. I know of your commitment to humanity. I am convinced that you were not aware of the presence of SS graves in the Bitburg cemetery. But now we all are aware of that presence. I therefore implore you Mr. President in the spirit of this moment that . . . you will not go there. That place is not your place.[4]

Wiesel could certainly have chosen to focus on another subject in that moment, or perhaps even spoken privately, but in so doing he would have betrayed who he was, and his sense of self.

When you have such moments and a voice, and in the face of injustice, then one must use one's voice and speak publicly. Rarely is there anything easy about this, but then in matters of substance and existential meaning, there is little that is easy. Likewise, with patience there are important moments in which one is compelled to be patient; at other times being patient is neither noble nor proper. Thus, in the face of injustices silence and patience are not virtues. This is not an invitation to be reckless, but rather to use one's voice on those occasions when it does not directly affect you, and on behalf of those who may not have a voice or those who have been silenced. This perhaps is the guiding principle of living justly. It is, as Thucydides, centuries ago clearly articulated. "Justice will not come . . . until those who are not injured are as indignant as those who are." This is the heart of being just; it is not waiting for a convenient time. Indeed, as Homer reflected, "Yet taught by time, my heart has learned to glow for other's good, and melt at other's woes." It is the human capacity to celebrate and be joyful over another fortune or goodness, and not simply wish that it were you or lapse into a state of jealousy. But to have the pain of the other also causes one pain. Homer's reflection points to the journey of arriving at a place where it is the heart that is moved. Perhaps it is the case that some people are naturally inclined to be moved by joy or sadness, but often it is a journey to get there. Yet, one must find the capacity to make that journey; to have the courage to change;

---

4. Wiesel, *From the Kingdom of Memory*, 176.

to be willing to live with a quality of an "inconvenience" if necessary. It is the heart that has to be moved; moved to act.

Breaking one's silence in the face of injustice and oppression is non-negotiable for all people, and certainly for people of faith, it is straight-forwardly a biblical mandate. Yet not all the breaking of silence is either desirable or constructive. The complexity of this tension in the United States is woven in the first amendment freedom of speech in the Constitution. In this context, *hate speech* is often allowed in both implicit, and in certain instances, explicit ways. There are moments when the latter may lead to, or incorporate violence, with tacit approval of leaders who ironically may choose to remain silent. We know that in notable instances when silence is broken, especially by the Hebrew Prophets, their words were met rejection and vilification by the government.

> And Amaziah said to Amos, "O seer, go, flee away to the land of Judah, earn your bread there, and prophesy there; but never again prophesy at Bethel, for it is the king's sanctuary, and it is a temple of the kingdom."[5]

> The days of punishment have come,
>   the days of recompense have come;
> Israel cries, "The prophet is a fool,
>   the man of the spirit is mad!"
> Because of your great iniquity,
>   your hostility is great.[6]

> [4] Then the officials said to the king, "This man ought to be put to death, because he is discouraging the soldiers who are left in this city, and all the people, by speaking such words to them. For this man is not seeking the welfare of this people, but their harm." [5] King Zedekiah said, "Here he is; he is in your hands; for the king is powerless against you."[7]

The biblical text is replete with clashes between authoritarianism and the prophetic voice. In a variety of circumstances this tension has made its way into contemporary society. The characters may differ, but the tension remains. Equally evident throughout is the fact that the prophetic voice, and the voice of the people must not be silenced. Every generation has a

5. Amos 7:12–13.

6. Hos 9:7.

7. Jer 38:4–5.

responsibility to those who come after, and every future generation must surely depend on their predecessors to make their voice known. The prophets and others who would dare to speak are vilified and threatened by death and expulsion from places of worship. The prophet Amos would remind the establishment that he is not a professional disrupter; he was not brought in to break the silence. There is consequential cost to keeping silent in the face of injustice, and whether it is the dramatic recognition of the psalmist, "while I kept silent, my body wasted away" (Ps 32:3a), or the persistent and lingering pulsing of one's moral conscience. Moreover, a significant effect of breaking one's silence is the ongoing effect it has on others. In this way, others who may have had a particular debilitating level of fear may in fact find in the community of others of like spirit, the capacity to use, and ultimately to raise one voice. Using one's voice and being indignant in the face of injustice on behalf of other might very well be inconvenient and even dangerous. Yet, it cannot be the case that convenience is the guiding principle in the face of injustice. Convenience might very well be another veil for delay or as Martin Luther King, jr. has said in his "Letter from Birmingham Jail," "A justice delayed is a justice denied" and in the face of injustice, "wait" means "never." One thinks of the prophet's Isaiah's words here.

> For the vineyard of the LORD of hosts is the house of Israel,
>
> and the people of Judah are his pleasant planting;
>
> he expected justice, but saw bloodshed;
>
> righteousness, but heard a cry!
>
> Ah, you who join house to house,
>
> who add field to field,
>
> until there is room for no one but you,
>
> and you are left to live alone
>
> in the midst of the land![8]

Cry in these texts stands as a turning point for justice. This is the fundamental tension. In justice, we have the essential undoing of cry. In both instances, it is YHWH as the architect, who not only observes equity, but acts. The cry of a people is such that the singular transformative absent quality is justice. "Justice is not deconstructible. When as totalism is committed to the status quo, and is always being deconstructed by the Spirit, the claims of justice situate us in the trajectory of the possible, beyond all present arrangements."[9]

8. Isa 5:7–8.

9. Brueggemann, God, Neighbor, 70.

On Wednesday February 12, 2003, the Late Senator Robert Byrd speaking to President George W. Bush and his Administration's decision to enter into a war with Iraq, pronounced the sobering words about the devastating danger of silence.

> To contemplate war is to think about the most horrible of human experiences. On this February day, as this nation stands at the brink of battle, every American on some level must be contemplating the horrors of war. Yet, this Chamber is, for the most part, silent, ominously, dreadfully silent. There is no debate, no discussion, no attempt to lay out for the nation the pros and cons of this particular war. There is nothing. We stand passively mute in the United States Senate, paralyzed by our own uncertainty, seemingly stunned by the sheer turmoil of events . . . On what is possibly the eve of horrific infliction of death and destruction on the population of the nation of Iraq, a population, I might add, of which over 50% is under age 15, this chamber is silent. On what is possibly only days before we send thousands of our own citizens to face unimagined horrors of chemical and biological warfare, this chamber is silent. On the eve of what could possibly be a vicious terrorist attack in retaliation for our attack on Iraq, it is business as usual in the United States Senate. We are truly "sleepwalking through history." In my heart of hearts I pray that this great nation and its good and trusting citizens are not in for a rudest of awakenings.[10]

One of the challenges that we encounter is the silence that surrounds us when we face voices that must be heard and words that must be spoken. Perhaps it is the case that out of sheer weariness and fatigue one is prone to collapse into silence, which by default then becomes the sustaining and support of the status quo. But there is also the more egregious issue, where one's voice is silenced, veiled under the guise of doing so for one's benefit. So, we might hear, "you can't go on like this" or "you need to move on." In these and other iterations, the silenced person is essentially told that this is the way things are, and always will be. It is a quality of fatalism. We must resist the temptation to silence others through our voice with an ill-conceived well-meaning notion of why certain events occur and delivering answers that effectively say, "move on," for there is nothing more to be said or done. Do not silence others and take away their stories through the sound of your voice.

10. Byrd, Speech in Senate, 2003.

Mandate to Refresh

> Six days you shall do your work, but on the seventh day you
> shall rest, so that your ox and your donkey may have relief, and
> your homeborn slave and the resident alien may be refreshed.[11]

> It is a sign forever between me and the people of Israel that in six
> days the LORD made heaven and earth, and on the seventh day
> he rested, and was refreshed.[12]

In the case of Exod 23:12, rest is for the entire household, including servants and animals. It is clear that it is the only way that one's *nephesh* can
be restored. What this time of rest intimates is an invitation to have a vision of hope beyond the present. It is the only way for the re-generation
and re-creation as the essential way for restoration to occur. Exod 23:12
makes clear that *nephesh* is not reserved only for one group; *nephesh* reminds us that it is the connecting force among all humans, God and the
rest of creation. There is no restriction. All have *nephesh,* and life is generated from *nephesh.* While the NRSV translates *nephesh* as *refreshed,* it can
easily be translated in a more complex way as *resouled.* Of course, it is not
a term that is typically a part of the common lexicon, and precisely because
of this, it does not engender an immediate and apparent understanding.
Thus, like the Sabbath itself, the very idea of *resouled* gives us pause to have
an understanding of what this means for us. So, we are aware that for a
variety of reasons, one may lose one's *nephesh*; most certainly as is the case
with God in Exod 31:17, for even God needs to have a time to be *resouled.*
There is a recognition that it is possible to have one's soul be wearied out,
and one cannot continue to live without it. (See, Isa 1:14) Here, surely
the *nephesh* of YHWH will need to be *re-nephesed* even as the prophets
call upon the people to ensure that their worship practices must be indelibly connected with the justice and righteousness for all in society. So, one
might argue that if *nephesh* in these two contexts is translated *soul,* the
centrality of rest is integral and essential for daily life. While it might seem
that *nephesh* is narrowly about the individual, it is fundamentally a relational term. One cannot be *soulless* and function in community. Moreover,
that God needs to be *re-nepheshed, and* given that humans are created in
the image of God, this means by extension, that we too as humans will, by
definition, need to be *re-nepheshed.* It is certainly not an abstract idea or
one that is locked into a time in the past.

---

11. Exod 23:12.
12. Exod 31:17.

David said to Abishai and to all his servants, "My own son seeks
my life; how much more now may this Benjaminite! Let him
alone, and let him curse; for the LORD has bidden him. It may be
that the LORD will look on my distress, and the LORD will repay
me with good for this cursing of me today." So David and his
men went on the road, while Shimei went along on the hillside
opposite him and cursed as he went, throwing stones and fling-
ing dust at him. The king and all the people who were with him
arrived weary at the Jordan; and there he *refreshed* himself.[13]

David's experience serves as a reminder that no one, in whatever
circumstance is exempt from the need to be *re-nepheshed*. In this instance
David and his entourage are spending time to be *re-nepheshed* after fleeing
from Absalom. With the weariness that comes with the expanse of life, it is
manifestly essential to be *re-nepheshed*, regardless of status or station in life.
Once again, this is not an abstract idea, as David and his entourage are fleeing for their lives; this is a matter of life d death. Arguably even more than
Exod 23:12, this instance is profoundly personal, and in a real way beyond
the particularity of David's situation. One can relate to this moment in one's
particularity of the need for rest and *resouling*. Aside from the gravity of the
situation with David and Absalom, the father-son dynamic, coupled with
David's corporate-private roles, experiences of fear and anxiety are common human realities. To *take heart*, by necessity means that we must have
restoration and replenishment of one's *nephesh*.

There is a further issue in this regard. While Sabbath might be the "festival of egalitarianism"[14] and collapses socio-economic barriers, it cannot
remain temporary and restricted. This could a time when a defining moment has the potential to become a movement. The danger here as always is
to celebrate the moment and then live lives as if such a moment is nothing
more than an appendix, and a fleeing asterisk. That is, there is an awareness
of its presence, but ultimately not of meaningful systemic transformation.
The challenge then for the person of faith, and for the society as a whole, who
might embrace the idea of the replenishing of the soul, is to have a counter
cultural voice, a voice that refuses only to be shaped by isolated weekly, occasional or annual moments. Instead, the voice must become the voice of
every day, every moment. The keeping of Sabbath is a ritual prescribed in
part to remember the importance of every corner of human existence. In
that moment, we are reminded of the whole, and the fractured parts of who
we are. However, as is so often the case, if we return to life as usual without

13. 2 Sam 16:11–14; my italics.
14. Brueggemann, *Mandate*, 175.

any meaningful transformation, then it is no more than a weekly or daily moment of self-indulgence. And this would be an indictment of our actions and the undermining of the integrity of the time of rest.

In ancient Israel, as indeed in contemporary society, we are often surrounded by public signs with words of virtue. It is not unusual to find signs extolling the virtues of the Ten Commandments or the ongoing admonition for Christians to keep Christ in Christmas, or others who remind society that war is not the answer or that there is no peace without justice. The point is that there is ample evidence of noble words, but often there is a conspicuous absence of the commensurate connection with actions. Ancient Israel was surrounded by such reminders of peace, from *Solomon* to *Jerusalem*, yet so frequently absent in the manner in which the persons and places lived out and manifested *shalom*. So, while surrounded by *shalom*, *shalom* is often absent. The prophet Jeremiah would dramatically challenge this self-indulgence, self-congratulatory certitude. As the people headed into exile in Babylon *shalom* in a painful dramatic nonnegotiable reality is understood and brought into focus. No more will the signs and names suffice for the very public display, for it was the mere repetition of virtuous ideas without the commensurate actions that led the people to collapse into a state of complacent satisfaction.

Resouling in Its Time

For everything there is a season, and a time for every matter under heaven:

² a time to be born, and a time to die;

a time to plant, and a time to pluck up what is planted;

³ a time to kill, and a time to heal;

a time to break down, and a time to build up;

⁴ a time to weep, and a time to laugh;

a time to mourn, and a time to dance;

⁵ a time to throw away stones,

and a time to gather stones together;

a time to embrace, and a time to refrain from embracing;

⁶ a time to seek, and a time to lose;

a time to keep, and a time to throw away;

⁷ a time to tear, and a time to sew;

a time to keep silence, and a time to speak;

⁸ a time to love, and a time to hate;

a time for war, and a time for peace.

⁹ What gain have the workers from their toil? ¹⁰ I have seen the business that God has given to everyone to be busy with. ¹¹ He has made everything suitable for its time; moreover, he has put a sense of past and future into their minds, yet they cannot find out what God has done from the beginning to the end. ¹² I know that there is nothing better for them than to be happy and enjoy themselves as long as they live; ¹³ moreover, it is God's gift that all should eat and drink and take pleasure in all their toil. ¹⁴ I know that whatever God does endures forever; nothing can be added to it, nor anything taken from it; God has done this, so that all should stand in awe before him.

¹⁵ That which is, already has been; that which is to be, already is; and God seeks out what has gone by.[a] ¹⁶ Moreover I saw under the sun that in the place of justice, wickedness was there, and in the place of righteousness, wickedness was there as well. ¹⁷ I said in my heart, God will judge the righteous and the wicked, for he has appointed a time for every matter, and for every work.

¹⁸ I said in my heart with regard to human beings that God is testing them to show that they are but animals. ¹⁹ For the fate of humans and the fate of animals is the same; as one dies, so dies the other. They all have the same breath, and humans have no advantage over the animals; for all is vanity. ²⁰ All go to one place; all are from the dust, and all turn to dust again. ²¹ Who knows whether the human spirit goes upward and the spirit of animals goes downward to the earth?

²² So I saw that there is nothing better than that all should enjoy their work, for that is their lot; who can bring them to see what will be after them?[15]

This is certainly a recognizable text, and in particular the opening eight verses. There is a good reason why we should not be allowed to edit, redact or selectively choose as we might be inclined to do from the statements in this text. But of course, we do. Why must there be a time for hatred and a time for war? But both of these are painfully present, and yet they are integral to the creation of the universe. These are very much a part of the human reality and condition. We all bring certain particulars to the reading of the texts, and the manner in which we interpret the words and their meanings and implications. So, we begin there and are reminded that claims

15. Eccl 3:1–21.

of objectivity are perhaps more of a shield to protect the status quo, and a privileged reading, than truth and possibility.

In this text, which over time has bridged the divide between the sacred and the profane, we have the many and varied defining moments in life. Certainly, one might not need to *take heart* in times of peace and love, but most assuredly one needs to *take heart* in times of pain and war, loss and despair. What is significant here is that this text brings together both the individual and the community; the nation and the world. War most clearly underlines this connection. It would be easy to conclude that the central message of Ecclesiastes is one of death and the futility of life. Perhaps a superficial reading of the text might suggest this. The idea is underlined by Qoheleth's one certainty, namely that death comes to all. However, a nuanced, and an intentionally careful reading, would also yield a message of hope and redemption. What Qoheleth invites us to see in its peculiar brutality is the complexity and the inevitable tension one finds in life. Qoheleth does not spare the reader the gravity of suffering and death, for he is qualitatively and assuredly affirmative about life as is encapsulated in the select texts below.

> [24] There is nothing better for mortals than to eat and drink, and find enjoyment in their toil. This also, I saw, is from the hand of God; [25] for apart from him who can eat or who can have enjoyment? [26] For to the one who pleases him God gives wisdom and knowledge and joy; but to the sinner he gives the work of gathering and heaping, only to give to one who pleases God. This also is vanity and a chasing after wind.[16]

> [12] I know that there is nothing better for them than to be happy and enjoy themselves as long as they live; [13] moreover, it is God's gift that all should eat and drink and take pleasure in all their toil.[17]

> [18] This is what I have seen to be good: it is fitting to eat and drink and find enjoyment in all the toil with which one toils under the sun the few days of the life God gives us; for this is our lot. [19] Likewise all to whom God gives wealth and possessions and whom he enables to enjoy them, and to accept their lot and find enjoyment in their toil—this is the gift of God. [20] For they will scarcely brood over the days of their lives, because God keeps them occupied with the joy of their hearts.[18]

16. Eccl 2:24–26.
17. Eccl 3:12–13.
18. Eccl 5:18–20.

> [7] Go, eat your bread with enjoyment, and drink your wine with
> a merry heart; for God has long ago approved what you do. [8]
> Let your garments always be white; do not let oil be lacking on
> your head. [9] Enjoy life with the wife whom you love, all the days
> of your vain life that are given you under the sun, because that
> is your portion in life and in your toil at which you toil under
> the sun. [10] Whatever your hand finds to do, do with your might;
> for there is no work or thought or knowledge or wisdom in
> Sheol, to which you are going.[19]

The importance of this tension is one that underlines the *reality* of life,
not the *futility* of life, as is often the instinctive and conclusive view. While
the Hebrew *hebel* in *Ecclesiastes* is most commonly translated *vanity*, its layered meaning, both literally and figuratively serves as a significant moment
for *taking heart*.[20]

While *hebel* literally means *vapor*, that which is fleeting and temporary, and that which evaporates, it is also what exists.

> The routines of our lives bear us along and absorb us, keeping us
> occupied with that next task or that next goal just ahead, even as
> we come round to where we started.
>
> Yet . . . sometimes it happens that an event or an experience,
> interrupts us in our accustomed round. It might be a story in the
> news, a tragic accident we witness, news of a schoolmate's death,
> a parent's sudden infirmity or an event quite insignificant in the
> face of it. We are brought up short and we ask, "what is it all for?'
> . . . This capacity to step back from our lives and to ponder our
> existence at a remove is unique to human beings. It is the quality
> that sets us apart from all living creatures. We alone have the
> ability to ask: is there value and meaning to what I do? What is
> the point of it all? Is this all that there is to living?[21]

In the manner in which the text begins, we are reminded that while
Qoheleth outlines defining moments in human journey, not necessarily
experiences that every human being will have, but rather a representation
of that which constitutes the human journey. However, the opening brack-
et of human existence is governed by God. So, humans do have choice, but
that which has ultimacy and finality are under divine auspices. "On the
bad day, one is to reflect. Times of suffering by their nature, call for some
critical distance or perspective. But on the *good day*, the only mandate is to

19. Eccl 9:7–10.

20. For a brief discussion of *hebel*, see Duncan, *Ecclesiastes*, 3–4.

21. Duncan, *Ecclesiastes,* 18.

be joyful . . . Strikingly, the literal translation of the Hebrew is '*be in good*.'"
[22] *Take Heart* allows the sufferer in whatever situation or circumstance
to know that there is a *safe space* beyond the conventional wisdom of *either or*. The *either or* binary in the description and interpretive conclusion
might be straightforward and easy, but it leaves a windowless reality for
truth and restoration, and in a safe space.

Following the direction of YHWH and further exploring what it means
to be in the image of God, it is particularly noteworthy that there is no
instance in the Hebrew Bible where there is a divine acknowledgement of
violence and punishment against the innocent. With respect to Genesis 18,
Ro suggests, "God tolerates or endures the guilt of a community because of
righteous individuals."[23] Yet, Lot as "righteous" is a dubious distinction and he
is woefully insufficient in his actions to save Sodom and Gomorrah. One of
the issues that persists in this regard is the idea that we humans are mandated
to acknowledge wrongdoing and *turn around*. Yet, if we are to take guidance
and formation from God, we are left in a state of unknown.

This is the broad scope of neighborly love. To live in the world and
seek the wellbeing of each person regardless of the qualities that we have,
and which have come to define us.

Mountain-Top Experience

On April 3, 1968, in Memphis Tennessee, the evening before his assassination, Martin Luther King, jr. delivered his last public speech. Among
the many things that Martin Luther King, jr. proclaimed that evening,
three in particular have had, and continue to have pointed relevance and
resonance for us as individuals, and as a society. First, perhaps one of the
most difficult things that King intimated is that while he has been to the
mountaintop, and has seen the promised land, he does not intend to stay
there. As King said in his speech, one cannot be compassionate by proxy.
Essential, as the mountain top experience is, it is not a place of permanent
dwelling. This too is notable, in large part because, figuratively speaking, it
is very tempting to remain there.

David Brooks in his very thoughtful and heartfelt volume that outlines
a platform for the moral life, suggests that such moral actions come from
what he designates, *The Second Mountain*, the title of the book. He suggests that "the second mountain is not the opposite of the first. To climb it

22. Duncan, *Ecclesiastes*, 50.
23. Ro, "Theological Concept," 407.

does not mean rejecting the first mountain. It is the journey after it.[24] What Brooks refers to as the *second mountain* is that deep rooted commitment that has to do with service, and what I propose as neighborliness. I have a different metaphor. As I reflect on the idea of mountain, it strikes me that historically the mountain experience has been one of notable significance that shapes the valley experience; given that life with all of the challenges, complexities and pain, occur in the valley. Transformation happens in the valley. We have seen this with Moses and Jesus and Martin Luther King, jr. The capacity to care, to love, to console, to act on behalf of others all occur in the valley. Life is not lived on the mountaintop, but being there allows a glimpse into what can, and will be. What can be, is seen over and against that which is. But there is also an additional quality to this experience. Sometimes one's experience on the mountaintop is not only for oneself, but for others, often for generations to come.

> [4] The LORD said to him, "This is the land of which I swore to Abraham, to Isaac, and to Jacob, saying, 'I will give it to your descendants'; I have let you see it with your eyes, but you shall not cross over there." [5] Then Moses, the servant of the LORD, died there in the land of Moab, at the LORD's command.[25]

In this case, the metaphor has biblical roots in that Moses was able to see the promised land but never entered, a reminder that the journey there may not guarantee entrance; it is not only for oneself but for others. Moreover, the road to the promised land is often not an easy road, but the journey has to be made even when there is no immediate chance to enter, or for that matter even when one cannot in fact see the land. Another biblical example, and perhaps even more compelling is the instance in which Jesus took Peter, James and John to a mountain, away from the busyness of everyday life, and there the disciples witness a transfiguration of Jesus and the presence of Moses and Elijah.

> Six days later, Jesus took with him Peter and James and his brother John and led them up a high mountain, by themselves. [2] And he was transfigured before them, and his face shone like the sun, and his clothes became dazzling white. [3] Suddenly there appeared to them Moses and Elijah, talking with him. [4] Then Peter said to Jesus, "Lord, it is good for us to be here; if you wish,

---

24. Brooks, *Second Mountain*, xiv.

25. Deut 34:4–5.

I will make three dwellings here, one for you, one for Moses, and one for Elijah.[26]

Here too is an example about the future, and with Moses and Elijah, Peter, James and John are reminded that the future is indelibly connected with the past, though also very distinct from each other. Peter's natural impulse is to build a tent for all present there and then remain there. And one might imagine what is there not to like about being on a mountain, and away from the vagaries and chaos of everyday life! Yet he is told immediately and clearly that staying on the mountain is not an option. Life does not live on the mountain; life lives in the complexities and ambiguities of the valley.

Second, in King's speech, he emphasizes a common theme found in many of his speeches and sermons, namely the inextricable connection that people have with each other. He calls this a "dangerous unselfishness." This is often a difficult road to travel, and yet, it is the only road towards the fulfillment of what it means to be each other's neighbor.

> In our era, it is not enough to be tolerant. You tolerate mosquitoes in the Summer, a rattle in an engine, the gray slush that collects at the crosswalk in winter. You tolerate what you would not have to deal with and wish would go away. It is no honor to be tolerated. Every spiritual tradition says love your neighbor as yourself, not tolerate them.[27]

We tolerate that which is a nuisance, large or small, animate or inanimate. It is the choice to act on behalf of the other when it might seem at times as if there are so many "good" reasons not to do so. Yet, not to act for whatever reason means that ultimately one will sacrifice the future, and disregard the past, for the sake of the present, and only one's limited vision.

> [25] Just then a lawyer stood up to test Jesus. "Teacher," he said, "what must I do to inherit eternal life?" [26] He said to him, "What is written in the law? What do you read there?" [27] He answered, "You shall love the LORD your God with all your heart, and with all your soul, and with all your strength, and with all your mind; and your neighbor as yourself." [28] And he said to him, "You have given the right answer; do this, and you will live." [29] But wanting to justify himself, he asked Jesus, "And who is my neighbor?" [30] Jesus replied, "A man was going down from Jerusalem to Jericho, and fell into the hands of robbers, who stripped him, beat him, and went away, leaving him half dead. [31] Now by chance

---

26. Matt 17:1–4
27. Wilkerson, *Caste*, 387.

a priest was going down that road; and when he saw him, he passed by on the other side. [32] So likewise a Levite, when he came to the place and saw him, passed by on the other side. [33] But a Samaritan while traveling came near him; and when he saw him, he was moved with pity. [34] He went to him and bandaged his wounds, having poured oil and wine on them. Then he put him on his own animal, brought him to an inn, and took care of him. [35] The next day he took out two denarii, gave them to the innkeeper, and said, 'Take care of him; and when I come back, I will repay you whatever more you spend.' [36] Which of these three, do you think, was a neighbor to the man who fell into the hands of the robbers?" [37] He said, "The one who showed him mercy." Jesus said to him, "Go and do likewise."[28]

Third, in citing the parable of the Good Samaritan, King asked the essential and single most constitutive question, echoing Jesus's change of the lawyer's question in the parable. King outlines the question in a precise and contextual manner. Being in Memphis, Tennessee to lend his voice and presence on behalf of the sanitation workers, he said that the question should be, "If I do not stop to help the sanitation workers, what will happen to them?" The lawyer testing Jesus wanted to know "who is the neighbor"? This is certainly a question that on the surface seems reasonable and has merit. It gives the impression that if one knew who the neighbor was, then one would seek to exhibit some kind of neighborly love to that person. But Jesus would have none of it, and he turns the question around. The point is not to know the identity of the neighbor, and thereby determine whether or not he or she qualifies for neighborly love. The point is not to focus on the object of the neighbor but on the subject of who one is. The world is the neighborhood and the identity of the other must not be the principle on which neighborly love is demonstrated. So, while the priest and the Levite choose to ignore and walk by the anonymous injured man on the road, for whatever reason, the Samaritan chooses otherwise, and in so doing chooses life for the unknown other. This is a matter of choice; it is about being neighborly in a way that does not pivot on religion, nationality, ethnicity, gender, station in life, status in society, etc. And certainly not as a legal requirement, neighborly love is a human quality that pierces the heart. Speaking of the need for goodness and human attachments, Marandiuc suggests:

> What kind of attachment practices and love disposition does it presuppose? Broadly speaking, such practices need to be rooted in an orientation of one's will and disposition toward the other

28. Luke 10:25–37.

in beneficence. Put differently, it is a will to love that acts to love. Such willing and acting are not yet either closeness or attachment, as one can show beneficence to strangers . . . [29]

Thus, as one reflects on the Trump administration's decision to separate children from their parents and the caging and internment of these children is not only policy to be followed, but such policy underlines and accentuates the inherent lack of beneficence. In the Administration's sweeping policy as administered through the Department of Justice at the direction of Attorney General Jeff Sessions and Acting Attorney General Rod Rosenstein that children are to be separated from their parents, there was no attention to the particularities and circumstances of their situation. Instead, as the Inspector General has reported, Attorney General Sessions mandated, "we need to take away their children." Surely, Hannah Arendt's striking and profound phrase, "the banality of evil" might very well apply to many of those who simply carried out pronouncements and policies generated by Donald Trump and the Trump administration, blurring the line between hate and blind loyalty. Marandiuc had argued, "the full flowering of all life's unfolding lies as far from a basic universality as one can be, and it blooms into inimitable particularity."[30] Suketu Mehta has made the point in a more unalloyed assessment. "I am not calling for open borders. I am calling for open hearts. The migrants are not likely to be rapists or terrorists than anyone else. They are ordinary people just like those who haven't had to move. But the ordeals they've had to face in their journey, and the sacrifices they made for family—both for children in their new country and the parents and siblings they support in the old—have made them into ordinary, everyday heroes."[31]

And, so for King, the question is not what will happen to him as he misses the time in his pastoral study, or for the other, who might say that he or she misses time in the office or some other activity, but rather what will happen to the sanitation workers if they do not stop and help. That is the issue; that is the governing principled question. In his incisive contemplation on this issue, Gustavo Gutierrez reflects: "Who is my neighbor? The neighbor was the Samaritan who *approached* the wounded man and *made him his neighbor*. The neighbor . . . is not he who I find in my path, but rather he in whose path I place myself, he whom I approach and actively seek."[32]

What will happen to the injured man if the Samaritan does not stop to help him? That is the question, and it is a question that that one carries

29. Marandiuc, *The Goodness of Home*, 71.

30. Marandiuc, *The Goodness of Home*, 102.

31. Mehta, *This Land*, 31

32. Gutierrez, *Seeds of the Spirit*, 78.

with oneself, because one's actions must be urgent and immediate. In certain defining instances, to be neighborly is to save a person; it is truly a choice between life and death. It would be easy, I imagine, to become cynical of that which is noble and virtuous when those with power, but with a moral nihilism as their compass unravel that which has been foundational for a caring and democratic society. Camus would remind us in these times that "one can be right and yet be beaten, that force can vanquish spirit, that there are times when courage is not its own recompense." "The heart is that piece of us that longs for fusion with others. We are not primarily creatures; we are primarily loving and desiring creatures. We are defined by what we desire. We become what we love. The core question for each of us is, Have we educated our emotions to love the right things in the right way?"[33] It is the statement, we become what we love, whether fully so or not, is the striking force in us. And this might be for good or ill. "The Buddha's enlightenment has been based on the principle that to love morally was to live for others. Unlike the other renouncers who retreated from human society, Buddhist monks were commanded to return to the world to help others find release from pain."[34]

After King was stabbed at a book signing event in New York, he received a note from a high school student in White Plains NY, who identified herself as a "white girl." She said that she was glad that he did not sneeze as that one fleeting moment would have caused the knife to rupture his artery, and likely he would have died. This was the note that left an indelible mark on him.

Rita Nakashima Brock points to the centrality of the heart. She sees the heart as the place of prominence in terms of what binds us to each other. It is the heart which "binds us to others . . . and empowers us to act."[35] King proclaimed repeatedly that he was glad that he did not sneeze! I have been thinking about that phrase, as innocuous as it is, and the depth of meaning it carried then, and what it might mean for us now. For most of us sneezing means being blinded for a fraction of a second, an almost throw away fleeting moment, but the consequences of such a moment might very well mean the difference between good and evil, life and death. Not only will a fraction mean that the broad landscape of many opportunities might be missed as King attests, but a moment missed might be a life for a person. As hackneyed as it sounds, it is to say that every moment counts.

33. Brooks, *Second Mountain*, 302.

34. Armstrong, *Fields*, 167.

35. Brock, *Journeys By Heart*, xiv.

In a contextually different example, what should self-evidently be a time of joy and celebration, the Hebrew slaves under Pharaoh struggles with their newly acquired freedom and deliverance from bondage. It might be easy to ridicule the people for not celebrating their freedom in the wilderness, but what cannot be overlooked, is the genuine fear of the unknown. This might be precisely why in the wilderness there is an evident longing for Pharaoh's world once more. It is certainly both incorrect and invalid to conclude that given the choice between freedom and slavery, the decision is for the latter. It is a false binary. Fear of the unknown is palpable, but it is not quantifiable. The people will need assurance, but this will be indelibly connected to the unwavering quality of trust. What the exodus event alerts us to is the inherent challenge that sometimes comes with freedom, particularly freedom that comes without a neatly crafted and outlined future. The future for the liberated and freed in the case of the ancient Israelites and in many respects for today's freed and liberated is one that will have to be shaped with the cornerstone of justice and neighborliness.

Majdanek

Sometimes it is the case that we simply do not want to face the reality of the other's pain, or even the memory of what caused such pain, or for some, even the acknowledgment of our own complicity. In theory, we might even espouse the centrality of neighborly love in all of this and the essential importance of not turning away; yet we often walk on the other side of the road or close our eyes, or purse our lips, attempt to disappear, and refrain from using our voice. But finally, those voices must be heard even though there are times when we choose to escape from them. We want to run far away, and not have to hear voices from the past or have glimpses of their stories, but we finally cannot run.

I really do not have the words to describe what it feels like, let alone what it *means* to step into a Holocaust concentration camp. I could perhaps be clinical in the description and speak about the physical appearance; the history, the buildings, the scent, etc., all of which might have some importance, but finally this all feels like a curtain behind which I am hiding. Yet, I cannot, as it bears down deep within the heart, and at the moment it seems that finally no words can adequately express the experience. Yet, one must find the vocabulary, as limiting as words sometimes are to capture that which far transcends the imagination. So, it is the case that as difficult as it might be to reflect on the experience, it must be done not only because it might be cathartic for oneself, but also for others.

On this particular journey, I had already gone to Auschwitz and Treblinka and Birkenau before I came to Majdanek. Each place bore a staggering testimony of the horror and evil that was perpetuated by the Nazis. The multitude of documentaries and books and even personal testimonies only begin to chronicle a narrative that can never be fully crafted, let alone envelop the magnitude of what occurred. While the shock of Auschwitz, Treblinka, and Birkenau erased all illusions that I had about being prepared, there was something in particular at Majdanek that struck such a difficult and painful chord that was impossible for me to fathom. There was silence and disbelief and horror. The camp itself was in sharp contrast to Auschwitz. While Auschwitz stood sturdy almost in readiness, built to last, Majdanek was battered and barren. The walls were flimsy and some of the buildings had walls that were so thin that for a while they seem transparent. The intense heat of the particular day was a mere hint of the devastation of the heat in the Nazi Summers and the brutality of the cold of the Nazi Winters. But then my imagination inevitably fell short of what the reality was. It was on entering one of the buildings that is now a memorial museum to the children where the children's voices relentless in their piercing cries emanated from the ground. These were voices that were surrounded by the memories of lives violently cut short, and in that a new and indescribably painful reality set in. Initially, I could not complete the visit and I stepped outside. Vivek Murthy in his thoughtful and medical, yet humane way reminds us of the importance of pausing to ensure that the heart is strong.

> Moments of pause are especially powerful when combined with gratitude and feelings of love . . . If we ever forget the power of pausing, we need only remember the lesson of our heart. The heart operates in two phases: systole where it pumps blood to the vital organs and diastole where it relaxes. Most people believe that systole is where the action is, and the more time in systole, the better. But diastole—the relaxation phase— is where the coronary blood vessels fill and supply life sustaining oxygen to the heart muscle itself. Pausing, it turns out is what sustaining the heart.[36]

There were the enclosures with tiny shoes, and hair and dresses and various items associated with children, and their innocence. But it was the sound that rose from beneath that simply pierced me and I walked back outside and sat in the heat of the day, knowing that it could not possibly end there. I could not run away, and so I returned and listened to the voices. I was again reminded that these painful voices must be heard.

36. Murthy, *Together*, 207.

Like the blood of Abel, so also the very ground will shout so as never to forget. For a while we may wish to run and seek to disappear but finally, the voices must be heard. As in the Cain and Abel episode, if God does not ignore, then neither can we.

4

Invitation to Choose and Resoul

"Since both the creator and the created are morally responsible for their behavior, the relationship between them is based on the consequences of choices." —Levine, 171

"I swore never to be silent whenever and wherever human beings endure suffering and humiliation. We must take sides. Neutrality helps the oppressor, never the victim. Silence encourages the tormentor, never the tormented." —Elie Wiesel

Choice is a gift and we have inherited that gift. We are given a choice to choose life and a choice of loyalty and belonging, in having or not having a relationship with God. Having a choice, is an act of grace and the biblical text is replete with examples of choice.

The language of choice and the manner in which it has been used and misused, and frequently misconstrued, is pervasive in everyday life. With few exceptions, we would all like to have the freedom to choose and not have decisions imposed on us, particularly those decisions that have a notable personal quality to them. Recently, I was having a conversation with a Holocaust survivor, and she related some of her experiences to me and my students. One of the statements that she made unequivocally was that she would not never forgive the Nazis for what they did.

She said that she inherited this quality from her mother who found it impossible to forgive them as well. So, what if one felt strongly about the importance, even the essential importance of forgiveness as a non-negotiable quality for oneself? Would one then impose this on the person who survived the Holocaust and who finds it impossible to forgive? *Choice* has taken on a remarkable politicized and very divisive quality in the American society and if one were to say that one is for choice or specifically, pro-choice, to use the more coded term, it immediately brackets one into a particular binary category. Particularly surrounding the issue of abortion, it is assumed that one is either *pro-life* or *pro-choice*. It is by any measure a false binary. Indeed,

I would argue that one might be both simultaneously, and one is able to hold such apparent contrarian positions with a discernment that is often missing in the contentious debate between pro-choice and pro-life. We do have a choice and indeed if we did not, we would be caught someplace between fatalism and being puppets. Given that most of the arguments by those who classify themselves as *pro-life* are generated from the perspective that their position is grounded in the biblical tenets, it would be helpful to explore the manner in which four biblical texts attend to this theme.

Choose Life (Deuteronomy 30:15–20)

First, arguably the most cited and well-known text with regard to choice is: "Choose life, so that you and your descendants may live" (Deut 30:19b). As is so often the case, texts are taken out of context simply to underline and strengthen a particular ideology. This is, of course, not uncommon for a variety of issues, regardless of where on the ideological spectrum one finds oneself. Not infrequently, the issue that is being argued, either for or against, often has little, if anything to do with the text and its context. So, according to Deut 30:19 should one choose life? The answer is unequivocally *yes*. But then one must ask, what is the text speaking about and how might that theme relate to the one for which it is currently applied. So, what is the broader context?

> See, I have set before you today *life* and *prosperity*, *death* and *adversity*. If you obey the commandments of the LORD your God that I am commanding you today, by loving the LORD your God, walking in his ways, and observing his commandments, decrees, and ordinances, then you shall live and become numerous, and the LORD your God will bless you in the land that you are entering to possess. But if your heart turns away and you do not hear, but are led astray to bow down to other gods and serve them, I declare to you today that you shall perish; you shall not live long in the land that you are crossing the Jordan to enter and possess. I call heaven and earth to witness against you today that I have set before you life and death, blessings and curses. Choose life so that you and your descendants may live, loving the LORD your God, obeying him, and holding fast to him; for that means life to you and length of days, so that you may live in the land that the LORD swore to give to your ancestors, to Abraham, to Isaac, and to Jacob.[1]

---

1. Deut 30:15–20, my italics.

In this section of Deuteronomy 30, the third part of a speech by Moses to the people, the people are told that they must choose. Indeed, choice is embedded as an important aspect of the freedom that Israel has. The choice is framed by the recognized brackets of "if . . . then" and the choice of life has to do with keeping Torah, and in so doing, the people and their descendants will be able to live in the land. It comes down to *obedience*, and life will thus continue in the land. The issue to be attentive to is obedience to what. What are the essential qualities that the people must attend to? In general, choosing has to do with loving God and neighbor. In this text, there are certain specifics that are outlined. Indeed, this is a matter of life and death. Life is to have a place of belonging in the land; death is to be in exile or to be in a state of landlessness. This is the central framework. Choosing does not mean that everyone must do *likewise*; some may choose to be, or do *otherwise*, and in so doing there will be consequences as well. Choosing does not mean that everyone must follow suit; but choice has to be made, and indeed it is divinely given to Moses and from Moses to the people. There is one additional matter in this regard.

First, the people are told to *obey*, the Hebrew in Deut 30:15 is translated *obey* but literally means *listen*. Herein lies one of the core messages for contemporary society. *Listen*. Without listening and hearing to what is being said and to the voice of those who must be heard, and the message that is spoken, then it is ultimately difficult to obey. But there is also the related issue of those who are compelled to speak either because they have a particular ideology, that is being promoted or peddled, or more simply because they do not wish to listen. It is instructive that depending on the context, the Hebrew *shema* may be translated, *listen*, *understand*, *obey*. There is something of an organic relationship among these terms.

Second, the phrase "life and prosperity, death and adversity" (v.15) certainly posits *life* versus *death* and the contrast is straightforward. The second pair of words, *prosperity* versus *adversity* can better be understood by exploring the Hebrew terms typically translated "prosperity" and "adversity," namely *ṭôb* and *rāʿ* respectively. We might more accurately and fittingly translate this mandate as choose between *life* and *goodness* versus *death* and *evil*. These are the fundamental choices. There is a quality of action associated with these terms. They are not static and at the base is the invitation to choose. This is not a mere suggestion but a mandate; we cannot simply repeat platitudes and ideologies, but actively choose. In so doing we will determine the landscape for now and the future. "The either-or of Deuteronomy is, of course, cast as a religious issue of true God or false gods. Attention to the text, however, makes clear that *religious claims* are deeply intertwined with *socioeconomic issues* so that the decision of life and death . . . is a decision that concerns money and possessions."[2]

The choice of life in Deut 30:15 brackets the opening promise in Deut 1:8. The life that is given is that of the land, and all that it entails. But it is a gift, and the qualities that are spelled out must be embraced.

> The land given must be a land taken: the life offered must be a life lived out . . . It has to do with the manner of Israel's worship, purity of life, justice and fairness toward the weak and the poor and the slave, honor of parents, respect of neighbors, administration of justice, leadership of the people, treatment of the natural order, the practice of war, the treatment of women.[3]

We are also reminded of Josh 24:14–24 where the freedom of choice is also given to the people. The hope here is that the people will choose YHWH the God of Israel; Joshua makes clear that he and his household have chosen, *but the people must choose for themselves.* There is such a temptation here to insist that if I have chosen in a particular way, determining what is right for me, then surely it has to be right for all others. That is to say *my* particular must become the universal. The biblical text belies such a position and makes such an interpretation untenable.

Choosing God or god

[20] So Ahab sent to all the Israelites, and assembled the prophets at Mount Carmel. [21] Elijah then came near to all the people, and said, "How long will you go limping with two different opinions? If the LORD is God, follow him; but if Baal, then follow him." The people did not answer him a word. [22] Then Elijah said to the people, "I, even I only, am left a prophet of the LORD; but Baal's prophets number four hundred fifty. [23] Let two bulls be given to us; let them choose one bull for themselves, cut it in pieces, and lay it on the wood, but put no fire to it; I will prepare the other bull and lay it on the wood, but put no fire to it. [24] Then you call on the name of your god and I will call on the name of the LORD; the god who answers by fire is indeed God." All the people answered, "Well spoken!" [25] Then Elijah said to the prophets of Baal, "Choose for yourselves one bull and prepare it first, for you are many; then call on the name of your god, but put no fire to it." [26] So they took the bull that was

---

2. Brueggemann, *Money*, 37.
3. Miller, *Deuteronomy*, 214.

given them, prepared it, and called on the name of Baal from morning until noon, crying, "O Baal, answer us!" But there was no voice, and no answer. They limped about the altar that they had made. ²⁷ At noon Elijah mocked them, saying, "Cry aloud! Surely he is a god; either he is meditating, or he has wandered away, or he is on a journey, or perhaps he is asleep and must be awakened." ²⁸ Then they cried aloud and, as was their custom, they cut themselves with swords and lances until the blood gushed out over them. ²⁹ As midday passed, they raved on until the time of the offering of the oblation, but there was no voice, no answer, and no response.

³⁰ Then Elijah said to all the people, "Come closer to me"; and all the people came closer to him. First he repaired the altar of the LORD that had been thrown down; ³¹ Elijah took twelve stones, according to the number of the tribes of the sons of Jacob, to whom the word of the LORD came, saying, "Israel shall be your name"; ³² with the stones he built an altar in the name of the LORD. Then he made a trench around the altar, large enough to contain two measures of seed. ³³ Next he put the wood in order, cut the bull in pieces, and laid it on the wood. He said, "Fill four jars with water and pour it on the burnt offering and on the wood." ³⁴ Then he said, "Do it a second time"; and they did it a second time. Again he said, "Do it a third time"; and they did it a third time, ³⁵ so that the water ran all around the altar, and filled the trench also with water. ³⁶ At the time of the offering of the oblation, the prophet Elijah came near and said, "O LORD, God of Abraham, Isaac, and Israel, let it be known this day that you are God in Israel, that I am your servant, and that I have done all these things at your bidding. ³⁷ Answer me, O LORD, answer me, so that this people may know that you, O LORD, are God, and that you have turned their hearts back." ³⁸ Then the fire of the LORD fell and consumed the burnt offering, the wood, the stones, and the dust, and even licked up the water that was in the trench. ³⁹ When all the people saw it, they fell on their faces and said, "The LORD indeed is God; the LORD indeed is God." ⁴⁰ Elijah said to them, "Seize the prophets of Baal; do not let one of them escape." Then they seized them; and Elijah brought them down to the Wadi Kishon, and killed them there.[4]

The prophet Elijah could not be any clearer with regard to choosing, when he says, "How long will you go limping with two different opinions?" The people who may seek to have it both ways, cannot do so, and it is the

4. 1 Kgs 18:20–40.

nature of choice that one must decide. Maybe it is the case that most of life constitutes gray areas, but there are defining moments when one must choose, and in those moments, the decision is not made for the people, but the people are given a scenario, and are invited to show evidence and make a choice. One of the components in this narrative is that there is a public display, with identical options in which to invoke the respective gods, and to display the power and presence of each. As we have discovered, there are troubling and violent consequences if one's god fails, and as devastating as the consequences might be, and indeed Elijah's actions are, nonetheless, the people are given an option to choose. The point is that the people are given a choice, and either way their choice will have consequences, both for life and death. Wallis notes, "The Biblical prophets were sometimes angry. And that prophetic anger is called for now in relationship to the divisive racial rhetoric from the President . . . The president of a country of immigrants infamously banned Muslim refugees and travelers because he claimed our country couldn't be sure they weren't terrorists."[5] Yet as recently as September 17, 2020, FBI Director Christopher Wray testifying before the United States Congress noted that, "within the domestic terrorism bucket, the category as a whole, racially motivated violent extremism is I think the biggest bucket . . . and within that racially motivated violent extremist bucket, people subscribing to some kind of white supremacist-type ideology is certainly the biggest chunk of that."

> Donald Trump has proved his identification with white nationalism from his demonizing of immigrants to making his anti immigrant lies the central message of his midterm election strategy, to deciding to make symbolic wall the heart of is vision and legacy, to his anti-Muslim ban, to his expressed hostility and falsehoods towards [Islam].[6]

With the completion of the 2020 presidential election, where Donald Trump lost by a wide margin, Mr. Trump's rhetoric has intensified and the list of enemies, including former loyal supporters has expanded. He has consistently scapegoated others not only for his countless failures, but also because such demonizing appeals to, and poisons the group of his unflinching supporters. "I believe the faustian bargain for power undertaken by the white evangelical religious right must be exposed and opposed on the basis of Donald Trump's support for white nationalism, which is in direct disobedience to the reconciling Gospel and person of Jesus Christ."[7]

5. Wallis, *Christ in Crisis*, 52–53.

6. Wallis, *Christ in Crisis*, 79.

7. Wallis, *Christ in Crisis*, 85.

In a most devastatingly vile way, the President and those of his supporters who are guided by his violent rhetoric, including those in position of power who either choose to remain quiet or by actively advocating the rhetoric of divisiveness have led to consequences that are calamitous.

This has been evidenced in the most profound way on January 6, 2021, where violent mobs stormed the US Capitol and sought to overturn the election and execute leaders.

Finding Oneself and Coming Home

One of the most well-known biblical texts and among those most cited when speaking about grace and belonging; love and forgiveness in the Bible, is the Parable of the Prodigal Son (Luke 15). Surely this is a title that stands as a sharp reminder that titles, names, and monikers all have the potential to shape the manner in which we read, hear and extrapolate from a narrative. Thus, the word *prodigal* which singularly has come to describe the younger son, is cast within a title that only relates the younger son to the father, with an overtone of self-indulgence. The title makes no reference to the older brother.

> 11 Then Jesus said, 'There was a man who had two sons. 12The younger of them said to his father, "Father, give me the share of the property that will belong to me." So he divided his property between them. 13A few days later the younger son gathered all he had and travelled to a distant country, and there he squandered his property in dissolute living. 14When he had spent everything, a severe famine took place throughout that country, and he began to be in need. 15So he went and hired himself out to one of the citizens of that country, who sent him to his fields to feed the pigs. 16He would gladly have filled himself with the pods that the pigs were eating; and no one gave him anything. 17But when he came to himself he said, "How many of my father's hired hands have bread enough and to spare, but here I am dying of hunger! 18I will get up and go to my father, and I will say to him, 'Father, I have sinned against heaven and before you; 19I am no longer worthy to be called your son; treat me like one of your hired hands.'" 20So he set off and went to his father. But while he was still far off, his father saw him and was filled with compassion; he ran and put his arms around him and kissed him. 21Then the son said to him, "Father, I have sinned against heaven and before you; I am no longer worthy to be called your son." 22But the father said to his slaves, "Quickly,

bring out a robe—the best one—and put it on him; put a ring on his finger and sandals on his feet. [23]And get the fatted calf and kill it, and let us eat and celebrate; [24]for this son of mine was dead and is alive again; he was lost and is found!" And they began to celebrate. [25] 'Now his elder son was in the field; and when he came and approached the house, he heard music and dancing. [26]He called one of the slaves and asked what was going on. [27]He replied, "Your brother has come, and your father has killed the fatted calf, because he has got him back safe and sound." [28]Then he became angry and refused to go in. His father came out and began to plead with him. [29]But he answered his father, "Listen! For all these years I have been working like a slave for you, and I have never disobeyed your command; yet you have never given me even a young goat so that I might celebrate with my friends. [30]But when this son of yours came back, who has devoured your property with prostitutes, you killed the fatted calf for him!" [31]Then the father said to him, "Son, you are always with me, and all that is mine is yours. [32]But we had to celebrate and rejoice, because this brother of yours was dead and has come to life; he was lost and has been found.[8]

This way of identifying the parable, namely the *Prodigal Son* has more to do with the Church and those who have determined the particular ideological trajectory of the parable, than the essence, of the text itself. This title is first found in 16th century English translations of the Bible.

The title likely came from the Vulgate—*de filio prodigo.* The German translation and title of this parable is *Der Verlersone Sohn*—the lost (forlorn) son, which is a preferable reflection of the parable, but still emphasizes only one element. As is so often the case with other titles and names, this one has come to be viewed as the standard, and the almost singular point of departure for the interpretive trajectory of the parable. One of the challenges for readers and hearers of this parable is to avoid the temptation of reading this parable in a binary way. In reading it in a binary way the younger son will inevitably be the *bad son* one who abandoned his father and squandered his inheritance, and the older son, the one who stayed home to help his father will be viewed as the *good son*. Once this designation is established, it is very difficult to undo, and despite the quest to ensure that one is not shaped by such tenuous distinctions, it becomes the defining direction of the parable. But there is most assuredly more to the story than simply pointing to the younger son as the *bad son*. And we are

8. Luke 15:11–32.

reminded that there are multiple layers of choice by all of the characters, father and sons. Everyone in this parable makes a choice.

Two examples will suffice in illustrating how we inherit these items, and the impact they have had on us. In English Bibles we have books such as Exodus and Numbers. In the Hebrew, we have *shemot* (*names*) *bemidbar* (*in the wilderness*) as opposed to Exodus and Numbers. Exodus from— *ex odos, from the road* or perhaps *out of the journey*; this is not necessarily a bad thing, it is simply that the entire meaning and emphasis on the text changes when the name *Exodus* is used. In the current vernacular exodus rarely carries a positive meaning, let alone an analogous narrative to the historic journey out of Egypt. And how does one compare a title such as *In the Wilderness* with imagination of all that might be captured in the idea of wilderness, and the layers of meaning in the narrative regarding journey.

As is the case with countless other instances, the title has been repeated so often that we do not reflect on its significance anymore; it is the standard that is universally embraced. The root of the word *prodigal* from the Latin *prodigere* has generated words such as prodigy and prodigious.

The word means extravagance—perhaps wastefully so. There is nothing inherently negative about this word, though it is typically used in this way. In fact, if we are able to dislocate its association from the Parable of the Prodigal Son, it will take on an entirely different and positive tone. There are a number of themes that we can identify in this parable.

Freedom and Responsibility

Estrangement

Longing and Return

Grace

Anguish

Reconciliation[9]

These are ever present themes, and one may explore any of these for universal implications. There is a central theme of divine forgiveness and unconditional love, including notably the distinct theme of *choice*. Before we arrive at the meaning of prodigal, there are choices that are made in the context of that which is lost. The quest for meaning and the prospects of loss, together with the perception of rejection are all interconnected. Regardless of the choice, there is both risk and vulnerability here. In this regard, it is the extravagant love of the father that is the focus. This is the theme, with a series

9. G. V. Jones *The Art*, 174.

of sub-themes. We are reminded that the parable begins: "There was a *man* who had two *sons.*" In order for the *one* to really matter, there has to be some cost, some risk, or it becomes cheap. Thus, one might say that the emphasis, while clearly on the loss, involves an element of risk.

The younger son has arrived at the age where he demands his inheritance. The father divided the estate *between* them, and we could be caught up in the clinical and technical aspects of the division, percentage, and the nature of biblical inheritance, etc., but it is the existential realities that are principal here; it is with these that we identify. It is often assumed that the father's property had been divided equally, but this too is absent from the text. For those of us who want to elevate "fairness" or to a privileged position in this parable, there is disappointment. The reality is that *grace* displaces *fairness* here—and we are left to struggle with the issue. As we listen to this parable carefully, it becomes apparent that there are certain conclusions to be drawn. Thus, in a way the issue is not to *explain* the parable but explore aspects that aid in our own understanding. There is no seeking out the younger son, he is gone, to a fate worse than death—he is lost—it is about a broken relationship, a displacement, an unknown, all by *choice.* And in the wake of *his* choice, there is loss and rejection. But in making the choice by the younger son to leave his father's house, there is no pursuit by the father. Simply because the younger son is not *successful* in his venture does not mean he should not have the freedom to choose. Life continues for the father and the older son, but, for the younger son, generated by a lifestyle that was prodigious in its own way, life drifted into the abyss. He drifted to the lowest point. There is, I believe, a dramatic transformative moment in this narrative. After the younger son reaches the lowest ebb in his life, the text proclaims that *he came to himself.* Choice allows us sometimes to have such a clarifying and defining moment. *He came to himself!* But this is not a matter of coming to himself in some kind of abstract way; this is not a theoretical issue. He *comes to himself* in a renewed vision of belonging, as the *son* of his *father.* This is his identity. Even though his father's love never left, never wavered he discovers this not in the context of being surrounded by love, but while in the depth of despair. Perhaps it is the case that the younger son needed to understand what it means to be human in relationship. In being bound in love, one is free to choose. He sets out by being human as defined by a kind of economy of material possessions.

The younger son leaves his father's *household* for the *household* of prodigious spending and pleasure. It is the economy of satisfying oneself with *stuff* that is construed as acute independence. But building one's life on the materials of the world invariably collapses. But that too is an element of choice. There is something tempting about creating a life based on the

economy of possessions and for a while might appear to be the life of ultimate choice. The alternative to such a gravitational temptation is an economy
of communion. The reality is that *economy of communion*, that is, the *household of communion* does not accidentally happen. For one to belong to such
a communion it necessarily means that one has intentionally embraces this
kind of belonging, and then importantly lives out the ideals.

When the younger son returns home, who runs to whom? Is there
hesitancy on the part of the son? In all likelihood, it is the father who runs,
and this invites imagination. The son comes to himself, and it is the father
who runs, embraces, kisses, welcomes him home. There is homecoming and
here the ideal is the invitation to *take heart* for in homecoming there is a
sense of redemption and restoration.

The older brother is still outside, physically and figuratively, for he
has not *come to himself* and in the context of the narrative, he never does.
But there is yet another issue with the older brother. There is no textual
evidence of fraternal love in this household. The older brother seems distinctly disinterested, and nothing is mentioned about the younger brother
in terms of his feelings for his brother. But we do know this much. The older
brother seeks to control the spectrum of paternal grace, and by choice he
remains at home. Yet, ironically, he discovers that in fact he is not at home
in his attempt to control grace. To the degree that the party and celebration
are expressions of grace and forgiveness, this then further creates angst
for him. *His* idea of choice is rooted in *his* idea of loyalty and hierarchy
of importance and entitlement. *His* sense of his brother's choice is that of
betrayal. The older brother is forced to come to grips with an understanding of belonging. Speaking angrily to his father, he says, "*This son of yours.*"
(v. 30) He certainly identifies one aspect of the equation correctly when he
says *that son of yours*, but he is missing another part of the equation. The father reminds him in his response: "that brother of yours." The fact that the
older brother uses the language of *this son of yours* does not nullify the fraternal relationship. They are inextricably linked one to the other. The son of
the father is also the brother; the lives of each are intertwined. The father's
response to the older brother is replete with heartbreaking poignancy. The
Greek term used here is τέκνον "my child." There are no recriminations; no
punishment for the older son's outburst, simply, "my child," you are always
with me! One might suggest that the father would gently tell his son to
take heart. That is to say then, either by circumstance or coercion, being
isolated undermines the very core of what it means to be human. "Without
dialogue, one's suffering is intolerable . . . We are especially susceptible to

borrowed shame when a person with whom we closely identify and care about harbors painful self-punitive shame."[10]

As is the case in everyday life, there is no immediate and *live happily ever* ending to this story. Words of familial significance are spoken and now the older son must choose. An overlooked aspect of this Parable is clearly the idea that the father's love is not constrained or conditional. Moreover, it is not enough as the older son is suggesting that he has kept all the commands; it is about the love of the repentant and forgiven one; it is about the love of the other. Keeping all of the commandments, void of love and empathy may harden one into a state of self-righteousness, where virtue is defined by the rigidity of keeping commandments. A foundational conclusion in this parable is that one cannot come home again unless one has found oneself. One cannot love the other as the father loves until one has found oneself. When this parable ends, we know what the love of the father is, it is unequivocal; it is unconditional. This is choice, perhaps born out of an inherent paternal love, but choice, nonetheless. The older brother did not *earn* his father's love by obeying commands. It was there; it is there; it will be there. We are left at the end to wonder. What will be the response of the older brother?

Shakespeare's *King Lear* suggested a reversal of the allegory: The youngest daughter is the *good daughter* rather than a *prodigal daughter*. She is exiled with no inheritance while the prodigal son leaves home with an inheritance and the good wishes of his father. When Cordelia returns, it is not because she has squandered her life, but rather she returns to save her father. Is it possible that like Cordelia, the younger son might be considered the *good son* for entirely different reasons from what tradition has dictated? Of course, we know that *prodigal*, which has so shaped the manner in which we read the text, is a designation that came centuries later than the original text. The *prodigal son* returns to save himself; he returns home to live with his father. Cordelia makes it home to die in her father's arms. Though, as it is, the prodigal son's *salvation* was not on his own accord but rather through his father's grace.

In Simon Wiesenthal's remarkable book, *The Sunflower*, where the existential issue of collective forgiveness dominates the narrative, protagonist Simon has to finally make a determination, a choice, as to whether he will tell the truth to the mother of Karl, the Nazi who is dying. He has to decide whether she should be told the true nature and actions of her son. He had promised to deliver the bundle of Karl's belongings to his mother; but in that moment, he must decide whether telling her the

10. Goldberg, "Concerning Madness," 18–19.

truth is a noble and virtuous act, or one of selfishness. The decision is not straightforwardly one or the other.

> I gazed at the lonely woman sitting sadly with her memories. I formed a picture of how she lived. I knew that from time to time she would take in her arms her son's bundle, his last present, as if it were her son himself.
> "I can well believe what people said—so many dreadful things happened. But one thing is certain, Karl never did any wrong. He was always a decent young man. I miss him so much now that my husband is dead . . ." I thought of the mothers who were also bereft of their sons. But her son had not lied to me; his home was just as he had described it. Yet the solution to my problem was not a single step nearer . . .
> I took my leave without diminishing in any way the poor woman's last surviving consolation—faith in the goodness of her son. Perhaps it was a mistake not to have told her the truth. Perhaps her tears might help to wash away some of the misery of the world.[11]

In that moment, Simon did an extraordinary thing, by being silent, when every measure of his experience might have suggested otherwise. Importantly, he does not dictate that his decision not to tell Karl's mother should be universal. We all live in East of Eden. We do have many choices in our lives and among those we can make choices for good. Perhaps Simon has still wondered, but in a defining moment, he chose a redemptive act, by withholding the truth that might have led to further grief and despair. Perhaps for a while, he ended the cycle of pain and grief.

Chaim Potok, in his deeply affective novel *The Chosen* has a father in conversation about his son Daniel with his son's friend Reuben. This might very well be about any son or daughter; any young man or young woman. It is about us! It is about you and me. This is what he said:

> Reuven, the Master of the Universe blessed me with a brilliant son. And he cursed me with all the problems of raising him. Ah, what it is to have a brilliant son! No, not a smart son, Reuven, but a brilliant son, a Daniel, a boy with a mind like a Jewel. Ah, what a curse it is, what an anguish it is to have a Daniel, whose mind is like a pearl, like a sun.
> Reuven when my Daniel was four years old, I saw him reading a story from a book. And I was frightened. He did not read the story, he swallowed it, as one swallows food or water.

11. Wiesenthal, *The Sunflower*, 94.

There was no soul in my four year old Daniel, there was only his mind. He was a mind in a body without a soul. It was a story in a Yiddish book about a poor Jew and his struggles to get to *eretz Israel* before he died. Ah, how the man suffered! And my Daniel enjoyed that story, he enjoyed the last terrible page, because when he finished it he realized for the first time what a memory he had. He looked at me proudly and told me the story from memory, and I cried inside my heart.

I went away and I cried to the master of the Universe, 'what have you done to me? A mind like this I need for a son?

A heart I need for a son, a soul I need for a son, compassion I want for my son, righteousness, mercy, strength to suffer and carry pain—that I want for my son, not a mind without a soul!'[12]

We do have choices in this world, perhaps not always easy and straightforward such as when powers may silence us in order to take away our freedom to choose. But we must choose, and the road we take, and the path we travel will make all the difference. To remain locked in the enclosure of our minds is to choose. To remain chained to walls that imprisoned us and live with the ultimacy of shadows is to choose as well (Plato, "Allegory of the Cave").

12. Potok, *The Chosen*, 276–77.

5

Sparing Cain and
The Destiny of Humankind[1]

The fiat of the Almighty, 'let there be light' has not spent its force.
No abuse, no outrage whether in taste, sport or avarice can now
hide itself from the all-pervading light. —Frederick Douglass,
July 4th, speech, Rochester, NY

The death penalty raises . . . ironies and inconsistencies to an
intolerable level, and not only because unavoidably it is resorted
to so unfairly and ambivalently. In moral logic, too, it fails,
for in the sameness, singleness, and finality of death, degrees
and kinds of wrong are erased. A person who in a rage kills a
faithless lover or a panicked, cornered robber who shoots a cop
receives the same punishment as the methodically sadistic serial
murder of score of victims. Deadly revenge is always too much
or too little. —Mendelson, 198

Now the man knew his wife Eve, and she conceived and bore
Cain, saying, "I have produced a man with the help of the LORD."
[2] Next she bore his brother Abel. Now Abel was a keeper of
sheep, and Cain a tiller of the ground. [3] In the course of time
Cain brought to the LORD an offering of the fruit of the ground,
[4] and Abel for his part brought of the firstlings of his flock, their
fat portions. And the LORD had regard for Abel and his offering,
[5] but for Cain and his offering he had no regard. So Cain was
very angry, and his countenance fell. [6] The LORD said to Cain,
"Why are you angry, and why has your countenance fallen? [7]
If you do well, will you not be accepted? And if you do not do
well, sin is lurking at the door; its desire is for you, but you must
master it." [8] Cain said to his brother Abel, "Let us go out to the
field." And when they were in the field, Cain rose up against

---

1. An earlier version of this section was published in *T&T Clark Handbook of Asian
American Biblical Hermeneutics*, edited by Uriah Kim and Seung Ai Yang (London:
T. & T. Clark) 211–19.

his brother Abel, and killed him. [9] Then the LORD said to Cain, "Where is your brother Abel?" He said, "I do not know; am I my brother's keeper?" [10] And the LORD said, "What have you done? Listen; your brother's blood is crying out to me from the ground! [11] And now you are cursed from the ground, which has opened its mouth to receive your brother's blood from your hand. [12] When you till the ground, it will no longer yield to you its strength; you will be a fugitive and a wanderer on the earth." [13] Cain said to the LORD, "My punishment is greater than I can bear! [14] Today you have driven me away from the soil, and I shall be hidden from your face; I shall be a fugitive and a wanderer on the earth, and anyone who meets me may kill me." [15] Then the LORD said to him, "Not so! Whoever kills Cain will suffer a sevenfold vengeance." And the LORD put a mark on Cain, so that no one who came upon him would kill him. [16] Then Cain went away from the presence of the LORD, and settled in the land of Nod, east of Eden. —Gen 4:1–6

A theme in a preliminary way that has for the most part remained unexplored, is one which does not particularly depend on taking vast interpretive leaps. Rather, it follows the trajectory of the text, and the manner in which it intersects with social, cultural and religious elements of society. There is an inherent invitation for interpreters to resist the temptation to settle for simple answers, and yield to the pressure of abiding by the established traditions that uphold long standing ideas that do not yield much that challenge the status quo. The point here is not to provide trajectories that are ultimate and which as a result cannot either be expanded or changed. Rather, in this case as with all others, the ideas are penultimate and as difficult as this might be for some to accept, it is arguably a foundational reality in all interpretation. We know that biblical texts have been interpreted and reinterpreted and have variously led to different conclusions (see Isa 2:1–4; Joel 2:1–5; Exodus; and Deuteronomy, inter alia). Below is a select example:

[2] In days to come

the mountain of the LORD's house

shall be established as the highest of the mountains,

and shall be raised above the hills;

all the nations shall stream to it.

[3] Many peoples shall come and say,

"Come, let us go up to the mountain of the LORD,

to the house of the God of Jacob;
    that he may teach us his ways
        and that we may walk in his paths."
For out of Zion shall go forth instruction,
        and the word of the LORD from Jerusalem.
[4] He shall judge between the nations,
        and shall arbitrate for many peoples;
they shall beat their swords into plowshares,
        and their spears into pruning hooks;
nation shall not lift up sword against nation,
        neither shall they learn war any more.[2]

Blow the trumpet in Zion;
    sound the alarm on my holy mountain!
Let all the inhabitants of the land tremble,
    for the day of the LORD is coming, it is near—
[2] a day of darkness and gloom,
    a day of clouds and thick darkness!
Like blackness spread upon the mountains
    a great and powerful army comes;
their like has never been from of old,
    nor will be again after them in ages to come.
[3] Fire devours in front of them,
    and behind them a flame burns.
Before them the land is like the garden of Eden,
    but after them a desolate wilderness,
    and nothing escapes them.
[4] They have the appearance of horses,
    and like war-horses they charge.
[5] As with the rumbling of chariots,
    they leap on the tops of the mountains,
like the crackling of a flame of fire
    devouring the stubble,
like a powerful army
    drawn up for battle.[3]

2. Isa 2:1–4.
3. Joel 2:1–5.

As Shulman has argued, "Insisting on openness to the manifold aspects of the Cain story is an act of fidelity not only to a text but also through that text to the city's message that openness and multiplicity are essential human values."[4] How does one begin to understand freedom in a foreign land? In the case of Cain, can one discover newness and new beginnings in exile when God is the one who placed the person there? Can one restore goodness in a radical way while living on, or beyond the margins of society? It is the case that more questions will be raised, ones that may linger for a while, but ones that should be asked and pursued. Cain makes a choice. Further, he is given choices by God, and what Cain does with such choices and the consequences of his choices will define his life and destiny. This is not a narrative that seeks to make universal moralizing axioms despite the fact that it is frequently used in this manner. As is so often the case, tradition has far superseded the text to the point where the text has gradually become secondary, and tradition is relied upon as the principal source for meaning and application. There are a multitude of pertinent questions that are generated from this narrative that I believe should, at the very least, be asked and pursued. So, for example: What do you think our destiny is? What or who will finally define our destiny? Are there limitations to forgiveness, human and divine? Is there always the possibility of redemption? What might this text tell us about being human or being God? What might it tell us about the death penalty as a punishment for the most heinous crimes? And specifically with regard to this text what might the parents be thinking at the loss of both of their sons? Are they aware of what happened? How might one answer the questions, "have you seen my son?" Which son? Whence does violence originate? Why might Cain think that the only option at his disposal is violence of the capital order? Why does God reject Cain's offering and not have a conversation with Cain? Is not the case at least in this instance that God imposes solitary confinement in the form of wandering alone in the East of Eden? The fact is, these are challenging questions, and one of the very things that one *must not do* is to be enticed and succumb to the temptation of discarding or too easily dismissing the questions.

In reading the narrative of Cain and Abel, there is the immediate and perhaps natural inclination to focus on the well-trodden path of the nature of the brothers' sacrifice, and the reason why God refused Cain's sacrifice and accepted Abel's. While these themes will continue to be important as part of the interpretive landscape, many interpreters no doubt will continue to take this narrative and cast it as a morality tale of good and evil; a tale of righteous versus unrighteous; a tale of innocent versus guilty. Yet, the layered quality of this narrative refuses to be collapsed into manageable ideological morality moments. There is much in this narrative that compels the

4. Shulman, "The Myth of Cain," 218.

reader to take seriously the layers and subtexts, and not reduce it to a binary lesson in morality. It is Cain's question, "Am I my brother's keeper" that has lingered in our consciousness, and it is clearly one that must be reckoned with. It is however the implied answer that Cain's question generates, not implied by God's response, that must be pointedly reckoned with. In many respects it is God's answer that we have inherited, and it is this answer that must be explored in all of its complexities.

In the Beginning: Sacrifice and the Advent of Sin

As difficult as it is to acknowledge, there is an arbitrariness to God's decision regarding which sacrifice or offering to accept, and which not to. We are never told in the text whether Cain or Abel knew what constitutes an "acceptable" offering. In the rejection of Cain's offering, given that there is no indication that Cain knew why, one can begin to understand why Cain would take God's action as a personal rejection. We are never told in the text as to the basis for the determination. While there has been any number of scholarly speculations regarding the reasoning behind God's actions, there is no definitive answer. In making the offering, we assume that offerings are a matter of course, but we are never told if *these* particular offerings were the first offerings, nor for that matter are we told if or what the guidelines and stipulations are for any offering. God does speak with Cain and while God questions and encourages, God never explains why his offering is rejected and what Cain must do in the future. With this, one might suggest that the focus is on God, and while Cain cannot directly punish God, by killing Abel he indirectly punishes God. Cain might have killed Abel to take away the joy from God, and thus the removal of the source of God's pleasure. For the sake of God, the first murder is committed.

Moreover, the text does not provide any idea as to the nature of the fraternal relationship, and in the singular moment where Cain speaks to Abel, the text is ambiguous; there is certainly no response by Abel. Textually, there is no evidence of a fraternal relationship, and nothing to suggest either a loving or an adversarial relationship. We know nothing about the character of Abel. The sum total is that he presented an offering to God and it was accepted. There is no indication of divine preference of one type of offering over against the other; rather there is an unfiltered, straightforward acceptance and rejection. As Byron and others have suggested, "the absence of an explanation for the rejection leaves a gap in the narrative that makes it impossible for the reader to learn from Cain's actions."[5] Divine favor does come with a devastating price, and equally devastating consequences that have gone beyond Cain and Abel. "Since the story makes it clear that God favored Abel over Cain, it seems peculiar that God never speaks to Abel. Rather than warn Abel or his parents of the upcoming tragedy, God chooses to speak to Cain in what appears as an effort to prevent him from committing fratricide."[6]

One must wonder if God ever attempted to keep Cain from killing Abel, given the warning. Why not speak directly to Abel? Why not address whatever the issue might have been, including a possible conflict between the brothers? Certainly, we are not privy to what might have transpired, but we do know God had spoken with Cain about sin. The possibility that Cain could conquer sin does not necessarily mean that this is in any way associated with the offering of Cain. God's admonition to Cain is that he has the capacity and the freedom to overcome sin, even as sin is described as lurking, waiting and ready to pounce. Clearly Cain has the freedom of choice and the will to conquer if he so chooses. "Cain's acrimonious speech and brooding thought intensify into furious savagery over time . . . God may be warning Cain of the potential in v. 7 when he cautions that sin lies לפתח at the opening. 'At the door' is the usual translation, but the word literally means 'opening' and is frequently used to refer to opening a mouth."[7]

While the intent here is not allegorize the character of Cain with that of the Donald Trump presidency, the actions of both and the consequences are striking. Reis's statement, "acrimonious speech and brooding thought intensify into furious savagery over time"[8] is an apt description of Donald Trump's character as he has made known, and the actions borne out of such quality. Mendelson has observed in a compelling manner the dangerous slide of those who veil their inner sense of worth with actions that are destructive.

> A nagging sense of inner worthlessness might very well set people off on a Hobbesian 'restless search of power after power" in a vain attempt to overcome it. Their lives are an endless struggle to keep a grip on the things that support their fragile sense of personal value, and they are prone to excruciating envy of those who have more than they and contempt for those who have less.[9]

5. Byron, "Cain's Rejected Offering," 4.

6. Byron, "Cain's Rejected Offering," 14.

7. Reis, "What Cain Said," 112.

8. Reis, "What Cain Said," 112.

9. Mendelson, *The Good Life*, 49.

The separation of infants and children from their parents is as notable an example among many where for the Trump administration was normalized. As Michele Goldberg has noted, "We still talk about American fascism as a looming threat, something could happen if we're not vigilant. But for undocumented immigrant, it is already here."[10] The detention of these children in cages is meant to discourage and dissuade refugees who are seeking shelter. The rhetoric for such abandonment of all noble ideals and morality has reached the pitch of calling on minority congresswomen to go back where they came from, a chant of dislocation that now spreads among the president's supporters.

> We are not so much in a 'culture war' as we are in search for cultural truth. And here's the truth: Trump's whole cultural narrative is based on a hostile lie, or what mimetic theory calls a 'myth' . . . [He] attempts to push this mythical narrative on almost every minority: Muslims, Mexicans, Africa Americans, journalists, immigrants, the transgender community . . . The mythical narrative (i.e. the lie) he espouses is that these minorities pose a significant threat to the American values.[11]

God's warning to Cain of לפתח (at the door) is apropos here for the president. *Sin* is here described as what one does against the other. And such action is frequently as a result of what comes from the mouth, as לפתח. Those in positions of power and who have a voice and who have not only actively but passively kept their silence have become inextricably complicit.

Even though Adam and Eve had disobeyed a divine mandate and suffered the consequence of that disobedience by being exiled from their life in the garden, the idea that they ate of the forbidden fruit is never described as *sin*. It is only in the Cain and Abel story that *sin* makes its biblical debut, and specifically only in relation to Cain. This is noteworthy not only for the distinction of being the first reference to *sin* in the Bible, but what is characterized as *sin* is an act by a human against another human; this is not a direct disobedience of a command by God, as is frequently posited as the fundamental expression of sin. God's affront to Cain's action is predicated on what Cain has done to his brother. What one does to the other, both the good and the evil, matters to God. And therefore, it is significant that it is the human violence against the other that establishes for the first time what is designated *sin* in the Bible.

---

10. Goldberg, *NY Times*, 06/11, 2018.

11. Ericksen, "Truth, Lies," 2017.

What is the proper balance between guarding the interests, rights, and autonomy of the individual on the one hand, and maintaining a strong sense of unity, shared purpose and common destiny on the other? . . . Many American political thinkers have argued that these two values are inherently in competition with one another, pitting social solidarity, equality, shared interest, shared destiny, mutual obligations, and shared values, against individual right, diversity, freedom, 'rugged' individualism and live-and-let-live tolerance . . . We reject that view that more freedom necessarily entails less equality and community.[12]

The poetic encapsulation by Martin Luther King Jr. of this shared destiny is captured thus: "We are caught in an inescapable network of mutuality, tied in a single garment of destiny."[13] The very act of bringing an offering to God, an act of virtue, doing that which is essential, reflecting a return of God's bounty, has become the reason for dissent and fratricide. One must at the very least wonder what role God has played and might have played in the aversion of such violence and divisiveness. "The problem is compounded by Abel's murder. Since Cain's act of fratricide is precipitated by God's unexplained rejection of the sacrifice which resulted in Cain's anger, God becomes complicit in the act."[14]

To what degree then might one argue that the responsibility for Abel's death lies in part with God? Wiesel has suggested, "Cain did not rise up against his brother, but against God, whose ways he found incomprehensible, intolerable. That he killed his brother to erase man's resignation and passivity."[15] Perhaps then in sparing the life of Cain and protecting him from others, might this be an act of divine remorse and regret? Is this divine admission of guilt? Or does God allow the fratricide to occur for something beyond human comprehension?

LaCocque takes the argument even further. He argues that in killing Abel, Cain has in fact killed someone who belongs to God, and so, while it is certainly fratricide, it is in LaCocque's estimation, more accurately deicide.[16] With the killing of Abel, this is the first human death in the biblical text. Prior to this only animals were killed. Is it possible that Cain is unaware of human death at the point of killing Abel? If to that point the killing of animals were for sacrificial purposes, Cain might have sacrificed Abel to show

12. Putnam, *The Upswing,* 339–340.

13. King, "Letter from Birmingham Jail"

14. Byron, "Cain's Rejected Offering," 4.

15. Wiesel, *Messengers of God,* 60.

16. LaCocque, *Onslaught,* 85.

God. Immediately after the first murder, we have genocide. Can one open the door for the other? In the aftermath of the Cain and Abel narrative, this would be a distinct possibility, and perhaps in the least cynical interpretation, an unintended consequence.

Am I My Brother's Keeper?

It is clearly the case that Cain's response to God's question, "where is Abel your brother?" acknowledges that both God and Cain know that that he *is* his brother's keeper. The absence of a divine response is not merely a non-answer to Cain's rhetorical question, but rather a clear expression that there is *no* need. Cain knows! Cain is suggesting that he has *no* responsibility for his brother, and as such he intentionally refuses to acknowledge the truth and essence of God's question.[17] The implication and inference in God's question is distinctly broader in scope than what Cain takes it to be. What Cain has done is not only failure in general as Abel's keeper, but rather he ended his fraternal role violently. *Brother* here, while literal, is broadly construed in the divine question, "where is your *brother, sister, neighbor*?" Moreover, killing here may be understood more broadly as well. Forced separation and loss, where being lost often becomes even more devastating than physical death. Cain's snide retort might in fact reflect Cain's challenge to God as one who has abandoned the responsibility as Cain's *keeper*? How could God, as Cain's ultimately *keeper* be unjust? When Cain finally pleads for protection, God promises to be his *keeper* by marking him. "The collective dimension of this motif in a primeval paradigmatic story is concretized in the cancellation of the law of talion . . . in spite of the fact that Cain's exclamation that he is not his brother's keeper (4:9) shows how the murder of one has broken the community of all."[18]

We function in community and each of us has an indelible relationship with the other; community regardless of geography either locally or globally. With this relationship among brothers and sisters across the globe, comes particular and inherent responsibilities.

> Radical empathy . . . means putting in the work to educate oneself and to listen with a humble heart, to understand another's experience from their perspective, not as we imagine we would feel . . . It is the kindred connection from a deep place of knowing that opens your spirit to the pain of another as they perceive

17. Craig, "Questions," 124.
18. LaCocque, *Onslaught*, 115.

it . . . The price of privilege is the moral duty to act when one sees another person treated unfairly.[19]

Wilkerson in this regard cites the poignant words of James Baldwin.

Because even if I should speak,

No one would believe me.

And they would not believe me precisely because

They would know that what I said was true.

We cannot speak of and understand the role of neighbor unless we understand and embrace the centrality of land, and all that it entails, including most notably, a sense of place and belonging.

More importantly, acknowledging and accepting one's ties to the larger communities in which one lives will give greater significance to each individuals actions and guide individuals in the choices they make. This is because one's identity and life purpose are derived from and nourished by larger narrative frameworks created and preserved by communities, not by autonomous individuals . . . Once individuals understand and affirm that our identity and life purpose are derived from larger communities, they will have an easier time clarifying and working toward the greater good of the larger human community. Indeed, it is time that we accepted the fact that we are our brothers' keepers.[20]

When President Trump speaks of nationalism, the seed of separation and the binary ideology of *us* and *them* is embedded in the consciousness of some. Yet, from the perspective of creation and neighborliness, the world is a global community, and we have come to know this in stark and challenging ways economically and racially. Notably it is the human and humane quality that have become casualties, as greed and superiority; racism and otherness, have taken shape in defining qualities. If, as Sarna has argued, everyone is the other's brother and keeper, then every homicide is fratricide.[21] Indeed if this is taken to another level, given that all humans are created in the image of God, and have the attributes and characteristics of God, then the killing of the other, might insinuate deicide. At the very least, one might argue by extension that all executions by the State would be fratricide.

Even though Cain's lament to God about his punishment and his fear of being killed is crafted in language of self-preservation, without

---

19. Wilkerson, *Caste*, 386.

20. Kaminsky, "The Sins," 328–29.

21. Sarna, *Genesis*, 35.

a modicum of remorse for killing his brother, he is nonetheless granted divine protection. Clearly such protection is not predicated on Cain's innocence, shame or repentance. Extrapolating from the particular to the universal, one might argue that a State execution of a person should not be based solely on the person's guilt or innocence, but on the general principle that systemic killing is both fratricidal and beyond the bounds of humanity. Moreover, what must be delineated here clearly in terms of a universal principle is the reality that systemic killing may be understood in a variety of ways, not only literally. When those who seek refuge are turned away or caged because the *country is full*, or children ripped from the arms of their parents or racial intimidation is stoked because of the rhetoric of racial supremacy, then the moral fabric of a nation and a people unravel. Cain's appeal to God is not about punishment, but rather about the nature of the punishment. "God not only spares Cain, but God also protects him from others, who might deem his punishment necessary."[22]

This very idea is precisely why systemic killing (outside of the confines of war) undermines the ideal of community. One of the consequences or effects of being exiled as a wanderer, presumably to be in some kind of solitary existence means that one is essentially excommunicated, that is, one is forcibly extricated from the community. Familial community will not be available, and not only is Cain left to be by himself, but this is likely what led to his pronounced fear for his life. It is possible that with enough time, Cain will be able to establish himself in a new community, but such a possibility takes time and trust, and for the present, there is neither. The idea of aloneness might strike a chord for some, but that also comes with challenges and often a loss that runs deep. The quality of social connections, empathy, compassion, care for the other, keeping the other, showing mercy would all be absent; these are the fundamental relational qualities of what it means to be human and community. If not, there's the real possibility of self-absorption, and worst, losing oneself. "One could also argue that Cain's crime and exile enable him to depend on others in a way not possible before; because of his crime, Cain acquires human sympathy; he shares the burden of every man's crime."[23]

22. Lohr, "Righteous Abel," 494.
23. Shulman, "The Myth of Cain," 226.

Human Destiny: Freedom, Punishment, Protection

"Violation of the brother is a deadly act. Yet, God's will for life is at work with the one under death sentence."[24] While this is clearly true with specific reference to Cain, this act has the potential to capture a range of what constitutes "life." God's conversation with Cain invites a critical reflection. God establishes and ensures that Cain *keeps* his brother; pronounces the punishment of wandering in the East of Eden; protects Cain from being killed. Protection against being killed is the last word in the conversation between God and Cain in this narrative. What Cain has to go on is God's spoken word. In this narrative cycle, God takes a definitive step by not punishing Cain with a death sentence, and thus preventing from what could have devolved into a cycle of violence. God stopped the killing of Cain as an act of retributive justice though there is no indication that Cain might not experience some form of physical backlash. Instead, a critical part of the punishment is that God removes Cain from his sight so that Cain would not see God. "Cain cries out in pain as he declares that his punishment is more than he can bear. He laments that outside the land, he will be hidden (סתר) from YHWH's face."[25]

If the response of Cain shows a level of despondency or distress, and he acts out of irrationality, then perhaps this quality of depression also precipitated the fear of being killed. One might surmise that God's decision not to punish Cain with death in the first place and then protect him from others might have reflected Cain's level of despondency. The "falling of one's countenance" reflects more sadness and not necessarily anger. "[I]t is not God's favoring Abel that will bring about the murder, but rather Cain's inability to accept a God who authors these mysterious and inequitable acts of choosing."[26]

Cain along with his parents will be in East of Eden. Evidently, after Adam and Eve are cast out from the Garden, Cain and Abel must still be able to dwell in the garden with God. Does this perhaps allude to the notion that the sins of the parents will not necessarily be carried on by the children? Yet, as we discover, God will protect them in a variety of ways while they are in the throes of banishment. "[T]he essense (sic) of being a free person is making choices and bearing their consequences. That freedom however, is

---

24. Brueggemann, *Genesis*, 63.
25. Craig, "Questions," 127.
26. Levenson, *Death and Resurrection*, 74–75.

deeply conditioned and bound. We are not free to do just anything, and we are not free if we do certain things."[27]

If indeed humans are created in the image of God, then the quest for freedom in relationship is part of God's character. While Cain in one respect had freedom to act violently against his brother, in so doing, that very freedom caused him to lose his freeing bond of family relationships. In sending Cain into exile, God also grants him a measure of freedom that allows him to function within certain constraints. Yet, he has the distinct possibility to create, an act that up to this point has been the exclusive realm of God. We are reminded that the wilderness somewhat counter-intuitively has been a place of renewal, and exile with all of its uncertainties and difficulties, still has the potential to bring about newness and new beginnings.

In the case of Cain, the wilderness will also be the place where the *polis* is birthed. In this regard it is not only the *idea* of the birth of a city, and the prospects of life not wholly dependent on the earth and its produce, but God's protection of this new future. God's protection of Cain from being killed is not only the *particular* protection of Cain, but a protection of what Cain's future will entail. In this way, then, God's protection is for the sake of humankind in general, and a new vision of life beyond the particularity of Cain's punishment. Newness then is a distinct possibility for those who are on the margin. And so, we are compelled to ask about those who may decide that those who flee from violence and seek a new like in a new place, within a new community, are turned away under the callous pretense, *we are full.* In the book of Ruth, Boaz did not turn away Ruth. Instead, there was radical empathy. He did not pronounce that his field was full or that the community was without a welcoming space. Yet, this was the essential pronounce by Donald Trump. "The clear call of Jesus to love the neighbor outside our path is seriously challenged and regularly compromised by our racial geography . . . which prevents people from finding their 'neighbors.'"[28]If our paths are narrow and we never step beyond the edges and margins, we will simply never be able to step onto a wider path, and in so doing discovering the neighbor in the broadest sense. Even as children were separated from their parents and placed in cages, many who preached "neighborly love" in the evangelical world, remained on the narrow path. Imagine staying in the narrow lanes even as toddlers and young children are taken into court for legal proceedings without a parent.

In leaving behind family, a land that was home and a place of familiarity and roots may be the only viable option for newness and a new beginning.

27. Shulman, "The Myth of Cain," 223.
28. Wallis, *Christ in Crisis*, 27.

In citing Cain as an example of one who is seeking a new beginning, not because he is noble or virtuous, or for that matter doing this by choice, but like the refugees from different parts of the world, there is no choice. The option for newness in their long journey in a quest for freedom and peace is the hope for open doors and arms. One of the principal concerns is the fear of leaving behind violence to be met with violence. Surely this was the generating fear of Cain; with the possibility of new life come the fear of violence. One might argue that like his father Adam, from whom a physical part of his body is sacrificed, that he, in his incompleteness, becomes complete, so also Cain, who in losing a significant part of himself, namely Abel, becomes a new person. Hannah Arendt has argued that radical beginnings such as city building do not eventuate without violence.[29] If this argument is to be sustained, then one might argue that equally important is the fact that the divine decision to protect Cain from being killed is foundational for the manner in which the *polis* will conduct its politics. It is thus both values and commitment that must be reckoned with. It is not enough to repeat the notion that we are a society of "values" but then not act on these when it comes to a moment of serious and existential reckoning.

This idea should be expanded beyond Cain, as his exile begins a journey that in part defines the destiny of humankind. This is in no way a suggestion that the murder of Abel be overlooked; indeed, God does not overlook the murder of Abel and the culpability of Cain. Yet, in the narrative, fratricide is not the last word. There is the further issue of "what now?" "God places himself as guarantor for Cain's life . . . Cain's life is guaranteed 'sevenfold,' that is to say, completely. God's final word to Cain is sealed with a sign, as if with a sacrament."[30] God makes a universal pronouncement after God promises to protect Cain. (4:15) God does not specifically only address Cain, but everyone. As Sarna suggests, "The reference is not a stigma of infamy, but to a sign indicating that the bearer is under divine protection."[31] "The divine intervention in human history does not tamper with human freedom even the freedom of unspeakably obscene acts, but the sign on Cain prevents his evil doing from being absolute, that is, an evil for which there is no forgiveness or reprieve because it has usurped God's unique absoluteness."[32]

Noteworthy here is the distinct notion that there is human freedom and in some instances such freedom is expansive. However, regardless of

29. Arendt, *On Revolution*, 10.

30. Peels, *The Vengeance of God*, 64.

31. Sarna, *Genesis*, 35.

32. LaCocque, *Onslaught*, 87.

the breadth of human freedom, including the capacity to create violence, the freedom is not infinite. In the case of Cain, it is still God who controls the boundaries and the contours of power. Despite President Trump's capacity to instigate and close doors to refugees and follow the dictates of those who counsel to create a nation of a particular type of persons, he will not have the final word. Human freedom, both for good and evil have inherent limitations. For a while, those who seek to divide and conquer might believe that the present represents all that is and all that will be, but history has shown otherwise. And most notably, God's protection is not reserved for the "good" who see themselves as living in Eden, but rather for all people including those who live on the margins, as wanderers and exiles in East of Eden. This is not only an assurance to Cain, but rather the spoken pronouncement becomes an event, not unlike other instances of God's spoken word such as in Genesis 1. In the encounter with God, Cain seeks two universal and essential divine/human acts. When he seeks justice, and there is no response by God. However, after the punishment is meted out, he seeks mercy, which is recognized and granted by God. But this is not any "cheap" mercy without consequences. This is not mercy that comes as an entitlement; this is divine mercy granted to one who has committed fratricide. What Cain seeks in the midst of justifiable punishment and despair, is precisely what every human seeks. These are qualities, both divine and human that must be held in tension. Together justice and mercy constitute life. As a society, we are always in the pursuit of the ideal, and the most notable ideal in this society is that of freedom, both the openness and the constraints. "Freedom only makes sense when situated in terms of values and commitment."[33]

God's world is on the terms that God has dictated; that is a challenge to live as humans, in addition to the idea that we must have a relationship of goodness and grace with other creatures, particularly with other human beings. What this narrative is ultimately about has to do with the destiny of the person and how that destiny is inextricably tied to the relationship with God. The issue here however is that Cain's brother has been violently violated and God must act, which God does and enacts punishment; yet this is the God who also saves. This is the necessary tension where one cannot be abandoned for the other.

> A good way to sharpen the point is to compare the individualist views of Ezekiel 18 to the more corporate theology espoused in Genesis 18:16–33, in which one finds the argument between God and Abraham over the fate of Sodom and Gomorrah. Comparing Ezekiel 18 to Genesis 18 one quickly notices that

33. Shulman, "The Myth of Cain," 224.

these two passages share many elements and that both contain arguments about divine justice versus divine mercy . . . In Genesis 18, Abraham appears to appeal to God's sense of justice (verse 25), but he, in fact is arguing for mercy. He wants a whole city to survive on the merit of a few righteous ones. And God accepts Abraham's reasoning as correct in principle, although Abraham fails to produce enough righteous men to merit saving the wicked inhabitants of these two cities . . . Not only does it stress the triumph of divine mercy over divine justice, but it also ties the concept of divine mercy to the idea that we benefit, as well as suffer, from other peoples' actions. Divine mercy is dependent on the idea of human relationality.[34]

This is a necessary, but complex relationship. God cannot ignore the cries of the brother, cries that arise from the ground. It is Cain's question that has lingered on, his rhetorical question unique on its own has assumed the correct answer as self-evident, but this is not the answer that we have inherited. Cain's question and God's response must be remembered and held together, as I did in the journey through Majdanek. What we also have in this text is the reminder that all humanity, certainly Cain and Abel, and all others live in East of Eden; no longer is it possible to live in Eden. Perhaps there are moments when we might glance into Eden, but we cannot live there, and our lives will have to be lived on the outside. In East of Eden the roads that we travel will not be straight and smooth. The roads in East of Eden are often fraught with blind corners; sharp curves; steep mountains; deceptive valleys.

God makes clear that Cain can do well, a straightforward reminder that nothing is impossible for God. As improbable as it might appear it is still possible for Cain to be redeemed. Redemption is possible though not inevitable. When God says that you can do well, then one must believe that it is possible. One can do well even after fratricide. As difficult as it is to fathom, let alone accept, this applies also to the Holocaust. Is there the possibility for redemption for everyone?

Can a person howsoever evil still do well? As in the Cain narrative, perhaps the answer lies in the reality that this will only ever happen in East of Eden where we all dwell.

The principal point here is that there is hope beyond despair, hope beyond the most excruciating pain; hope beyond the boundaries of the imagined. This is the platform for the assurance of hope in the face of Donald Trump's decision to undo the *Affordable Care Act*, separate

34. Kaminsky, "The Sins," 325–26.

families; rescind the DACA decision; sow seeds of hatred and discontent; discord and disunity. In the present, hope in such despair seems beyond a reasonable, perhaps inconceivable horizon. Cain can in fact choose and act in ways that are good, the choice is clearly there as sin lurks at the door, and ready to pounce. There is a stark contrast here, between sin and doing what is good. It is important to note that God does not say *think* and *reflect*, but rather *do good*. I want to be clear here. We must think and reflect and use the vocabulary of care and love. But in this instance the emphasis is unequivocally on acting. This is about doing. In the case of Donald Trump, the devastating failure in this regard is threefold. First, the exaggerated word that have consistently crossed the margins of truth have led to beliefs that are unfounded and deceitful.

Like the false prophets in Jeremiah's time, as we witness in Jeremiah 29 who shamelessly proclaimed "peace" "peace" when there was no peace or prospects for peace, so likewise Donald Trump shameless and proudly proclaimed that "Mexico will pay for the wall"; Mexico will pay for the wall"; "I will protect Medicare"; "windmills cause cancer," the election was fraudulent, among others. The President has betrayed the people with words that constantly made truth a casualty. Truth in the Trump administration has been a widespread casualty and has generated the belief on the part of those who perpetuated the lies, as becoming the truth. Wallis noted that from Kellyanne Conway to Rudy Giuliani; from Sarah Huckabee Sanders to Kayleigh MacEnany, where the "alternative facts" and "truth isn't truth" harkens to Pontius Pilate's "what is truth"?[35] The issue is not whether there were or are lies that related misstatements or misinformation. Presidents and leaders have done this in the past and most assuredly will do this in the future. But with President Donald Trump and his administration, the propensity to lie is widespread, instinctive and serves as a default. So as shocking and immediately proven to be false is Sean Spicer's loud and insistent pronouncement that Donald Trump's inauguration crowd was larger than that of Barack Obama's. As Leonhardt has noted, the president of the United States, "has lied about, among other things, Obama's birthday, John Kennedy's assassination, Sept 11, the Iraq war, ISIS, NATO, military veterans, Mexican Immigrant, anti-Semitic attacks, the unemployment rate, the murder rate, the electoral college, voter fraud, and his groping of women."[36]

Second, the President's words are frequently, conspicuously absent or diluted in times of grief, particularly grief generated by gun violence. One thinks of the devastating gun violence in Parkland and his inability

35. Wallis, *Christ in Crisis*, 84.
36. Leonhardt, "All the President's Lies," March 20, 2017.

to express empathy and the kind of compassion that ought to be natural. Third, the aspect of doing good has eluded the President repeatedly. He has withdrawn the United States from the Paris Accord; he has undone the clean air regulations; he has sought to ban persons from predominantly Muslim counties from entering the United States among other acts that pivot toward destruction and despair. Thus, while the divine assurance that one can still do good; be good in East of Eden, the President has chosen otherwise and has continuously created fear and pain; grief and despair. "Sin, he reflected, is not what it is usually thought to be; it is not to steal and tell lies. Sin is for one man to walk brutally over the life of another and to be quite oblivious of the wounds he has left behind."[37]

Belonging and connecting are essential for the very existence of life. The act of separation and detention where there is no connection and belonging intensified the sense of desolation and aloneness. Vivek Murthy has observed:

> We're wired to associate belonging with the sharing of stories, feelings, memories, and concerns. That's why our bodies relax and our spirits lift when we connect in genuine friendship and love. Strong personal relationships not only add joy and meaning to our lives, but they have positive effects on our health, mood, and performance . . . The stronger our connections with each other, the richer our culture and the stronger society become.[38]

Sin has a desire for Cain; sin hungers for Cain. This hungering is active and thus cannot be left alone less it consumes and leads to acts that are destructive. The hungering here has a universal human quality in that the most instinctive human impulse is for revenge, to return pain for pain. The fact that this is the impulse means also that not to do so, to look and move beyond such impulse must take great will, see beyond what is, and most of all, to choose. The impulse is to do *likewise* but we must do *otherwise* and bring the cycle, whatever the nature of the cycle of pain, to an end. In the mark of Cain there is both guilt and grace, inextricably connected.

The text makes a pronouncement but then proceeds to go under the words. Before one comes to God one must first reconcile with each other. Because we reach skywards, we must look across and around, and reconcile with the other, whoever the other is. The very notion of reconciliation by definition presupposes that there was already a relationship, and this vertical relationship must be reckoned with and healed before there is a quest for divine reckoning. Loving and caring for the other may be different in

37. Endō, *Silence*, 86.
38. Murthy, *Together*, 32.

the regard, for it would not be reconciliation, but an invitation to be conciliatory to the other. We cannot simply repeat this as a mantra, but rather make it an active endeavor. Reconciliation works on the recognition that a relationship already exists. There must have been something conciliatory, there must have been a relationship that has been fractured through whatever circumstances, and that must be restored. There is nothing that is evidently easy about this, but it cannot be cast aside. To cast aside is a marked indication that one does not take God seriously, even though all of the outward signs and ritual proprieties suggest that one does. It is not so much that one does not take the other seriously, that would certainly be true, but when the mandate is divinely instituted, then it is the principal focus is ultimately about the divine. Heschel has so rightly observed that one must *go through the secular to get to the sacred*. Therefore, the secular cannot be discarded as a shortcut to the sacred! Fraternal reconciliation comes very close to giving us an understanding of new life. When death lurks and there is fear of death, God steps in, and places a mark and the prospects and possibility for new life dawns. God simply does not let go of the guilty one, and this too is an act of grace.

The text raises questions for every generation rather than clearing a path of moralizing which is often the easy, legalistic and less effective way to proceed. There are certainly many in our society, who in the face of tragedy, draw instant moralizing conclusions. This has been the case with such extraordinary tragic events such as 9/11, hurricane Katrina, Sandy Hook and Parkland school massacres, and Tsunamis, among many others. The temptation to "play God" must be resisted and preying on the suffering, and those who are in pain, must cease. It is a time to tell others to *take heart*, to know this is not the last word, to be reassured not with platitudes but with knowledge.

6

Sacred Belonging and Resouling

"The struggle to reach the top is itself enough to fulfill the heart of man. One must believe that Sisyphus is happy." —Albert Camus, *The Myth of Sisyphus*

"Work for something because it is good, not just because it stands a chance to succeed." —Václav Havel

"Our memory is our coherence, our reason, our feeling, even our action. Without it we are nothing." —Luis Buñuel

There are any number of defining moments when one's journey does not lead to the *promised land* from Moses to Martin Luther King, jr. and scores in between. But this is also a reminder that the very journey here matters precisely because those who come after us will have to continue the journey, and lead others into that place called home. Both Moses and King together with many others in between, and since, from Dietrich Bonhoeffer to Oscar Romero; Nelson Mandela to Václav Havel have travelled difficult and painful journeys: generations after these individuals have stepped onto paths and continued to pave the way for others. Home as the promised land is elusive. Bart Giamatti's reflections come to mind.

> Why is home plate not called fourth base? As far as I can tell, it has never been thus. And why not? Meditate upon the name. *Home* is an English word virtually impossible to translate into other tongues. No translation catches the associations, the sense of security and autonomy and accessibility, the aroma of inclusiveness, of freedom from wariness, that cling to the word *home* and are absent from *house* or even *my house*. *Home* is a concept, not a place; it is a state of mind where self-definition starts; it is origins—the mix of time and place and smell and weather wherein one first realizes one is an original, perhaps

like others, especially those one loves, but discrete, distinct, not to be copied.[1]

Unlike Sisyphus whose repeated journeys to the mountain top was a punishment, some will travel to the mountain top to give hope to others, to *take heart* that the *promised land* does exist, and it is indeed possible to journey there. Occasionally, the journey might seem unimaginable, even impossible, but to have one choose that path and have a glimpse of the *promised land* is enough for others to *take heart*, for others to know that the journey is not in vain, and they do not have to abandon hope. It is to continue and further clear a wider path for others to follow and not allow the path to become covered and unseen and unclear again. Sometimes it is the case that some might need to walk in the footsteps of those who have journeyed before us and carry on forging a path that has already begun. There will always be the necessity for one to end a cycle: violence, injustice, oppression or whatever it is that pivots against the freedom to live one's life fully. Ending a cycle in this regard is invariably difficult, and perhaps for a while it might even seem insurmountable. Yet, it must be if indeed we are to believe that injustice and violence and revenge are not to be inscribed as the final words in humanity's destiny. It might be asking to go against what one might believe to be one's natural impulse.

Sophocles's *Antigone*, is a classic Greek tragedy of monumental proportions and yet a tragedy of remarkable redemption as well. While redemption, perhaps is not a theme conventionally associated with *Antigone*, it is one nevertheless that is at the heart of the drama. In this regard, one thinks of the unmistakable parallels between Shakespeare's Cordelia and Lear and Sophocles' Antigone. Redemptive justice is not only for the instant or immediate, but for those inheritors of the redemption that is born out of the tragedy. So, like Lear and Cordelia, Antigone does die, but in death there is both present and future redemption. The actualization of redemption only for the present subverts the essence and scope of redemption. "Lear and Cordelia are defeated, it is true, but their efforts help put an end to the casualties practiced by Goneril, Regan, Cornwall and Edmund."[2] When Antigone says that she will share her love not her hate, she makes a pronouncement that transforms the entire narrative from one of ongoing tragedy to one that has the prospects of bringing the cycle of violence and pain to an end. Here, Antigone is perhaps reflecting the axiom that to hate another is to drink poison and expect the other to die. It does take an inordinate level of moral courage, and the requisite action to accompany

1. Giamatti, *Take Time For Paradise*, 91.
2. Benson, "Materialist Criticism," 445.

such courage. If one claims to have courage and it is not acted out in the face of violence and injustice, then it is a vacuous courage. As dramatic as the plot of this tragedy is, it is also a juxtaposition of two very different worldviews with equally dramatic implications for contemporary society. The logic of Antigone's sister Ismene is well grounded. She has seen, and her family has experienced far too much violence, tragedy and death, and so to pursue the path that Antigone has embarked on does not seem wise in Ismene's eyes. Ismene's arguments are multi-dimensional, each arguably with some merit. She has witnessed unparalleled violence within her family with a quality of horror that no one person should experience. Thus, to have a father who gouged out his eyes, dying in shame and disgrace, and a mother who committed suicide, and brothers who killed each other, one is forced to pause and take note and listen.

Ironically both Antigone and Ismene seek an end to the family's pain, but the perspectives could not be more diametrically opposed to each other. The death of their brother Polyneices, whose dead body is desacralized by being left in the street for the world to see, as a sign of betrayal of the throne and state serves to create a powerful existential crisis for the sisters. As king, Creon has the power of the throne to dictate the law on which to lean, and the basis for protection. And perhaps most of all he has the history of violence to ensure that he remains in power. The moral dilemma however comes with Creon's public shaming and desecration of the body of Poly-neices by leaving his body on public display without the sacred protocol of burial. This decision by Creon is both a personal and private one; it is a decree handed down that is expected to be followed as all decrees by the king are absolute and beyond question. His action makes it clear that loyalty is expected and is absolute and those who dare to challenge the throne will pay a price, even in death. In speaking to Ismene, Antigone lays out her plan to give their brother a proper burial. At the outset, the issue is not to focus on the rightness or wrongness of each other's perspective, but rather to do what is decent and proper, in the burial of her brother. And while it is likely that Ismene wants a decent burial for her brother and understands the importance of this act, she is unwilling to embrace Antigone's plan. Her arguments are not frivolous or superficial. Like Antigone, she has witnessed the violence, and indeed has suffered the violence in the family. For Ismene, it is not for her to challenge the crown's decree and in any event, she does not believe that it is really within her nature to challenge such authority. She has decided that in fact there has been enough violence, and in her estimation to challenge Creon's decree would only lead to more violence; likely, she is right. For Ismene, the only recourse such as it is, is to obey the decree. Yet, beyond her personal grief which cannot be discounted or underestimated, Antigone sees a disgrace of such proportions that it cannot be overlooked or cast aside. As is so often the case, what begins as a matter of principle on a personal level, takes on a much more universal quality. What must be noted as well, is that Antigone's defiance for what is just is not against some "far off foe" to use Thoreau's phrase, but rather against King Creon, her betrothed's father. But in a matter of moral conscience those with conventional power may not have the final word.

While it is entirely possible that Antigone understands her sister's concern, ultimately, she views Ismene's objections as acquiescing to Creon and the power of the crown. Ismene's concern and the loss that both she and Antigone feel is intense. However, Antigone sees her proposal as a challenge to power that is predicated on revenge and abuse. What might be considered state decree and legal, must on occasion give way to that which is proper and life giving, moral and even vulnerable and essential. It is where finally *moral* and *essential* must take precedence over *legal*. Despite what the *Chorus* and the trusted prophet Teiresias would say to him, Creon is bent on revenge, and thus an opportunity to rule with a moral compass, gives way to a rule with force and fear.

President Trump and King Creon

While the corresponding parallel between King Creon and President Donald Trump may diverge at certain points, the principal characteristic quest for infinite power and unquestioning loyalty and the insistence on punishment for perceived disloyalty is evident in both. I cite briefly four representative instances in the Trump presidency in this regard. First, following Special Counsel Robert Mueller III's report on the Russian interference in the 2016 Presidential election, and possible complicity between the Trump campaign and Russian operatives, President Trump extrapolated that he was fully exonerated and there was no obstruction of justice on his part, repeating such a verifiable untruth at every turn. In fact, neither of these statements is true, though he repeatedly said and tweeted such. It is consistently the case for Mr. Trump that he views himself to be above reproach. He remarked on April 22, 2019, in response to a question as to his reaction to the Special Counsel's report that members of his staff refused his orders to obstruct the investigation, he said, "nobody disobeys my orders." Second, before the President dismissed the FBI Director, James Comey, he alluded to the importance of loyalty. Even though this kind of expectation of loyalty between a President and FBI Director is known to be inappropriate and indecorous, the President sought to normalize it. And when James Comey

did not act at Mr. Trump's behest, he was summarily dismissed as FBI Director. Third, within days of the Special Counsel's redacted report being made
public, the President verbally ridiculed those whose testimony outlined the
many ways the President sought to undermine the law and Constitution.
One such person who declined to follow his orders was the White House
attorney, Donald McGahn. Once McGahn's verbatim testimony was made
public and his scorching and unflattering portrayal of the president, the
services associated with the law offices of McGahn were immediately dis-
continued. Fourth, and perhaps most notable is the February 27th, 2019
testimony before Congress of Michael Cohen former Attorney and self-
identified "fixer to Donald Trump." In a brutal expose´ of the President's
narcissistic impulses, Cohen laid bare his former boss's dishonesty and
self-indulgence. The significance of Cohen's testimony to Congress months
before he began serving his prison sentence is the fact that Cohen not long
before his agreement with the Special Counsel, he had publicly proclaimed
that he would willingly "take a bullet" for President trump. Cohen's loyalty,
blind to the core was extolled as a matter of virtue. Trump's ridicule and
quest for vengeance was swift and unyielding.

In a way despite King Creon's acknowledgement that he has always listened to Teiresias, when the prophet warned him on the impending disaster,
he refused to imagine or believe that any such disaster could happen to him.
Antigone, unlike Ismene does not express concern for herself, the fear of protecting herself from any further violence at the hands of the crown. And as is
so often the case with those who challenge the convention, the norm and the
well-established worldviews of power, they are vilified and not infrequently
killed. The world is often very hard on dreamers and visionaries, and ultimately Antigone would also be killed. Yet, there are instances that the death
of one might be the moment when a cycle of violence and the perpetuation
of injustice and abuse will end. A Minneapolis police officer Derek Chauvin
pinned his knee on George Floyd's neck and for nine minutes and twenty-
nine seconds kept his knee there and thereby killing Floyd.

With the ensuing intense protest and demonstrations in more than
200 cities, there were also scattered instances of violence. Instead of speaking to the nation to bring about the calm, President Trump would instead
seek photo opportunities in front of St. John's Episcopal Church in DC
where protesters were cleared off from the path with tear gas. He would
further call the governors and mayors to use force. He expressed the need
to dominate the street. And so, the cycle of violence would continue. Antigone's death certainly does this. As is so often stated, love will finally overcome hate and even though for a while it might seem to be a promethean

struggle, love will win. The cycle will end, and it is clear that with the violent end will also come redemption.

This unflinching and abiding quality that Antigone displayed was certainly in the first instance about the indecency and vengeful act against Polyneices by Creon. But beyond that particularity lies the greater implications for every person who might face the drama of challenging a force of considerable magnitude. The clash between the power of the state and one's moral conscience will certainly point to a markedly unequal balance of power; yet herein lies hope. Despite Ismene's concern that she has no power given that she is seeking to survive in a male dominated world, nonetheless, as she discovers, that world of power will ultimately disintegrate in the face of moral fortitude and rectitude. Prometheus's suffering for the sake of doing what is noble for humanity, and that which is good and essential, cannot be kept only for those who have the power to do so. There is no indication that he was aware of the consequences. But it is a choice nonetheless, for the greater good of humanity. And the narrative of Jephthah's daughter is positioned as a pointed example as well.

Jephthah's Daughter: Ending the Cycle of Violence

Now Jephthah the Gileadite, the son of a prostitute, was a mighty warrior. Gilead was the father of Jephthah. [2] Gilead's wife also bore him sons; and when his wife's sons grew up, they drove Jephthah away, saying to him, "You shall not inherit anything in our father's house; for you are the son of another woman." [3] Then Jephthah fled from his brothers and lived in the land of Tob. Outlaws collected around Jephthah and went raiding with him.

[4] After a time the Ammonites made war against Israel. [5] And when the Ammonites made war against Israel, the elders of Gilead went to bring Jephthah from the land of Tob. [6] They said to Jephthah, "Come and be our commander, so that we may fight with the Ammonites." [7] But Jephthah said to the elders of Gilead, "Are you not the very ones who rejected me and drove me out of my father's house? So why do you come to me now when you are in trouble?" [8] The elders of Gilead said to Jephthah, "Nevertheless, we have now turned back to you, so that you may go with us and fight with the Ammonites, and become head over us, over all the inhabitants of Gilead." [9] Jephthah said to the elders of Gilead, "If you bring me home again to fight with the Ammonites, and the LORD gives them over to me, I will be your head." [10] And the elders of Gilead said to Jephthah, "The LORD will be witness between us; we will surely do as you say." [11]

So Jephthah went with the elders of Gilead, and the people made him head and commander over them; and Jephthah spoke all his words before the LORD at Mizpah.

[12] Then Jephthah sent messengers to the king of the Ammonites and said, "What is there between you and me, that you have come to me to fight against my land?" [13] The king of the Ammonites answered the messengers of Jephthah, "Because Israel, on coming from Egypt, took away my land from the Arnon to the Jabbok and to the Jordan; now therefore restore it peaceably." [14] Once again Jephthah sent messengers to the king of the Ammonites [15] and said to him: "Thus says Jephthah: Israel did not take away the land of Moab or the land of the Ammonites, [16] but when they came up from Egypt, Israel went through the wilderness to the Red Sea and came to Kadesh. [17] Israel then sent messengers to the king of Edom, saying, 'Let us pass through your land'; but the king of Edom would not listen. They also sent to the king of Moab, but he would not consent. So Israel remained at Kadesh. [18] Then they journeyed through the wilderness, went around the land of Edom and the land of Moab, arrived on the east side of the land of Moab, and camped on the other side of the Arnon. They did not enter the territory of Moab, for the Arnon was the boundary of Moab. [19] Israel then sent messengers to King Sihon of the Amorites, king of Heshbon; and Israel said to him, 'Let us pass through your land to our country.' [20] But Sihon did not trust Israel to pass through his territory; so Sihon gathered all his people together, and encamped at Jahaz, and fought with Israel. [21] Then the LORD, the God of Israel, gave Sihon and all his people into the hand of Israel, and they defeated them; so Israel occupied all the land of the Amorites, who inhabited that country. [22] They occupied all the territory of the Amorites from the Arnon to the Jabbok and from the wilderness to the Jordan. [23] So now the LORD, the God of Israel, has conquered the Amorites for the benefit of his people Israel. Do you intend to take their place? [24] Should you not possess what your god Chemosh gives you to possess? And should we not be the ones to possess everything that the LORD our God has conquered for our benefit? [25] Now are you any better than King Balak son of Zippor of Moab? Did he ever enter into conflict with Israel, or did he ever go to war with them? [26] While Israel lived in Heshbon and its villages, and in Aroer and its villages, and in all the towns that are along the Arnon, three hundred years, why did you not recover them within that time? [27] It is not I who have sinned against you, but you are the one who does me wrong by making war on me. Let the LORD, who

is judge, decide today for the Israelites or for the Ammonites." [28] But the king of the Ammonites did not heed the message that Jephthah sent him.

[29] Then the spirit of the LORD came upon Jephthah, and he passed through Gilead and Manasseh. He passed on to Mizpah of Gilead, and from Mizpah of Gilead he passed on to the Ammonites. [30] And Jephthah made a vow to the LORD, and said, "If you will give the Ammonites into my hand, [31] then whoever comes out of the doors of my house to meet me, when I return victorious from the Ammonites, shall be the LORD's, to be offered up by me as a burnt offering." [32] So Jephthah crossed over to the Ammonites to fight against them; and the LORD gave them into his hand. [33] He inflicted a massive defeat on them from Aroer to the neighborhood of Minnith, twenty towns, and as far as Abel-keramim. So the Ammonites were subdued before the people of Israel.

[34] Then Jephthah came to his home at Mizpah; and there was his daughter coming out to meet him with timbrels and with dancing. She was his only child; he had no son or daughter except her. [35] When he saw her, he tore his clothes, and said, "Alas, my daughter! You have brought me very low; you have become the cause of great trouble to me. For I have opened my mouth to the LORD, and I cannot take back my vow." [36] She said to him, "My father, if you have opened your mouth to the LORD, do to me according to what has gone out of your mouth, now that the LORD has given you vengeance against your enemies, the Ammonites." [37] And she said to her father, "Let this thing be done for me: Grant me two months, so that I may go and wander on the mountains, and bewail my virginity, my companions and I." [38] "Go," he said and sent her away for two months. So she departed, she and her companions, and bewailed her virginity on the mountains. [39] At the end of two months, she returned to her father, who did with her according to the vow he had made. She had never slept with a man. So there arose an Israelite custom that [40] for four days every year the daughters of Israel would go out to lament the daughter of Jephthah the Gileadite.[3]

Judges 11 is a rare narrative that has a devastating and dubious trilogy, namely: hypocrisy, sex, and violence, and it seems for a while as if the theme of violence will simply continue unabated at so many levels. Over time a disproportionate amount of attention and scholarship has been devoted to Jephthah, while the anonymous daughter has for the most part remained in

---

3. Judges 11.

the shadows. Yet, it is the daughter who finally brings the cycle of violence to an end, and it is through her that there is redemption. Jephthah, according to the story, was born to a prostitute, and as is typically the case with a prostitute who becomes pregnant, one may not be sure as to who the father is, without DNA, etc. So, who is the father? The father is anyone who might have consorted with prostitutes, used and abused them. Any of these men could have been the father of Jephthah. Later, when the leaders (the fathers), invite him, in a manner of speaking, to return home, it is for ulterior motives. What we do know is that the half-brothers of Jephthah who do not wish to have him present as a member of the family, unceremoniously cast him out. "You will not have any inheritance in our father's house, for you are the son of another woman." They expel him. The Hebrew term used here for "expel" is the same word typically used for divorce, and so it has the force of that which is legal and formal. The so-called propriety of the community is such that they cannot be tainted by one who is the offspring of a prostitute; yet this was not his choice to such an identity. But those who have cast this shame on him have also expelled him, legally severing all rights. *Shame* by association is perhaps a vexatious reminder of their own culpability. Thus, Jephthah became an outlaw; there is really no great way in which to characterize what he did, except to say that he was the leader of a group of bandits. We know that at the time, there was no centralized government in Israel, and much of the leadership was regional, often by Judges who were primarily military leaders. So, when a tribe of Gilead was being threatened, the leader of Gilead realizing that they had no military leader of distinction to lead them against the Ammonites, the leaders sought out Jephthah. This decision started a series of events that would lead to devastating results and consequences. Memory is an important and powerful quality: an essential aspect of our lives. Jephthah remembers and he ensures that the men of Gilead know that he remembers and knows.

After Jephthah is contacted and the request is made, he reminds those who had banished him: "Are you not the ones who hated me and expelled me from my father's house? Why have you come to me now when you are having trouble?" The intentional loss of memory; the neglect to reflect and know the past that have brought us to where we are. The men have lost their memory or pushed it into the recesses of their consciousness. Nevertheless, he agrees to lead them against the Ammonites, and they further offered to appoint him their natural leader, and this is agreed upon. Given that he has been a bandit and mercenary, it is somewhat surprising that first thing he does is negotiate, telling the Ammonites that he does not have an issue with them. A defining moment that is often lost in the discussion comes when Jephthah makes a vow to God, an uninvited vow, an unexpected vow, and ultimately, I believe a calamitous ill-advised vow that would lead to devastating consequences. We have already been assured that Jephthah will defeat the Ammonites, and yet, unsolicited and unnecessary he makes this extraordinary vow. A vow is not always redemptive in nature. A vow might very well be predicated on fear and unfaithfulness and a vision that only focuses on the immediate and the present.

We know of the tradition in Israel, where women have come out to welcome their victorious heroes. So here, a newly minted leader makes a choice; makes an unnecessary vow, one that demonstrates more unfaithfulness, than faith, and returns home to a joyful greeting by his daughter. And on seeing her and recalling his vow, he blames *her* for *his* demise! He makes a self-indulgent choice with devastating consequences, and arguably this situation would warrant a conversation about the vow with both God and Jephthah's daughter, but that never occurs. But instead, the daughter has only one request. "Let me have two months so that I might go to the mountains and bewail my virginity, I and my companions." There is no argument, and the father simply allows his daughter to be sacrificed. She will depart to "bewail her virginity." So, can we think of anything redemptive about his daughter's actions? Maybe bringing to an end the cycle of violence? The irony is that the war is won, and thus, the ongoing military violence at least for a while has abated, but violence still lurks at many levels, and it is only with the daughter's decision that this particular cycle will end. It is the daughter and not Jephthah or the leaders in the country who end violence. What the daughter brings is an end through personal sacrifice. The "sacrifice" that the leaders made is a matter of relinquishing some of their monopoly on power for the sake of victory, but not ending violence.

A Time for Homecoming

[25] Just then a lawyer stood up to test Jesus. "Teacher," he said, "what must I do to inherit eternal life?" [26] He said to him, "What is written in the law? What do you read there?" [27] He answered, "You shall love the Lord your God with all your heart, and with all your soul, and with all your strength, and with all your mind; and your neighbor as yourself." [28] And he said to him, "You have given the right answer; do this, and you will live."

[29] But wanting to justify himself, he asked Jesus, "And who is my neighbor?" [30] Jesus replied, "A man was going down from Jerusalem to Jericho, and fell into the hands of robbers, who stripped him, beat him, and went away, leaving him half dead. [31] Now by chance a priest was going down that road; and when he

saw him, he passed by on the other side. [32] So likewise a Levite, when he came to the place and saw him, passed by on the other side. [33] But a Samaritan while traveling came near him; and when he saw him, he was moved with pity. [34] He went to him and bandaged his wounds, having poured oil and wine on them. Then he put him on his own animal, brought him to an inn, and took care of him. [35] The next day he took out two denarii, gave them to the innkeeper, and said, 'Take care of him; and when I come back, I will repay you whatever more you spend.' [36] Which of these three, do you think, was a neighbor to the man who fell into the hands of the robbers?" [37] He said, "The one who showed him mercy." Jesus said to him, "Go and do likewise."[4]

Likely one of the most well-known biblical texts, the Parable of the Good Samaritan is replete with a litany of acts of grace together with challenges. As is so often the case, because the parable so well known it also poses the problem that familiarity typically does. We often do not attend to the story because there is a sense that we know it well enough. Because of this, invariably details and nuances are overlooked, and significant trajectories of the story are neglected. We typically hear about the Samaritans only when we hear the *Parable of the Good Samaritan* or a story of the *Samaritan Woman* at the well.

In the late Second Temple period, the Samaritans lived in an area between Judea and Galilee that had been the Capital and the surrounding lands of the Northern Kingdom. In 721/722 BCE Assyria conquered the Northern Kingdom and exiled many of its people.

[24] The king of Assyria brought people from Babylon, Cuthah, Avva, Hamath, and Sepharvaim, and placed them in the cities of Samaria in place of the people of Israel; they took possession of Samaria, and settled in its cities. [25] When they first settled there, they did not worship the LORD; therefore the LORD sent lions among them, which killed some of them. [26] So the king of Assyria was told, "The nations that you have carried away and placed in the cities of Samaria do not know the law of the god of the land; therefore he has sent lions among them; they are killing them, because they do not know the law of the god of the land." [27] Then the king of Assyria commanded, "Send there one of the priests whom you carried away from there; let him go and live there, and teach them the law of the god of the land." [28] So one of the priests whom they had carried away from

4. Luke 10:25-37.

> Samaria came and lived in Bethel; he taught them how they
> should worship the LORD.[5]

Second Kings 17:24–28 provides an idea of how the Samaritans who were
not members of Israel came to have a copy of the Torah. We also have an
idea of why they were allowed to live in the land even though they were not
Jews. Even though the Samaritans had their own Torah, they also brought
with them their own gods, and this became a seriously divisive issue. The
Samaritans did not view the Temple in Jerusalem as the center of worship,
and they consequently built a temple at Mt. Gerazim at Shechem.

Thus, the *Good Samaritan* should strike us as particularly shocking.
The parable begins with a fairly straightforward question: What must *I*
do to inherit eternal life? This is a personal concern, and there is clearly
nothing wrong with such a concern. The lawyer who poses the question
makes certain presuppositions. It is what one *does*, to inherit eternal life.
For the questioner, it is about *doing*. The response of Jesus in the first instance is instructive. It is the appeal to the great commandment. Love the
LORD, with all your heart, all your soul, and all your mind, and with all
your strength! And your neighbor as yourself! (Deut 6:4–5) We may be
able repeat these words fairly easily from memory, but there is little that
is easy about them. So, for example, what does it mean to love with one's
soul (*nephesh*)? What does it mean to love with one's mind? Or what does
it mean to love with one's strength?

In this text the LXX translates the Hebrew *me'od* as δυνάμεώς and the
Vulgate translates it as *fortitudine*. Both the Greek and the Latin rendering have inherent limitations. As we can also see from the lawyer's questions he is interested in the future, beyond the concreteness of the present.
When Jesus responds, he mandates that what needs to be done is in the
present. That is what is necessary in order to live. To *take heart* for the future, what is necessary is to live fully in the present, and this means to love
God, self and neighbor with the fullness of who one is. And thus, follows
the question, "Who is my neighbor?" That is the question that the lawyer
asks after he hears the story. That is the question that we have inherited.
But is that really the principal question? As the parable ends and Jesus
asks the all-important question, we notice that the question changes, and
as the question changes, so does the answer. This is frequently where we
overlook the change in direction.

The problem with the lawyer's question at its very core, is that it does
not seek to understand what it means for him or anyone to be a neighbor, but
rather simply getting a definition. He looks for an easy and straightforward

---

5. 2 Kgs 17:24–28.

answer to an existential question. What does it mean to be a neighbor, and for that matter to make a choice of being neighborly? Jesus does not focus on the lawyer's interest but redefines and expands the question. We should not be surprised that we are not given the identity of the injured man on the road. The definition of the neighbor is in fact *anyone*, regardless. The person on the road is simply "a person." Finally, that is all that matters. We do however have something of the identity of those who walk by the injured man and crossed to the other side. What defines "neighborliness" for us is not the person on the street, but who *we* are. To be a neighbor is defined not by the identity of the one who is the object, but rather the nature of who we are.

> Thus says the LORD to his anointed, to Cyrus,
> whose right hand I have grasped
> to subdue nations before him
> and strip kings of their robes,
> to open doors before him—
> and the gates shall not be closed:
> ² I will go before you
> and level the mountains,
> I will break in pieces the doors of bronze
> and cut through the bars of iron,
> ³ I will give you the treasures of darkness
> and riches hidden in secret places,
> so that you may know that it is I, the LORD,
> the God of Israel, who call you by your name.
> ⁴ For the sake of my servant Jacob,
> and Israel my chosen,
> I call you by your name,
> I surname you, though you do not know me.
> ⁵ I am the LORD, and there is no other;
> besides me there is no god.
> I arm you, though you do not know me,
> ⁶ so that they may know, from the rising of the sun
> and from the west, that there is no one besides me;
> I am the LORD, and there is no other.

7 I form light and create darkness,

I make weal and create woe;

I the Lord do all these things.[6]

We are most assuredly reminded in this text that YHWH will identify and use whomever YHWH desires. Thus, in the realm of hope and redemption, transformation and deliverance, we are reminded that we cannot and must not dismiss anyone on the basis that he or she might be unworthy or beyond the scope of helping. It is not uncommon to see on television or more so on the Internet to have stories of individuals who are set apart for doing something extraordinary, or the subject of an act of goodness to an unlikely person. But this is not the biblical norm. One should not be surprised by such acts of the heart. In other words, noble acts, redemptive acts, etc., should not be relegated to the margins. Moreover, not only should everyone to be included in those called to act, but there must be no barricades as to who is included.

Are you not like the Ethiopians to me,

O people of Israel? says the Lord.

Did I not bring Israel up from the land of Egypt,

and the Philistines from Caphtor and the Arameans from Kir?

8 The eyes of the Lord God are upon the sinful kingdom,

and I will destroy it from the face of the earth

—except that I will not utterly destroy the house of Jacob, says the Lord.[7]

In this text from Amos, these are words that must have been shocking to the ears of the "insiders." There is an equivalency made between Israel and Ethiopia, representative of all nations. This is reminiscent of Jesus healing the ten lepers, where Jews and Samaritans walked together with shared pain and are healed with no distinction. God, and thus by extension humans, will free and save anyone regardless of religion or national identity. Often, in a world where such qualities are commonplace, separate or united, this parable is unequivocal in the pronouncement by Jesus, "who will you be a neighbor to?" This is the question that continues its pointed relevance and currency in today's society. Two ideas are of particular note here. First, the neighbor is anyone, and we are the ones who regardless of all identity

6. Isa 45:1–7.

7. Amos 9:7–8.

markers, must act. Second, in the case of the Ten Lepers, neither ethnic nor religious identity mattered, or for that matter were these identifying factors required for healing and restoration. And we may legitimately extrapolate on healing as being both physical and also as a metaphor.

7

Resisting Inheritance and Resouling

"A premoral culture, or culture of narcissism, reemerges when morality collapses. When premoral thinking becomes culturally dominant, moral values begin to seem unconvincing and uncompelling . . . Compassion is seen as weakness, mercy as injustice. Eventually the narcissistic goods—wealth, power, success—replace moral ones." —Mendelson, p. 68

"There is no spiritual conversion or reconciliation. Jonah is coerced by God, not convinced." —Levine, p. 175

Where I wander—You Where I ponder—You

Only You, You again, always You! You! You! You!

When I am gladdened—You! When I am saddened—You!

Only You, You again, always You! You! You! You! —Levi Yizchak

Growth is demanding and may seem dangerous, for there is loss as well as gain in growth. But why go on living if one has ceased to grow? And what more demanding atmosphere for growth than love in any form, than any relationship which can call out and requires of us our most secret and deepest selves. —Sarton, *Journal of a Solitude,* p. 80

1 Hear this, all you peoples;
     give ear, all inhabitants of the world,
2 both low and high,
     rich and poor together.
3 My mouth shall speak wisdom;
     the meditation of my heart shall be understanding.
4 I will incline my ear to a proverb;
     I will solve my riddle to the music of the harp.

5 Why should I fear in times of trouble,

when the iniquity of my persecutors surrounds me,

6 those who trust in their wealth

and boast of the abundance of their riches?

7 Truly, no ransom avails for one's life,

there is no price one can give to God for it.

8 For the ransom of life is costly, and can never suffice,

9 that one should live on forever

and never see the grave.

10 When we look at the wise, they die;

fool and dolt perish together

and leave their wealth to others.

11 Their graves are their homes forever,

their dwelling places to all generations, though they named lands their own.

12 Mortals cannot abide in their pomp;

they are like the animals that perish.

13 Such is the fate of the foolhardy,

the end of those who are pleased with their lot.

14 Like sheep they are appointed for Sheol;

Death shall be their shepherd;

straight to the grave they descend,

and their form shall waste away;

Sheol shall be their home.

15 But God will ransom my soul from the power of Sheol,

for he will receive me.

16 Do not be afraid when some become rich,

when the wealth of their houses increases.

17 For when they die they will carry nothing away;

their wealth will not go down after them.

18 Though in their lifetime they count themselves happy

—for you are praised when you do well for yourself—

19 they will go to the company of their ancestors,

who will never again see the light.

20 Mortals cannot abide in their pomp;
        they are like the animals that perish.[1]

W hen one sees those who are not only wealthy, but where their riches
        and opulent life have reached a height where they feel compelled to
boast of their worth and grandeur, then one might not only feel slighted,
but also a sense of distinct and impenetrable inequity and unfairness in the
world. In Psalm 49, the psalmist reminds us that the magnitude of such
wealth and the boasting however is not the last word. The last word is not
wholly for humans to determine. Instead, even with all the wealth, there is
no ransoming that is available. One cannot, through one's wealth, negotiate
with God for a longer or never-ending life.

What we know is that ultimately wealth and power are finite. For a
while, wealth, and its enormous deceptive importance of ultimacy might
appear to make one invincible, but such a lack of reality of both history
and a vision that goes beyond the present, will not be determinative of life.
President Donald Trump has repeatedly referred to his wealth and power
as definitive and central to who he is, and in this regard the public has also
come to realize that the president has been less than truthful about his finances and actions he has taken. Without a modicum of shame, he boasts of
his greatness. His sense of greatness is self-focused, always with superlatives
in defending his wealth, business acumen, talent, memory, genius status,
etc., rather than on his national and societal responsibilities.

> Moral individualism is something psychologically distinct and
> opposed to the 'individualism' of egoism and unrestrained
> greed. Those who develop the moral mind enjoy a sense of self
> that enables them to resist and moderate the temptations of
> wealth, rank, power, fame, status and beauty and, in some cases,
> to enjoy the happiness even in their absence. Moral characters
> seek such goods with less appetite than others, and when they
> acquire them, especially wealth and fame and rank, they are less
> likely to be harmed by them and inflated with them."[2]

Among the many areas of the unconscionable lack in care and justice
is, the horrific treatment of refugees, encaged without the basic need such
as soap, toothbrushes and kept in cold conditions. In Jeremiah 9, steadfast
love, justice and righteousness bring joy to the Lord. For President Trump,

---

1. Psalm 49.
2. Mendelson, *The Good Life*, 43.

praise from himself and others about himself bring him immeasurable satisfaction and joy.

The psalmist is very clear that all of the external pomp and evidence of wealthy splendor and opulence will ultimately not help and save a person. For those who believe that wealth and opulence are their permanent state of being, such foolhardy attitude has led them to an ultimate state of self-indulgent pleasure. Verse 16 reflects both the reality of fear but also assurance of a future that will not simply echo the status quo. There are clearly reasons to be fearful of those who are driven and shaped by wealth and power, particularly if such impulse for wealthy power comes at all costs, for invariably with this comes the oppression of sections of society. Thus, the assurance not to fear is predicated on a real concern that there *is* something to fear. An important factor in this assurance is the twofold perspective that the present will not remain forever and the equalizer for all of life is death. The manner in which the Psalm ends is emphatic in the repetition of v. 12. *Mortals cannot abide in their pomp.*

In the common vernacular the phrase "the reversal of fortunes is widely known." This might be broadly cast as figurative language, but it can be viewed equally as literally true. Fortune, literally or otherwise, wealth, power, status, station in society or any such is not the last word, and those who have pinned their hopes on this notion, and who have continued to imagine this to be the case, do so at their own peril. No one necessarily wills this reversal to occur, but it points to a larger and more existential issue, namely those inherently fleeting things to which we tether ourselves and imagine that this will continue *ad infinitum.*

On Job and Fleeting Power

One of the principal threads woven throughout both the poetry and prose of the book of Job is the journey from wealth to poverty and then to wealth once more; from a happy closely knitted family to a solitary existence; from health and societal regard to debilitation and dissolution of friendships; and finally, an opportunity for redemption. Though for the most part neglected in biblical scholarship, this theme of fullness/emptiness is pivotal. Throughout his life, Job had always known that God is the architect of all of life, and so even when viewed as the greatest man in the East, with massive wealth, he never believed that God was unnecessary or immaterial to his life. Indeed, it seemed to Job that the celebratory lifestyle of his children, never described as decadent or reckless, nevertheless needed particular ritual attention to ensure that if they had done anything that was sinful, they would be sanctified. This was of singular concern to him and so he offered sacrifices on their behalf. What Job's journey makes clear is that being at either end of the spectrum of health or weakness, wealth or poverty, full or empty, is never the final word.

Rather than casting blame on Job, and seeking to make him responsible for his suffering, the friends, Eliphaz, Bildad and Zophar could have more wisely and compassionately told him to *take heart*. Instead, they saw his suffering, and determined that God had justifiably punished him. They did not imagine with Job the possibility that there might be life beyond sitting with sores on an ash heap. The friends never asked or wondered about whether there could be life beyond the depth in which Job found himself. In light of the previous forty-one chapters of the book, the dramatic and unexpected Epilogue suggests either a remarkably unrealistic and simplistic ending, or at the very least it leaves readers with a litany of existential questions on theodicy. Certainly, it would be presumptuous to conclude that either of these conclusions is entirely inappropriate, but what is equally clear is the fact that these conclusions do not exhaust the possibilities. Both the Prologue and Epilogue invite us to the highest summit and the deepest valley of human existence, and in both instances, we are reminded that neither is the last word. And not surprisingly, a series of essential questions arise.

What might we learn from the friends of Job? What happens when the "right" answers are wrong? What happens when what we have been taught, and perhaps inherited, do not fit a particular situation? In this regard, we might be wise to learn from the mistakes of the friends of Job, who despite their tenacious resistance to Job's questions, personal and existential, got it wrong, and insisted on universal prescriptive answers. They evidently learned the "right" answers to explain and justify the suffering of Job or anyone else. Their answers are unfiltered and universal in application; they believed with certitude that all suffering can be explained by established templates. Given that we are privy to the reasons for Job's suffering we know that these answers are wrong; at the end God makes it abundantly and unequivocally clear that the friends were wrong about both Job and God. It is as stark and straightforward a moment in the narrative as to the wrongness of their "right" answers, so much so that they would have to depend on Job for their lives. What the friends had at their disposal, was *textbook* answers and these are applied to all questions, answers that are forcibly made to fit the questions. The reality about textbook answers is that one does not have to think about situations and circumstances, the realities of the cause or particularities. Even though they were unaware of the circumstances that led to his suffering, the friends nonetheless insisted on their justification. What is particularly startling about their answers is that Eliphaz, Bildad and

Zophar were friends; they cared deeply about Job and came to be with him in the time of his trauma and grief. They did not set out to hurt him or be self-righteous or derisive, but in fact what we discover is that their friendship was not enough to withstand their judgment. That is, no amount of friendship or love could dissuade them from believing that their answer to human suffering was universal in scope and application.

The confidence of the friends of Job in their theological perspective regarding the reason for human suffering is such that they see no particular value in appealing to God. They see Job's understanding as more belligerence and guilt; their position is that their theological position is not only true in particular instances but universally true. One of the issues with existential overtones such as human suffering is that it cannot be attended to with sweeping explanations. Invariably such generalizations undermine and belittle those who suffer. Not only are such generalizations futile, but they cast aside the particularity of the sufferer's situation and circumstances. The point is not to generalize and simply reduce the sufferer's reality as one that generates pity.

Nussbaum suggests that pity is in reality insulting and dismissive, and is granted under the guise of care, compassion and consolation; in reality, however it is not so subtle distancing of one for the other. Thus, when the friends of Job demonstrate their *caring*, it has the outward appearance of seeking to help, but in fact such words are no more than self-serving and a form of righteous indulgence. Consolation should not be about explanation, and most certainly not to be employed as a means to justify, which the friends of Job are on the cusp of doing. But rather, it should be about hope in both the present and a vision for the future. Words do matter, but not at the expense of the sufferer. "Dealing successfully with trauma essentially involves establishing a sense of the world as benevolent, meaningful, and safe, and the self as significant and valuable, even in the face of the traumatic event."[3]

If as typically is the case that human suffering does not always have an immediately obvious answer, and neither platitudes nor clichés are helpful, then one must have the confidence to rely on the question. The question must be asked of God and each other, but *sans* the haste of providing answers. This is as much a factor to be reckoned with for those who seek to care or provide consolation. The point in listening to the other is not to be the repository of all answers.

Is it possible that that God could be involved in idolatry? Could God have idolized relationships, including covenant relationships to the point where divine punishment is meted out when the idolized iteration is not

---

3. O'Kane, "Trauma and the Bible," 50.

met? Conversely, could the idolizing of Job have led to his horrific suffering? In fact, in *Job*, it could be argued that God so idolized obedience to the relationship that God was willing, and readily agreed to challenge the Satan, which by any reasonable measure served to vindicate God. The result is Job's calamitous suffering.

> Job is experiencing a cruel investigative process. His suffering is intimately committed to the fact that he is now subject to the violence of God's law . . . Are Job's actions in the story in any way connected to the fact that he is being tortured . . . The tortured lie to stop the torture. The assumption that torturers must torture to ascertain the truth camouflages the real reason that torturers torture, which is to realign the thinking of the tortured with that of his or her torturer . . . The torture that Job endures is theocratic violence of the greatest magnitude. The friends are God's police force. Schökel demonstrates that the point of the friends' activity is not Job's wellbeing. The point is, instead, the triumph of a theological doctrine that purports a specific divine legal system.[4]

In this regard, *torture* may not necessarily be construed narrowly as only physical. Rather, in addition to physical torture, others such as emotional, psychological, mental, etc., are equally significant and violent to the individual, community or nation. Thus, as a leader of a nation, one's insistent actions to forcibly ensure that everyone should think, do, and be like him or her is assuredly destructive. "The assumption that torturers must torture to ascertain the truth camouflages the real reason that torturers torture, which is to realize the thinking of the tortured with that of his or her torturer."[5] President Trump relentless vilifying of anyone or any institution that reports or suggests *otherwise* stands as a principal example. The President's idea of *likewise* is the only option; there is no other alternative. As Magdalene notes above, everyone must realign with the President's ideology. I use the term ideology rather than principles in large part because the latter is invariably bolstered and undergirded by ethical qualities. As the Special Counsel testified in Congress on July 24th, 2019, the President's actions have been unethical. As has been the case already in the course of Donald Trump's presidency, punishment in a variety of ways is meted to those who challenge or disagree with him including most recently FoxNews which he believes should always be loyal to and supportive of him.

---

4. Magdalene, "Job's Wife," 225–31.
5. Magdalene, "Job's Wife," 227.

Moreover, the President has surrounded himself with loyalists at all costs, who have pledged allegiance in words and actions, and thus there is a tone of protection often at the cost of truth and decency. Like the friends of Job who purport to demonstrate care, they simply dispense platitudes and defenses of the president's torture. In the midst of such tortuous behavior, those who are the objects of punishment may imagine that this will never end. But it does end, and such inevitability must be repeated until it is on the foreseeable horizon, and it can be emblazoned on the hearts of those who are tortured.

Did God shame *Job* in the face of the community? There is reference to the community in chapter I, and the pronouncement that Job is the greatest man in the East. Yet, there is no further reference to the community regarding Job. No member of the community comes to Job's aid or comfort. Is Job effectively excommunicated? Why the absence of community members? Does the "shaming of Job" by God's punishment in effect casts Job beyond the margins of society?

The only ones who come to comfort Job are from afar—from different directions. What this tells us is that the word about Job's suffering, and what had transpired had spread far and wide. "[Job] repudiated the dominant biblical explanation for adverse experience: indicating that whereas he can accept the deprivations and losses visited upon; he will not tolerate inaccurate and unfair descriptions of him as immoral. It is the mislabeling of his behavior and intentions that cause Job to suffer, not the painful experience themselves."[6]

Much of the issue in *Job* is not the suffering per se, important as that is, but the *why* question. Therein lies the critical issue. Why is God setting this in motion? In Job God seems to care more about Satan than he does about Job! Yet, as the narrative moves inexorably to something of an improbable denouement, there is the appropriate assurance of *take heart*. This provides for Job a hopeful platform for a new future and hints at the possibility of a universal hope. One of the frequently neglected ideas in Job is the notion that while Job was relentless in the pursuit of an answer from God, instead of receiving the hoped-for answer, he received one that came in the form of an informed personal relationship. An important part of entering into dialogue with God even if the dialogue takes the form of an intense complaint/questioning, the foundation is being established for a relationship of substance, perhaps even one of intimacy.

---

6. Goldberg, "Concerning Madness," 20–21.

Hope in a Liminal Time

As the days and months have drifted into years into the twentieth anniversary the images of the unimaginable horror of September 11 have been permanently etched deeply into the world's consciousness. In the days following that extraordinary tragedy, it seems that our hearts were broken again and again at the sights, sounds, and the narratives of personal experiences that have been related. The very landscape smoldering in its embers has become part of the fabric of the nation's consciousness individually and collectively. We now must live with both the particularities of this tragedy, and the memory that persist, and continue to reflect on the manner in which this moment shapes our future.

In the midst of this national sorrow, there were those who have sought to capitalize on the pain and vulnerability of the people, from those who inflated gas prices to exorbitant levels, to those who made dishonest solicitations for help, preying on the unsuspecting and the vulnerable. The very decency, generosity and compassion of many Americans, qualities now sharpened before our eyes, were viewed by some as an invitation to further pillage. As disturbing as both the temporary elevation of gas pricing, and the indecency of false solicitations were, they were quickly attended to. Yet, I believe there was another and more insidious attack that was launched. Many were utterly alarmed by the perspectives of the Reverends Pat Robertson and Jerry Falwell regarding the horror of September 11. Theirs was a word of stinging indictment. It was the timing, the spectacular insensitivity, and the unwitting alliance with those who challenge, and seek to perpetuate violence and the ideals of this nation that was striking. Robertson and Falwell entered the fray with a word of hopelessness that spewed hatred and cast derisions against a wounded and pained people. What is this word that was announced with such urgency and thoughtless immediacy?

In his September 14, 2001 statement, the Reverend Pat Robertson announced that God Almighty is lifting his protection from the United States because of secularism, pornography, abortion, and the pursuit of health, wealth and material pleasure. These are the reasons that he outlined for this divine withdrawal of protection. The very God who has protected the United States thus far has now decided to use this extraordinary expression of evil to deliver what Falwell deems "a wake-up call."

The Reverend Jerry Falwell appearing on Televangelist Pat Robertson's *700 Club* television show said that the United States had this coming, and that indeed there would be more. In such a time of profound distress and pain, the blame for the terrorists' actions is cast upon particular groups of people. According to Falwell, the people brought this upon themselves, for God has allowed this evil to come upon us, and it is a foretaste of what is likely to happen in the future if "God continues to lift the curtain and allow the enemies of America to give us probably what we deserve." Is this the God in whom we believe? Is this the message that is borne out of the biblical tradition? For Falwell it is the "the pagans and the abortionists, and the feminists, and the gays and the lesbians . . . the ACLU and People for the American Way who have brought on this horrific disaster." How are Robertson and Falwell different from those who artificially elevated gas prices and preyed on the innocent during the early days of the tragedy? They are not, though markedly more dangerous. They have continued to have an unflinching loyalty. Almost two decades later, Robertson announced to his followers and the nation that God told him that President Donald Trump would be reelected President of the United States. As is his typical manner, his proclamation had certitude. When Donald Trump lost the election, Robertson proclaimed that Go had called Trump for a particular time and purpose. Yet, Robertson's earlier word had succeeded in damaging the sacredness of the electoral process.

They not only submerged and stifled the pain of those who now suffer but added a further layer of guilt. Preying on the innocent and suffering has no place in our society; it is a radical departure from the biblical tradition, which both Falwell and Robertson purport to follow. They view themselves as self-appointed prophets of our time, yet two striking considerations are overlooked. There were prophets with questionable credentials and motivations within the biblical tradition (e.g. Hananiah, with his own agenda, in the time of Jeremiah) and second, the biblical prophets do not hurriedly recant in the face of opposition. In light of September 11, and perhaps as a counter to these positions we must have a different word. But what word?

We live in a society where it is not uncommon to seek instant answers. Immediacy is critical and with the continued advances in technology, the urgency for answers has generated voices and agencies that are more than willing to provide such answers. But answers at what cost? There are three observations and three biblical visions from which we might proceed with an eye to *take heart* as one way of attending to the issues and questions surrounding the horror and tragedy of September 11.

Rarely has the word been shown to have such transformational power as it does today. The very drama of the word, the importance and centrality of the word also means that it cannot be summarily uttered, and then retracted as Robertson and Falwell did. The word in a particular place and under particular circumstances has the capacity to be transformative. The pronouncement must come with some level of demanding intellectual rigor that is grounded in the present, imagines the future, and in every case, appeals to memory. Moments such as September 11 do indeed have the distinct possibility to define a people. It is precisely a moment such as this that calls for words that transform, daring, yet not reckless. We have witnessed such an extraordinary confusion of reckless pronouncements mistaken for daring speech. Robertson and Falwell most notably, but others such as Franklin Graham as well, have engaged in reckless speech under the guise of prophetic testimony. In times of historic proportions where there is piercing proclamation, the word, often spectacularly painful, enters the heart of a people and holds together in tension, hope in the face of suffering, and pronounces the benedictory note of *take heart*. In the United States where *freedom of speech* holds such a prominent and privileged place as a cornerstone expression of freedom, the often, misguided assumption is that speech does not have constraints. We have somehow assumed that words may be freely spoken without moral, political, or even emotional encumbrances. Words have power, and thus, they must be uttered with care and thoughtfulness at the very least. Moreover, this issue of the potency of words is not to be reduced to a generation gone by, but in our time, we are acutely aware of the power of words. A now common occurrence is the ubiquitous daily tweets of President Donald Trump, often with language and tone that are accusatory and derisive. They have invariably caused immeasurable damage to the civic fabric of society until his account was suspended.

Second, while it is the word that is featured prominently, crucially it is also about the timing of the word. That something is true does not in itself invite pronouncement. There is a season for the right word to be spoken, and a season for silence in the face of suffering that pains the soul. Here too, some voices have wondered aloud whether the United States and its relationship with other countries might have precipitated such horror. Is it possible that we as a society have not always with care and sensitivity, attended to the fragile nature of our relations with global societies? I am certain, that, as in all things, there is some truth here. Yet was that the right time to lavishly reflect on such truth? One might reflect on an incident as Simon Wiesenthal relates in the book, *The Sunflower*. In that moment when the deeply aggrieved Simon has the opportunity to tell the mother of Karl what an evil and deeply racist person her son was, and the immeasurable horror he inflicted on the innocent, Simon chose to do otherwise. Maybe at a different time, the mother might discover or be told, but for Simon, that was not the time, even though the memory of the torture and the wounds were fresh. Occasionally, when one feels the surge of indictment that might be borne out of such a cause and effect scenario, it may be that *silence* is the wisest word. The power and freedom to speak even when the word might have truth in all of its particularity, does not mean that one should make pronouncements. Timing and context do matter.

Third, in the quest for answers, it is the case that sometimes broad and general sweeps are made. Generalizations about people have the uncanny ability to lead ultimately to dangerous dimensions. Surely there is a place for anger, for pain, for suffering, but hatred destroys from within, and with it violence and death lurk. Generalizations are facile, and invariably reflect a disdain for intellectual and personal engagement. Broad strokes of wounding indictment have taken the place of more painful, but intellectually thoughtful particularities of the moment. Chris Matthews formerly of MSNBC's *Hardball*, in his quest to understand what might be the appropriate response of President Bush to the 9/11 terrorists' attack, suggests that the President is guided by an Old Testament approach to justice. This remark like others with its broad, sweeping and astonishing limitation seeks answers that are sharp and well defined in a binary way. But such sweeping assessments are dangerous when the questions continue to unfold with all of their complexities. At best this is a caricaturing of the Hebrew tradition, at worst it is perhaps even a reduction of the Divine to the scope of the human comprehension.

More than anything else, I would propose that a response of integrity for such a tragedy is one of liminal hope. Those within this society who wish to make concrete pronouncements of certitude either liberally or conservatively, are invited to imagine a new biblical creation. Certitude lends itself more to a sense of order rather than hope and justice, though they are not mutually exclusive. Hope dwells in liminality, not in the certitude of order. What is therefore necessary is to create a tension that attends to justice that must be meted out, and the challenging testimony of hope borne out of the biblical tradition.

> Thus says the LORD:
>
> A voice is heard in Ramah,
>
> > lamentation and bitter weeping.
>
> Rachel is weeping for her children;
>
> > she refuses to be comforted for her children,
> >
> > because they are no more.[7]

Even as Rachel weeps for her children her grief becomes a model for all who grieve and are broken hearted. There must be grief and the word spoken in the midst of such devastating grief cannot be one of indictment or the insinuation of divine withdrawal. Rather, hope dispels the arrogance

---

7. Jer 31:15.

and the self-indulgence of a community of present and provisional power and opens the possibilities of a liminal future. The peculiar paradox of hope is that it emerges most notably out of times of grief and suffering, though ultimately it transcends both joy and suffering.

> Ahab told Jezebel all that Elijah had done, and how he had killed all the prophets with the sword. 2 Then Jezebel sent a messenger to Elijah, saying, "So may the gods do to me, and more also, if I do not make your life like the life of one of them by this time tomorrow." 3 Then he was afraid; he got up and fled for his life, and came to Beer-sheba, which belongs to Judah; he left his servant there.
>
> 4 But he himself went a day's journey into the wilderness, and came and sat down under a solitary broom tree. He asked that he might die: "It is enough; now, O LORD, take away my life, for I am no better than my ancestors." 5 Then he lay down under the broom tree and fell asleep. Suddenly an angel touched him and said to him, "Get up and eat." 6 He looked, and there at his head was a cake baked on hot stones, and a jar of water. He ate and drank, and lay down again. 7 The angel of the LORD came a second time, touched him, and said, "Get up and eat, otherwise the journey will be too much for you." 8 He got up, and ate and drank; then he went in the strength of that food forty days and forty nights to Horeb the mount of God. 9 At that place he came to a cave, and spent the night there.
>
> Then the word of the LORD came to him, saying, "What are you doing here, Elijah?" 10 He answered, "I have been very zealous for the LORD, the God of hosts; for the Israelites have forsaken your covenant, thrown down your altars, and killed your prophets with the sword. I alone am left, and they are seeking my life, to take it away."
>
> 11 He said, "Go out and stand on the mountain before the LORD, for the LORD is about to pass by." Now there was a great wind, so strong that it was splitting mountains and breaking rocks in pieces before the LORD, but the LORD was not in the wind; and after the wind an earthquake, but the LORD was not in the earthquake; 12 and after the earthquake a fire, but the LORD was not in the fire; and after the fire a sound of sheer silence.[8]

This text, well known in some circles might very well be recalled for its sudden proposition of silence. Often in our society, the virtue of silence may be extolled in the abstract, but it may be that silence is necessary as

---

8. 1 Kgs 19:1–12.

a particular and concrete response, and not in a broadly universal way. When God does not reveal God's word through the established and expected conduits of wind and fire; earthquake and shattering mountains, silence unexpectedly becomes the conduit that transports the word. Sometimes it is precisely in a speechless moment that one hears, and divine utterance invites us to do likewise.

The prophet Elijah functioned in an imperial environment of grave danger, where the truth of his word stood in sharp contrast to imperial speech. His actions were not enough to guarantee his security. Prophetic truth clashed with the machinery of royal power and for a while the latter appeared unassailable in its relentless capacity to inflict violence. It was a matter of conflicting words; the word of YHWH or the word of the Empire, both with power, and both with pronouncements that hovered between life and death. The immediate word from Queen Jezebel is a challenge of terrifying power. Despite the truth of Elijah's ministry, the prophet will nonetheless face death; death by the persistent imperial hand of power. In the face of such unimaginable fear, Elijah flees beyond the boundaries of the Empire, and for a while in this state of barrenness, he sees death as the only viable alternative. He is unable to move beyond his present circumstances and that which his vision allowed him to see. In a truly desperate moment where he oscillates between life and death, Elijah hastily retreats to the wilderness, an odd, and literally an outlandish place of safety, and there he seeks a sign from YHWH. The wilderness is typically a place of death, yet in the life of ancient Israel it is the place where relationships were formally constituted and sealed, and where life in this rugged world of unprotective boundaries, was established in new and astonishing ways.

One cannot underestimate the threat of punishment in whatever form, when the punishment is pronounced and meted out by one who has the capacity and power to do so. Institutional power, whether through the monarch or president may cast lengthy shadows of fear. The natural impulse for those who are being targeted and tortured as Elijah was, is often to retreat and perhaps disappear. In so doing, as instinctive as this may be, particularly as a matter of self-preservation, is also to leave a vacuum of moral reckoning. It would take YHWH's still voice to send the prophet back to challenge Ahab and Jezebel. Royal power in the case of Ahab, dispensed in greed and egotistical ways, in threats and bullying is always at best, penultimate. Yet, in the moment, such power while not ultimate and lasting often creates devastating despair. When it is clear that no moral code or institutionalized laws be regarded, installed or followed, the impulse is to despair, and in certain defining moments, provoked into violence.

The word given to Elijah is that despite the vision of barrenness; despite the depth of despair this is not the end, for God chooses life, and it is a moment of divine reminder to *take heart*. In the face of a seeming unerring declaration of death by the Empire, or the request for death by those who assert the infallibility of "I" and abandon the essential "thou," comes the pronouncement of life. The divine response is radically communal and forms the very foundation of life as there is the immediate provision of daily sustenance. Elijah is invited to do that which is most difficult in times of despair and suffering, namely, to *eat, drink, sleep*. Even in times of despair, perhaps particularly in times of despair, that which is essential for both survival and health cannot become casualties. It is to ensure that life will continue even as the darkness of despair ends. For survival, without question, he does. Thus, the cycle continues as life goes on even as death lurks in the air, and fear causes anxiety about a diminished future. The concern by God is for the whole journey. As definitive as this moment was, yet the journey was unfinished and must be continued. Elijah who retreats and seeks assurance is told to continue with life and look to the greater scope of the created order. This is the challenge for human finitude so sharpened by the necessity for immediate procurement of answers, and the somewhat persistent impatience that accompanies this quest. In the face of such established convention, Elijah in two different ways is made to dwell in a state of divine liminality. "O Lord take away my life" he pleads, and instead he is given the necessary rationing of daily sustenance, *food, drink and sleep*. In the face of justifiable debilitating fear, he awaits the divine word. The word was not in the wind; the word was not in the earthquake; the word was not in the fire. At least for a while these structures will not be conduits for the word.

The experience is an invitation and reminder that while historical and established modes for providing resolution may be important, they cannot be viewed as absolute and resolute. As challenging as it might be when unimagined or unprecedented circumstances present themselves, conventional solutions may no longer work or be applicable. Even though the focus in the narrative is on Elijah, he is more than an individual, for he represents YHWH and therefore must be a voice for the community and espouse and live with words and actions that are just and humane. He must stand sharply in distinction to what Ahab and Jezebel represent. Does Elijah have the capacity to wait and imagine? Do we have the capacity to imagine a radical new word that is not as yet defined that breaks away from the well-worn conventions? This is exactly part of the challenge; do not imagine the present and its conventions as final. The invitation and challenge is to imagine what lies beyond.

Occasionally in the face of unimaginable suffering well-worn conventions may need to give way to new constructs. Weeks after September 11, 2001, indeed new constructs were being devised as there was the reluctant recognition of the radical landscape that we now face. As is the case in the story of Job, the most profound expression of poignant empathy and shared grief comes in the expression of prolonged silence. When the spoken word is uttered, it does not necessarily always have the quality that understands the magnitude of the grief, and thus those who seek to help dwell on the well-worn and narrow road may miss the mark. Job's experience was anything but representative. Even Job is bewildered by the depth of the suffering, and in this way, the established conventions could no longer apply.

καὶ ἀπέστειλεν Ιεζαβελ, πρὸζ Ηλιου καὶ εἰπεν Εἰ σὺ εἰ Ηλιου
καὶ ἐγὼ Ιεζαβελ τάδε ποιήσαι μοι ὁ θεὸζ καὶ τάδε προσθείη, ὅτι
ταύτην τὴν ὥραν αὔριον θήσομαι τὴν ψυχήν σου καθὼζ ψυχὴν
ἑνὸζ ἐξ αὐτῶν.[9]

This LXX text of 1 Kgs 19:2 adds a phrase that is absent in the Hebrew, and in this context it is instructive. It reiterates the power construct. "If you are Elijah, I am Jezebel." This phrase seeks to remind Elijah that there should be no misunderstanding of the levels of power, and for that matter the embodiment of the power. Elijah already knows the word of the Empire, a subversive word. He has experienced it personally. Jezebel the royal designee speaks the word as she has established herself as the one most capable of killing. Could prophetic testimony rooted in divine initiative stand in the face of imperial power? Elijah knew what the traditions dictated; he knew the conduits of divine announcements, all loud and typically with an explosion of nature. He made his claims; he reported his activities and waited. He listened; he heard; he saw what he expected, but the word was not enveloped in such anticipated drama; the word as he expected and imagined, never came. Elijah came with certitude as he had lived through the traditions of generations before him. He had reason to be certain with regard to the varied expressions of theophanic manifestations. He was, after all, the prophet of God, and had been obedient to the point of immanent death. But there was a word, not a word that allowed for the sort of order that he sought, beyond the boundaries of the Empire, but a word that transcended the norms of the day; a word that resisted the scripted conventions that he and the other prophets had come to know and assumed to be definitive and exhaustive. When the word finally came to Elijah it was captured in "a sound of sheer silence." Occasionally, there are no words. To

9. 1 Kgs 19:2.

intimate otherwise particularly under the guise of absoluteness, would be, among other things, to cast blinders on the breadth of divine initiative. Certitude evinced either by those who cast derision on particular groups with whom they may have ideological and theological differences, or by those who have evidence regarding American global policies, must ultimately acknowledge as Job and Elijah did, that they do not fully understand the scope and intricacies of the divine order.

Certitude brings with it a particular level of arrogance that is rooted in a narrowly defined exclusivity, and which is often contrived and lacks veracity. At other times, it is a certitude that takes on divine qualities that purport to be infallible and speaks on behalf of God and seeks to determine who needs to repent. The Reverend Franklin Graham who over the years has claimed to know the reason for, and justification of certain natural disasters, such as Hurricane Katrina in New Orleans that devastated a city and killed over eighteen hundred people or the tsunami in Indonesia in 2004 that killed over a quarter million people. Recently, Reverend Graham publicly called on Mayor Pete Buttigieg to repent because he is gay as once again, he claims to know the heart of God. Katrina was a punishment for the lifestyle in New Orleans or the tsunami in Indonesia a punishment against Muslims. Yet, Reverend Graham is firmly allied with President Trump on whose side he is an unflinching advocate despite the President's well-documented countless immoral and unethical actions. Certitude, particularly by those who have a public voice often has a note of finality to it, and the effect is to influence and also silence others.

> ¹ I give you thanks, O Lord, with my whole heart;
>
>> before the gods I sing your praise;
>
> ² I bow down toward your holy temple
>
>> and give thanks to your name for your steadfast love and your faithfulness;
>>
>> for you have exalted your name and your word
>>
>> above everything.
>
> ³ On the day I called, you answered me, you increased my strength of soul.
>
> ⁴ All the kings of the earth shall praise you,
>
>> O Lord, for they have heard the words of your mouth.
>
> ⁵ They shall sing of the ways of the Lord,
>
>> for great is the glory of the Lord.
>
> ⁶ For though the Lord is high, he regards the lowly;

but the haughty he perceives from far away.

⁷ Though I walk in the midst of trouble,

> you preserve me against the wrath of my enemies;

you stretch out your hand,

> and your right hand delivers me.

⁸ The LORD will fulfill his purpose for me;

> your steadfast love, O LORD, endures forever.

Do not forsake the work of your hands.[10]

Second, I propose a construct predicated on an exploration of Psalm 138. More than any other collection within the biblical corpus, it is, I believe within the Psalter that we encounter most profoundly the passionate heart to heart divine-human engagements. These encounters catapult emotions from the very depth of our being: joy and sorrow; fear and hope, appealing to God in language that is frequently explosive in its honesty and integrity. As ancient prayers, these psalms form the core of both individual and communal angst and praise. The psalms are the astonishing words of assurance and constancy that we inherit from the memory and dramatic legacy of those who have gone before us. We ought not be surprised that we embrace these assurances and words of hope in varying states of liminality. Words of assurance arise and have particular meaning in moments of suffering and despair. Now in the drama of our own lives, rooted in a world which at moments seems self-destructive, we are invited by these psalms to reach within the very depths of our being for the courage to express unconstrained lamentation and genuine emotional affectation.

Psalm 138 in its setting within the canon is conspicuously and meaningfully cradled between Psalm 137, that well known communal psalm of such despair and anger that finds the people of ancient Israel within the hostile, exilic barricades of the Babylonian empire, and Psalm 139 that elevates divine grace to a level of infinite magnitude. Psalm 137, poses the question whether there could be life again when the land is razed and lost, and the people scattered? There is no precedent. Can one sing songs in such a wretched prosaic, exilic existence? Such are the questions, and the horizons of hope disappear into a future, and thus brings no comfort. Yet, there is memory. And with this memory comes the seemingly improbable assurance of *take heart.* "Remember, O LORD . . . remember and pay them back."

The anger and the quest for vengeance strike terror into the hearts of those of us who read this psalm today. This psalm should never strike a chord

10. Psalm 138.

of ordinariness. It ends on a note of such horror that we would like to redact the last verse. Perhaps it is the case that the injustice that is perpetuated, the pain that is borne, and the utter insensitivity and belligerence of the captors that propel such violence in the shattered hearts of the people.

"Happy shall they be who take your little ones and dash them against the rock." This is the concluding sentiment of Psalm 137, yet not the last word. This image of such horror emerges from the passionate core of the community's being, and yet, it is left into the hands of God. To take these words out of context is to engage in madness of a sort that would be utterly unpropitious and calamitous. No one seeks to dash the heads of infants against rocks, but within the troubling confines of an exilic experience, and the tenacious belief in a resilient God, it allows us to remember and know that we are not alone. Passions unharnessed, runs deeply. I have noted elsewhere the devastating experience of exile.

> Revenge and pain are born out of the depth of suffering and a sense of betrayal and abandonment in the exilic experience. As much as any other text of Lamentation, it is Psalm 137 that provides a backdrop of what exile is like in Babylon. The qualities of life; the range of emotions; the grasp of a lost existence; the evaporating of hopes and aspirations; the loss of belonging and home, have all left an indelible mark on the exiles . . . Yet, this psalm is not only about unrestrained violent revenge, but in the midst of extraordinary and life transforming despair, the exiles' memory will not allow them to neglect or forget the history of their relationship with God, and Jerusalem.[11]

Bracketing Psalm 138 on the other side Psalm 139 is perhaps the most reassuring psalm of divine indulgence and persistent grace. This is the portrayal of God who never abandons, whose very creative power allows for the distant navigation and negotiation of treacherous waters into the far reaches of darkness. This is a psalm of such exquisite praise that one has to be careful not to overlook the very places that cause us to drown in grief or become disoriented in the geography of our existence.

Thus, between these two psalms, Psalm 138 exposes the profound juxtaposition of deep-rooted, complex emotions. The perspective of this psalm is global; it is for everyone; it is for the world; it is addressed to both the powerful and powerless; to the particular and universal. It is a psalm of personal thanksgiving. This might seem like an odd text to embrace at a time like this, thanksgiving for what? How might one sing songs in the midst of mourning? How might we give thanks and praise at a time of

11. Gossai, "The Babylonian Empire in the Bible." NP.

ruins? Can we imagine Spring-time in the midst of wintry days? We must, for it is about hope, and *taking heart* precisely when it appears improbable. Paradoxically, this is a season of hope though not hope as a last resort as it is so often understood. Psalm 138 refuses to believe that we must close our hearts to the pain, and equally refuses to imagine that the only recourse is vengeance. Instead, the psalmist insists on publicly acknowledging that this moment is not to be isolated. It is within the scheme of all creation and indeed all other gods that the God who is sought is acknowledged. There are other gods, those elevated into places of prominence in the lives of the people, consistently asserted throughout the biblical tradition. We know that other gods exist; they did in ancient times, and they have been multiplied today. There are other gods that vie for attention and loyalty, but there is a persistence to this God, YHWH who is not seasonal.

Presidential Adulation

The existence of other *gods*, those elevated to a principal place of promi-nence, where loyalty and worship are deeply ingrained and mandated, is not to be relegated to a historical biblical era. The message and allusions in Psalm 138 have a particular currency in the era of the Donald Trump presidency. The idea of idolatry is not to be narrowly construed as hav-ing only to do with divine beings. Rather, the critical power and force of idolatry may very well focus more on what preoccupies the center of one's consciousness. Donald Trump's unbridled preoccupation with power and wealth, self-importance and perhaps being adulated and adored is the very definition of idolatry. What Psalm 138 in the Donald Trump presidency environment points to is an understanding that loyalty, wor-ship and idolatry cannot be narrowly construed as religious concepts. By any measure, even as some national evangelical leaders such as Franklin Graham, Robert Jeffress, Jerry Falwell, jr. among others, and by some data, as many as 80% of evangelicals support President Trump. There is wide-spread adoration even as President Trump's words and actions are deeply and profoundly antithetical to core biblical truth and mandates such as mercy, justice, righteousness, compassion, care for the other, welcoming of the stranger. In his ongoing quest to support President Trump, the Rev-erend Robert Jeffress on a television show suggests that there is a biblical justification for building the wall on the southern border, suggesting that Heaven will have a wall. One could certainly challenge Jeffress's guiding interpretive principles, but more importantly, it is the interpretive leap to support the President that would essentially dismantle fundamental mores

of ethical guidance and humane principles. Recently Laura Mohsene, an
ex-evangelical Christian in an open letter to evangelical Christians points
to the systemic unraveling of the principles that were once core.

> So, the current coterie of evangelical pastors who support and
> encourage their congregations to support Trump are doing what
> they've always done. Church members are discouraged from
> thinking for themselves or questioning the doctrines or decla-
> rations of their group. If they hear rumors of sinful behavior
> against their pastors and the pastor denies it, then they side with
> the pastor against those Christians or outsiders who tell them
> the truth.
>
> This is why Trump's lies and denials are accepted by his
> flock of followers. Trump is not unlike the fictional Elmer
> Gantry. In spite of his personal immoral life, he draws people
> in and controls them by using their beliefs and prejudices. His
> charisma is more persuasive than his morals so they ignore his
> lack of them.[12]

The very idea of building a wall has become much more than a literal
physical barricade, but rather a metaphor of division and fear; for despair
and anguish. For far too many, including the majority of white evangelicals, have abandoned the vision of tomorrow for a longing of what was, a
retreat to yesterday. Former member of Congress Michele Bachman re-
marks that Donald Trump is "the most godly president" or the Reverend
Franklin Graham who says of Donald Trump, "he is a changed man and
a defender of the faith." Graham goes on to conclude that since his immoral behavior was before he became president, that does not matter. He
will have to answer to God. All the while the President dismantles and
abandons core biblical values and the basic ethic of empathy and care for
the other who is not in the image of the president. And I believe therein
lies the fundamental discord. A biblical and humane ethic is being crafted
in the image of Donald Trump and supporters are creating and re-creating
themselves in Donald Trump's image.

Donald Trump has rendered himself something of a contemporary
bone fide manifestation of Henrik Ibsen's Gregers Werle in *A Wild Duck*. Like
Werle, Donald Trump has bestowed on himself the role of crusader of truth
in a variety of issues, and instead he has unleashed a particular level of venom
on individuals, institutions, communities that either oppose or challenge *his
truths*. Like Gregers Werle, Trump trades in insults and at the very core, for
all his crusading for *truth*, it is apparent that like Werle, Trump is neither a

---

12. Mohsene "Letter to Evangelical Christians," Oct. 26, 2018.

good nor a decent man. Indeed, like Gregers Werle Trump sets out to seek vengeance against those he has perceived as having *wronged* him. Like Werle, despite the ruin he has brought on Americans and those who seek refuge in the United States, he insists on his righteousness, and has as his unlikely followers a sizeable majority of evangelical Christians. The gospel that Donald Trump preaches, like Werle has led him to become the acknowledged purveyor of falsehoods. No amount of religious rhetoric or adamant political divisiveness will last forever or save Trump from himself. Like Werle, ultimately those have been ardent and loyal in their unwavering support will retreat. Like Werle, whose righteous canvassing end in infamy and shame and a dismantling of friendship and support, so the slope exits for Trump as he journeys in a similar trajectory and traffics in pseudo-righteous indignation. In the face of such enticing idolatrous preoccupations, the Psalmist noncoercive, invitational word comes. It appeals to what has been, for a hope of what will be, and in a way, one might say it has more to do with the ultimate and not the fleeting and temporary. It has to do with permanence, and in this regard, there is an invitation to *take heart*.

The psalmist begins by giving thanks with all the heart, a thanksgiving that is neither superficial nor contrived; it is not merely an external fulfillment of some kind of societal expectation; but gratitude from the heart. It is gratitude that is deeply embedded within the person. Moreover, it is inherently an acknowledgment of the other, human or divine. Underlying this is the idea that we are shaped by community, and we function in community. This is a psalm that brings us face to face with political and social realities, as expressed through the juxtaposition of the haughty and the lowly, and an acknowledgement that not only do they exist side by side, but that they do co-exist. There is a social awareness that counters the posture of the enemy, and the God of the psalmist understands this, and attends to it. This is a God who may be enthroned on high, but who watches and keeps the inhabitants of the earth, not only for a few, or for the select, but *all* the inhabitants of the earth. The biblical tradition speaks of God with language that takes us in faraway reaches of the universe, and then leads us back in the trenches, where the wounds of the earth appear. This is a God who, when we speak, even with broken hearts, perhaps particularly with broken hearts, hears and listens. The psalmist was confident of this and invites us to enter into that state of confidence. But we who live with technology and the advances of our time, and who expect answers within time frames defined by our finite vision, must now lament and wait, be restored through a hope that is not able to be confined into our spaces. Finitude and the circumspection of time and space must not be viewed as setbacks or impediments. It is the reality that shapes the landscape of human capacity. What it brings with it is the knowledge and certainty that the present is penultimate. So, we wait, hope and *take heart*.

> In days to come the mountain of the LORD's house
> > shall be established as the highest of the mountains,
> > and shall be raised up above the hills.
> Peoples shall stream to it,
> ² and many nations shall come and say:
> > "Come, let us go up to the mountain of the LORD,
> > to the house of the God of Jacob;
> > that he may teach us his ways
> > and that we may walk in his paths."
> For out of Zion shall go forth instruction,
> > and the word of the LORD from Jerusalem.
> ³ He shall judge between many peoples,
> > and shall arbitrate between strong nations far away;
> > they shall beat their swords into plowshares,
> > and their spears into pruning hooks;
> > nation shall not lift up sword against nation,
> > neither shall they learn war any more;
> ⁴ but they shall all sit under their own vines and under their
> > own fig trees,
> > and no one shall make them afraid;
> > for the mouth of the LORD of hosts has spoken.[13]

Third, I propose a vision of hope in the prophet Micah that stations itself firmly within the creation matrix, where the created order is to be a place of peace. As much as any place in the biblical corpus, the Hebrew Prophets make it abundantly clear that military might and boasting of military prowess, and the accumulation of wealth and land at the expense of the poor will never be sustained. History has crystallized the fact that for a while loud claims to invincibility will rule, but it never does forever.

> Alas for those who devise wickedness
> and evil deeds on their beds!
> When the morning dawns,
> they perform it, because it is in their power.[14]

13. Mic 4:1–4.
14. Mic 2:1.

Alas for those who lie on beds of ivory,

    and lounge on their couches,

    and eat lambs from the flock,

    and calves from the stall;

⁵ who sing idle songs to the sound of the harp,

    and like David improvise on instruments of music;

⁶ who drink wine from bowls,

    and anoint themselves with the finest oils,

    but are not grieved over the ruin of Joseph![15]

For you have forsaken the ways of your people,
    O house of Jacob.

Indeed they are full of diviners from the east

    and of soothsayers like the Philistines,

    and they clasp hands with foreigners.

Their land is filled with silver and gold,

    and there is no end to their treasures;

    their land is filled with horses,

    and there is no end to their chariots. [16]

Look at the proud!

Their spirit is not right in them,

    but the righteous live by their faith.[17]

What is pervasive in the prophets is the vast divide between those who have power and wealth, and the ongoing disconnect with those who do not. The Mic 2:1 text is striking in its indictment of those who may even use their time of rest to devise ways of doing evil, perhaps while lying in their opulent settings as Amos 6:4 outlines. We note that with numerous other prophetic texts, Mic 2:1 and Amos 6:4 begin with הוי which often with affectation and refinement is rendered *alas* or *ah*. Yet, the more powerfully expressed *woe*, may better capture the breadth of indictment and punishment. And the reason why any of the expressions of evil would come to fruition following the planning in darkness is straightforward: power and the abuse of power.

    Peace is perhaps the most challenging vision to articulate at this time, and it is one which has been embraced repeatedly over time, but almost

---

15. Amos 6:4–6.

16. Isa 2:6–7.

17. Hab 2:4.

always as an elusive ideal. Yet is there a better time to speak of, reflect on, and pursue peace than at a time when it seems that the established power constructs all point to war. This is also a word that must be heard alongside other pertinent words. As is the case with the prophetic word, there is no timeline, no deadline that is set. Indeed, there is no prescriptive outline of "how to." The language is that of hope, and those who hear this word are invited to embrace such radical hope in the face of a time that refuses to be quarantined by human constraints. "Do we dare?" is the underlying question in this prophetic text.

There will come a time, pronounces the prophet in Mic 4:1–4 when peace will be established with God as the architect of such peace. Clearly not only is there widespread disaffirmation of such a vision today in the world, but for many it appears so inconceivable, that they seek to find interpretive avenues to explain it away. There is a sustained sense of arrogance in this regard, even as human vision becomes the measure of what may be. Mic 4:1–4 presupposes certain elements, followed by a radical vision. The reality of the text remains undiminished by the historical framework. The prophet acknowledges the presence of war, the instruments of war, and the divisiveness that comes from war. What is the alternative divine word? Four pronouncements form the foundation of this stunning prophecy. First, there will come a time, beyond human inclination and imagination, where peoples will indeed gather together with a common purpose, namely, to learn. Second, there will be a divine arbiter, for clearly there is inadequacy in human arbitration. Or in any event, the present construct led by human presuppositions of power that sees war as the final arbiter, will give way to divine initiative. Third, there will need to be a dramatic reversal of directions. The very instruments of war will be re-created into instruments that sustain and keep creation, rather than dismantle it. But it is more than simply destroying the implements of war; this vision announces a dramatic change in mindset. It is not enough to change external arsenal, but a season of unlearning war must now be embarked upon; that which has long ago been interiorized within the heart must now be excised and be replaced by a new learning. Fourth, this divine word will cause a return to a life of simplicity, and perhaps most notably, there will be no fear. Such is this radical vision.

Almost twenty years ago, September 11, 2001, brought with it a defining moment for the United States and the world. Old constructs do not have the capacity to attend to such a moment. It is a time of invitation to think and reflect anew, perhaps to live vulnerably in a state of liminality, rather than settle for constructs that undermine and collapse our hopes, or worst, embrace platitudes that deepen the wounds. And after thousands of years of recorded history, we have witnessed the cycles of war and peace; violence and redemption. One can certainly advance the argument that in many devastating instances of war, literal and figurative, comes a horizon of peace and tranquility that may appear distant. I write these words at a time when national tension in the United States regarding racism, hate speech and anti-Semitism have risen in unprecedented ways. Yet, in the face of such fear and trepidation, hope emerges and beckons. Fear and hope in tension. Perhaps, no greater example than the widespread hate filled gun violence in churches, mosques, synagogues in recent months where fear and hope reside side by side. This is a new season for hope in a liminal state. Liminal states also allow us to take time and be refreshed and reflect and act. One might argue that without this moment of refreshing and reaction, we are not able to function and live fully.

8

Hope Beyond Despair: Ruth

"If you can, convert him. If not remember that kindliness was given to you for this reason. It is indeed humanity's unique quality to love even the transgressors, and this love emerges as you remember that such men are your kinsmen. That soon both they and you will be dead, and above all that, they cannot hurt you." —Marcus Aurelius, *Meditations*, VII 22, and IX, 11

In this brief but resonant quote from Marcus Aurelius' *Meditations*, there are three essential ideas that one should reckon with in the context of hope from despair. First, Aurelius advocates the possibility of conversion; the possibility of change. Certainly, he acknowledges that while that possibility exists, it is also conceivable that it might not work. The importance of this is precisely the belief that everyone is capable of change and should be granted the opportunity to do so. Even when words and actions crafted with noticeable deficiency in moral mooring or grounded in a code of ethics, but rather are shaped by racial or ethnic or national identity, there is nonetheless present such a possibility for change. Second, if such conversion to a place of virtue and compassion is not possible, and is met with repudiation or rebuff, one must not lose one's capacity for kindness. It is to say that above all else we must not lose who we are in the face of disenchantment and rejection. Whether Aurelius is right in his argument that humans were given kindness for this reason, it is the fact that those who have the quality of kindness must not be bracketed and reserved only for those who espouse similar qualities. As difficult and challenging as it is likely to be, such kindliness must be meted out to all people, including the transgressors even as we are reminded of the human connection. This would not be necessary to argue here, were it not for the inherent challenge that it poses. Third, Aurelius' reference to death is not only about finality, but more broadly about human finitude and mortality. An important part of this idea of death is that mortality will in its inevitable way brings an end to all suffering. Aurelius underlines the idea that those who are the architects and principals in causing suffering and despair will in time die. This is not an invitation to wait, but to know that when all virtuous possibilities are exhausted, there is still hope beyond the present.

> But Naomi said to her two daughters-in-law, "Go back each of you to your mother's house. May the LORD deal kindly with you, as you have dealt with the dead and with me. ⁹ The LORD grant that you may find security, each of you in the house of your husband." Then she kissed them, and they wept aloud.[1]

> Her mother-in-law said to her, "Where did you glean today? And where have you worked? Blessed be the man who took notice of you." So she told her mother-in-law with whom she had worked, and said, "The name of the man with whom I worked today is Boaz." ²⁰ Then Naomi said to her daughter-in-law, "Blessed be he by the LORD, whose kindness has not forsaken the living or the dead!" Naomi also said to her, "The man is a relative of ours, one of our nearest kin.[2]

Simply mentioning *God* in every statement intending to reflect one's religious conviction does not necessarily grant greater legitimacy to the actions or words. Such use of the name of God as a rhetorical device undermines the essence and nature and ultimately is seen for its disingenuity. One thinks of Jeremiah's cautioning of the repetition of, "the Temple of the LORD, the Temple of the LORD, the Temple of the LORD" (Jer 7:4) as a protective and exclusive device as opposed to the intent of Temple as a place of worship; inclusion and community gathering. The book of Ruth mentions God *twice*. Yet, there is a clear, and ever-present evidence that God is actively involved in the lives of the people. Simply mentioning God or the name of God is not to be a substitute for acting with compassion and care and doing that which is neighborly. Is appeal to God to provide, characteristic of both Naomi's and Boaz's prayers in that they regard blessing as God's natural response to human faithfulness and goodness? One should note that while God is referenced several times in *Ruth*, God does not speak in the book, and while not as dramatic as *Esther*, here too we have an unavoidable synthesis between God and humankind. There is a clear picture of the fact that God works through human beings, regardless of the artificial boundaries that we have so often erected. What is equally significant is the fact that the characters appeal to God, question God, blame God; and bless in the name of God. In all of this, it is unnecessary to repeat the language and name of God. Finally,

1. Ruth 1:8–9.
2. Ruth 2:19–20.

in all circumstances, it is understood that God is present and active, even as human actions unfold. "The book of Ruth presents God hidden and mysterious, like yeast at work in a loaf of bread, until all is transformed. God is at work through the everyday actions of faithful people seeking to manifest divine loyalty in the loyal interactions with those around them."[3]

Naomi prays that God would grant her daughters-in-law security in marriage, and that Yahweh will bless Boaz. Though having said this, it seems that there is Naomi's follow up in sending Ruth into the fields to glean. In praying to God, there is an expectation that God will act through humans. There is an unavoidable and organic connection between prayers to God and human action, and this is most notable in the actions of Boaz.

> The most refined example of the hidden interplay between human action and God's control is in chapters 2–3 where Boaz prays that Ruth may receive her full reward from the God of Israel under whose wings she has sought shelter. Little does he know that Ruth will shortly ask *him* for shelter under his own "wings." (Cf. the wordplay on wings and the corner of Boaz's garment in 2:12 and 3:9) It soon turns out that it is Boaz himself who is to fulfill his own prayer for Ruth, for thus the will of God of Israel show his faithfulness toward the family of Elimelech.[4]

The centrality of *hesed* in *Ruth* extends the manner in which we think of neighborliness and care for the other. This is not fulfillment of the expected, but beyond both the conventions and defined legal requirement. We witness this as Boaz invites Ruth to be a part of his community, repeatedly removing her from the margin, closer to the center. In *Ruth* one cannot overlook the significance of Moab as a place of plenty, granting life to a family coming from the devastating famine of the *house of bread* that is now defined by the quality of scarcity. The further significance is that Israelites are told Moab is a city to be avoided. Yet, after the history of Lot and his daughters, it is clear that the possibility exists for something good in Moab; there is generosity and plenty, and the capacity to welcome and share with outsiders. As is frequently the case in the biblical narrative, the story of Ruth begins in a state of barrenness (broadly construed as a metaphor) or as Neilsen has said, "Ruth takes as its starting point a situation of want, in this case the famine that forces the family into exile . . . Hunger and death thus become the negative conditions for a significant leitmotif in Ruth."[5]

---

3. Sakenfeld, *Ruth*, 15–16.

4. Neilsen, *Ruth*, 31.

5. Neilsen, *Ruth*, 43.

Why will Orpah and Ruth want to leave the comforts of their homeland to take a chance on a deity who had so heartlessly spurned Naomi? . . . The author of the book of Ruth has set the situation up this way in order to accentuate the supernatural dimension of Ruth's decision to enter the land of Israel. By painting Orpah's choice to remain in Moab as eminently reasonable, the author sets in bold relief the audacity of Ruth's decision to go up to the land of Israel.[6]

We are never told exactly why Ruth clung to Naomi, though we are able to extrapolate and draw conclusions that would allow Ruth's actions to stand in contrast to Orpah's. But what we *do* know is that choices are made, and in this narrative, neither choice can be construed as wrong or in negative tones, though they are surely to be contrasted. Indeed, the decision by both Ruth and Orpah are made after Naomi's heartfelt reflective suggestion that they return to their mothers' house. Both daughters-in-law decline and proceed to make their respective determinations regarding their future. Moreover, the anonymity of the *goʾel* is not looked down upon or ridiculed. The anonymous *goʾel* is given an account of this reality of which he is a principal actor, and he chooses not to undertake his role as *goʾel*. Whatever one feels about his decision, it is his, and it is accepted without quarrel, argument or recrimination.

In terms of the narrative, we hear no more of Orpah or the principal *goʾel*, yet according to *Ruth Rabbah*, Orpah is brutally punished for her decision to return to her mother's house; she is raped by a hundred men and even a dog! This is what one commentator would like readers to believe, though Orpah does what Naomi in the first instance proposes, caringly and thoughtfully. Once again this is a reminder that one's ideology or worldview may invariably shape or redesign a narrative to reflect what imagines or believes it should say. Particularly noteworthy here is the fact that Naomi urges Ruth to follow in her sister-in-law's footsteps and return to her mother's house. Naomi clearly viewed this option and choice to be significant and perhaps even the most appropriate for the future of the daughters-in-law and their welfare. Thus, *Ruth Rabbah's* depiction of the brutal rape of Orpah reflects the author's view that Orpah's decision was so improper as to deserve such extraordinary punishment, reflecting a striking depth of moral depravity. Or does Naomi's forceful suggestion betray the sense of difficulty that Ruth is likely to face as a Moabite in Judah? One is not sure. But perhaps this too reflects the history between the two countries, and the strict admonitions that there is nothing good about

6. Anderson, *Charity*, 100.

Moab; indeed, even getting close to Moab is forbidden. Yet, the mitigating circumstances in life are such that in the face of famine, certain boundaries, ancient and current must be circumvented. There is practically no response or reaction by Naomi to Ruth's extraordinary decision. Only much later is there any indication of Ruth's positive presence when Naomi seeks to have an heir through her. So while Ruth binds herself to Naomi, in God, land and community through a divine oath, Naomi is conspicuously unmoved, at least initially, as they began their journey to Bethlehem in Judah. Indeed, Naomi's response to the women who welcome her back to Bethlehem is one filled with the language of emptiness, with no acknowledgement or mentioning of Ruth and a pronouncement that she is being punished by God. Like Job, she has no idea why, and the circumstances as she understands them, except that God is almighty and inscrutable, and as her understanding dictates, God is responsible. Unlike Job however, the audience is equally aware of the divine reasoning. One option for the punishment might be the family's journey to Moab. Yet, if this is the case, and it is Elimelech's decision to do so; then why Naomi's punishment?

The unexpected new information that a relative of Naomi owns land propels the narrative through Ruth's initiative. It is something of a surprise that Boaz the Redeemer, and Naomi never meet in the text. That would have been the conventional course, but as we have witnessed throughout the narrative, the journey to a place of belonging and hope frequently travels a non-conventional road. One might justifiably surmise that Ruth did not know what to expect in her journey to Judah; indeed, she is genuinely surprised by Boaz's gracious acceptance, and in the response casts herself in prostration at the feet of Boaz. Whether it is the history between the two countries, or simply the extraordinary kindness of a wealthy stranger, Boaz's actions by any measure is unencumbered by ulterior motives. The cynic might readily conclude that Boaz must indeed have some element of personal self-interest. Yet, there is no *quid pro quo*, but simply the act of unexpected grace. Boaz's action is in no way only the fulfillment of the bare minimum in keeping with the biblical provision for the care of the poor or refugee. In itself, this would be life giving, but Boaz goes noticeably beyond such prescribed boundaries. It might have been such an extravagant act that propelled Ruth to bow and prostrate herself before him. Boaz in meeting Ruth is clearly aware of her circumstances and points to the fact that he has heard of her loyalty to Naomi. Evidently this is instrumental in his decision to aid Ruth and Naomi beyond the established expectations.

> When you reap the harvest of your land, you shall not reap to
> the very edges of your field, or gather the gleanings of your

harvest. [10] You shall not strip your vineyard bare, or gather the fallen grapes of your vineyard; you shall leave them for the poor and the alien: I am the LORD your God.[7]

[19] When you reap your harvest in your field and forget a sheaf in the field, you shall not go back to get it; it shall be left for the alien, the orphan, and the widow, so that the LORD your God may bless you in all your undertakings. [20] When you beat your olive trees, do not strip what is left; it shall be for the alien, the orphan, and the widow. [21] When you gather the grapes of your vineyard, do not glean what is left; it shall be for the alien, the orphan, and the widow. [22] Remember that you were a slave in the land of Egypt; therefore, I am commanding you to do this.[8]

Gleaning as is outlined in the texts above are not a matter personal goodwill, as important as that may be, but it is an expectation born out of a particular relationship. When Boaz comes to the field and sees Ruth among the gleaners, whether she was gleaning or resting, he does two very particular things that have defined/should define the landscape of how we treat and accommodate the outsider. Boaz could have been entirely hospitable by fulfilling the "letter of the law" in providing gleaning opportunity for Naomi, but instead he extends his personal magnanimity in two significant ways. First, he invites/encourages Ruth to remain in his field. There is no need to go looking elsewhere; there's no need to be concerned about overstaying her welcome. Perhaps more than this is the significant role of providing a sense of place; a sense of belonging.

Second, this sense of inclusion and belonging in the community is more than a pronouncement, important as that is, but rather what such belonging means for functioning in community. Boaz's response gives shape to a platform that could be a template for the manner in which *outsiders* are welcome and incorporated into society. In welcoming Ruth, Boaz does not make his decision on whether Ruth will add to his economic gains or whether her presence in the community will *fit*. Rather, she is welcomed for one principal reason, and because of one immeasurable attribute: kindness. The measure, therefore, by which refugees are accepted or rejected in the United States through the Trump administration is that of nationality and status and economic status and ideology of exclusion of the *other*. Ruth demonstrates none of the above, but rather kindness, sacrifice, grace. She comes as a widow, childless accompanying an elderly widow from a nation classified as enemy. Decision for those who seek refuge should be predicated

7. Lev 19:9–10.
8. Deut 24:19–22.

on qualities of empathy and compassion, kindness and community and always the acknowledgement of the human condition. Boaz, as a resident and
a *worthy man* of Bethlehem is aware of the potential dangers that Ruth is
likely to face, both as a young widow and as a foreigner. Much of the advice
given to Ruth indicates that she is the one who takes the initiative. What
Boaz reminds us is that providing the "legal minimum" and functioning
on the assumption that is well and sufficient, is not good enough. Boaz's
words would certainly classify as seeking the *shalom* of Ruth, her welfare,
her entire well-being, beyond bare sustenance.

> The story from start to finish illustrates the ways in which loyal
> action, kindness and good will produce a surplus that can both
> break down dividing walls of hostility and open horizons to
> shattered lives . . . Boaz's generosity is evident, but it is not suf-
> ficient to reverse Naomi and Ruth's economic hardship. They are
> better off than a day ago, but the future remains bleak unless
> longer-term solution can be put into place.[9]

As Sakenfeld notes, *goodness* and *kindness* do not only serve in a particular case but have the potential to influence and shape other acts. In general, those who seek refuge do so in large part because of their fragmented
and fractured lives, experienced in a variety of ways. What is also significant
and noteworthy here is the fact that there may not be an immediate correla-
tion between an act of kindness and economic gain. Yet, we see that in the
case with Ruth, such a sense of settledness and belonging, takes ongoing acts
of kindness, inclusion and time. To further illustrate this reality of hope in
migration that transcend time and place, geography and nationality, Mehta
speaks to its significance today in the midst of nationalistic policies and
impulses. "When migrants move, it's not out of idle fancy, or because they
hate their homelands, or to plunder the country they come to, or even (most
often) to strike it rich. They move—as my grandfather knew—because the
accumulated burdens of history have rendered their homelands less and less
habitable. They are here because you are here."[10]

And in the case of Naomi, the reasons are twice over. In a way she
returns to her homeland from a place she once called home because of loss
and hopelessness. And as Mehta notes, because "you are here." The cycle
in *Ruth* reminds us in vivid relief that there are distinctions of importance
and priorities to be made between all that is necessary for life. So, in going
to Moab the principal and most urgent need was that for food, and that
is spelled out immediately as the famine in Bethlehem is the precipitating

9. Sakenfeld, *Ruth*, 45–46.
10. Mehta, *This Land is our Land*, 61.

factor. It is following this immediate need that the narrative announces that both Mahlon and Chilion husbands to Orpah and Ruth are dead, in addition to Elimelech. Of course, this immediately underlines the precarious reality of the three women who are left with varying states of hardships and significant challenges. But this unexpected reality has two interconnected components, both the present, and significantly the prospects of a future without an heir. As Ruth has found favor with Boaz, and with his gracious invitation and protection, the narrative turns to the future. The distinction between life in Moab where the present is fulfilled, and the women seem to be heading into a state of barrenness, as Naomi and Ruth return to Bethlehem, is striking. Will there be an heir for Naomi? Unlike the seemingly insurmountable challenges in Moab, Bethlehem also presents complications, though none is insurmountable. There will be a future, but once again, not as the convention would dictate. "[I]n both Ruth's and Tamar's stories, it is when Boaz and Judah truly see the face of the young woman in all vulnerability that they act for the other's good. In this regard, it has been argued that a common theme in these two narratives regards the notion of seeing and not seeing, or concealing and revealing."[11]

At the risk of oversimplification, one might argue that a face to face encounter is always a better moment for empathy and understanding. At the very least, this precludes the distinct possibility of generalizing. To look into the eyes of the other and see not only the other, but oneself will certainly establish a platform for the empathy at a distance when it is not possible to physically look into the eyes of the other. In his superb historical record of an era of darkness for American immigration, Daniel Okrent brings to life not only the clinical actions of many, but in so doing underlines the parallels with the Trump administration's policies and directives.

Moreover, the parallels point disconcertingly to the basis, namely one of prejudice and bigotry. Specifically, Okrent recounts Henry Cabot Lodge's *literary* test to be used to determine immigrant suitability for entrance into the United States. Based on this principle, a bill was sent to President Taft to sign. When Taft reluctantly vetoed it, evidently not out of a principled position, his veto was overridden in the Senate and barely sustained in the House.[12] Okrent notes Lodge's comment, which with very little difficulty, one is able to draw a line directly from Lodge to Trump, except the geography has changed and now has the issue of color. "This country was settled and built by the people from Great Britain and Ireland, from Scandinavia, from Holland, from Germany and from France . . . But now . . . for more than two maddening,

11. Claasen, "Resisting Dehumanization," 669–670

12. Okrent, *The Guarded Gate*, 183–184.

frustrating decades, the immigrants coming in this from Eastern and South-
eastern Europe . . . offspring of a different civilization."[13]

This is precisely one of the aspects of the Trump administration's
policy and action on refugees that has been, and continues to be so profoundly painful and lacking in kindness; namely the intentional separation
of children from parents to discourage migration. Moreover, such separation and encampment and the scattering of the children to unknown parts
of the country has been executed by orders, and thus the president or the
secretary of Homeland Security do not have to look into the eyes of those
who seek refuge. It is to look at the face and into the eyes of the person
that reveals life's experiences, and perhaps something of the journey that
the person has travelled, by choice or circumstances. One thinks of Oscar
Wilde's A Portrait of Dorian Gray, where the author suggests that the story
of one's life is seen in one's face; one's eyes.

While the possibility of change may occur from a distance, it is distinctly more possible when one sees the face of the other and looks into
their eyes. Perhaps in looking into the face and eyes of the other, much may
be revealed that also underlines what the other seeks to conceal. Yet, none
of this may be possible if one makes decisions and acts from a distance and
casts out refugees through deputies.

Emanuel Levinas argues that in fact one cannot be ethical unless one
sees the face of the other and takes it seriously. The ethical quality of the
person is predicated on encountering the face of the neighbor. "The face
of the neighbor signifies for me an unexceptionable responsibility, preceding every fee consent, every fact, every contract."[14] One aspect of Levinas's
philosophy in this regard makes evident the reality that there is a path that
may be paved beyond enmity or difference into neighborliness and accord.
Beyond the inhumane disconnect of not looking into the eyes of the other is
a grounding for generalization. In this way, broad groups of persons could
be discarded, and invariably such generalization become acceptable, here
the empathy for the person becomes a casualty, as does the person.

All humans want to belong; to be seen; to be heard. "[T]o be human
means, first to resist those forces that seek to violate and obscure one's dignity; and second, to be able to see or recognize the plight of another."[15] As
is typically the case with every seemingly indisputable idea, this too likely
has exceptions. Yet, even the ascetic or the one in solitude by choice, wants
to belong; even those who have chosen "silence" as a quality of life, want to

13. Okrent, The Guarded Gate, 184–185.

14. Levinas, Otherwise, 88.

15. Claasens, "Resisting Dehumanization," 660.

belong. Perhaps a religious virtue to be pursued is that of the inalienable right to be heard. When a person is silenced by another, an inherent aspect of who he or she is, is taken away, and this invariably leads to, or reflects a power imbalance. "Equally important though, is the ability to see the other, to show empathy—to take up one's responsibility to act for the well-being of the other—regards the ability to see the face of the other, to forge a common connection, between oneself and the other."[16]

One of the self-evident factors in Ruth is that Boaz is wealthy and both Ruth and Naomi are dependent. Yet, the narrative is not defined entirely by this dichotomy. What we witness is the vision of the women, a vision that pivots on the importance of their future welfare. The presupposition is that the reality in Moab with the death of sons and husbands may be the last word. Instead, at every step Ruth and Naomi refuse to imagine that their present will always be the way life will be. Boaz's power, wealth, and kindness, are all in play within the narrative, though not at the expense of the women. Ruth's proposal of marriage to Boaz is perhaps the most striking reminder that such initiative typically is the prerogative and domain of the man, and in this instance, is taken without any due regard by a vulnerable woman. Why is Chilion not considered in terms of progeny and descendant? Is the concern entirely only for the future of one to carry on? Had Orpah returned with Naomi and Ruth, would there have been a similar concern/interest?

In the narrative leading to Boaz being the *go'el*, we are again struck by the fact that even when choices/decisions are made, the role of the community remains central. While Boaz already holds Ruth in high esteem because of her loyalty, now the community elders also express their regard for Ruth, noting again, her loyalty. This all fits with the overall orientation of the narrative. As loyalty, steadfast love, etc., exist in the relationship between Ruth and Naomi, nonetheless, the overarching concern is for the future legacy, an issue that moves beyond the individual. As is so often the case in the Bible, divine promises or human hopes and dreams are not always, immediately, or routinely and smoothly fulfilled, but invariably, there are obstacles to overcome. Whether it is Sarah or Rebekah or Rachel or Hannah's barrenness, or as is the case in Ruth, the *go'el* ahead of Boaz who declines to marry her, obstacles exist. "Rachel, Leah and Tamar represent typical female destinies: the infertile but beloved Rachel; the fertile but unwanted Leah; and the deceived Tamar who had to secure her rights herself before she could become pregnant."[17]

16. Claasens, "Resisting Dehumanization," 668.
17. Nielsen, *Ruth*, 92.

An underlying theme in this narrative is the idea that while Moab was able to provide for the present, it had no prospects for Naomi's future. So, Naomi's comment about returning to Bethlehem "empty" might indeed not so much be a slighting of Ruth, but her understanding of what she experienced in Moab; a recognition that there is little prospect for a future with her in Judah. She gained a present and lost a future. Finally, the place of rootedness, Bethlehem in Judah, despite its time of famine is a reminder that famine is not the last word. Rootedness, sacrifice and belonging all do matter in the great scheme of life.

In Naomi's suggestion that Ruth return to her mother's house, Naomi knows that she has no future to offer Ruth, and perhaps Ruth knows that she could not in good conscience abandon Naomi in her present state. There is no evidence in the text that would intimate that Ruth accompanied Naomi for ulterior motives. In many respects, Elimelech, Naomi, Ruth and Boaz broke with societal conventions, and did what they thought was most beneficial for the family. There is no real evidence to suggest that any of the actions were generated by personal creed or greed.

> The portrait of the community may be regarded as a microcosm of the peaceable kingdom envisioned by the prophetic tradition. It is a human community in which the marginalized person has dared to insist upon full participation; in which one in the center has reached out beyond societal norms to include the marginalized. It is a community in which children are celebrated and the elderly are attentively cared for. It is a community in which all are fed, a community in which joy is the dominant note.[18]

In particular as we reflect on the realities of children and the elderly, the most vulnerable in our society, we are also reminded that there is hope beyond despair, and therefore the exhortation to *take heart*. In *Ruth*, beyond the significantly held focus on empathy, mercy and compassion, is the very notable social component. The narrative begins with a socio-economic crisis, wrapped in the complexity of cultural and national prohibitions, and ends on an unambiguous note of socio-economic and cultural fulfillment, which envisions, if only for a while, a society where boundaries between center and margin are collapsed.

While the specifics of the story must not be overlooked or relegated as props, nonetheless, it is the broad metaphorical sweep of the narrative that underlines the dramatic vision of a future where certain conventions are cast aside for the hope of a new ideal. It is where it is possible for one to *take heart* that origins and the nature of the journey do not necessarily

---

18. Sakenfeld, *Ruth*, 10.

dictate how the future should or will unfold. We have witnessed this in great moments in the quest for freedom, from civil rights in the US to the end of apartheid in South Africa, to independence in India from imperial Britain, among others. What King, Mandela and Gandhi brought has been indelibly etched in our consciousness. But we know that the journey to these defining moments is invariably noted in the shadows or in the footnote of history. It is abundantly clear that the future for Ruth and Naomi is inextricably tied to Boaz and a patriarchal society. But herein lies a vision of what is possible and what could move beyond the isolated footnote.

In the relationship between Naomi and Ruth, and later between Ruth and Boaz, we are made aware that most of the qualities that have come to define who we are, are those that are defined by society, instituted by humans. In the Ruth/Naomi, Ruth/Boaz encounters and relationships, marital status, nationality, religion, are all noted, but finally none would come to define the reason and foundation for the relationship of care and empathy. So, after the identity qualifiers are stripped away, it is the common and shared humanity that becomes the basis for the relationship. It does not mean that patriarchal traditions have been dismantled, but relationships and acts of virtue and caring are done beyond the conventions.

Rather, this is a vision of a larger world, a world in which the outsider, the stranger, the marginalized are all welcomed into the community and a future is forged together. Beyond the significant developments for the family, immediate needs and future prospects, the narrative serves as a vision for a world of inclusiveness where ancient divisions and historical boundaries collapse under the weight of human kindness. Of further note in this narrative is the natural gift of praise regardless of identity or status. They are praised for doing not only what is expected, but for doing what is beyond the ordinary, beyond the convention. In this regard, the most noteworthy action is that of Ruth accompanying Naomi, where in the latter's state there is no hope or prospects for Ruth's future. Yet, Ruth proceeds to a land and people who have within their history, a strict prohibition against all that is Moab.

> [S]urvival for one woman means survival for both . . . A relationship that began in tensions moves towards solidarity.[19]

> Each of the principal characters—Ruth, Boaz and to a lesser extent Naomi—chooses to act in ways that promote the well being of others. The praise accorded to Ruth and Boaz, validating their actions and choices, lies generally on the lips of other characters

---

19. Sakenfeld, *Ruth*, 14.

in the story, rather, than in the words of the narrator . . . Ruth's continuing care in seeking food for the despairing Naomi and her willingness to cooperate in the risky visit to the threshing floor are recognized by Boaz as evidence of this special category of extraordinary commitment.[20]

The two women who are brought together in an unexpected way as mother-in-law and daughter-in-law, are bound by circumstances beyond their control. Their identities will henceforth be inextricably tied to each other. They would come to define themselves as independent and inter-dependent where one is in despair, the other acts; where one is weak, the other is strong. They come to epitomize solidarity that transcend race or nationality or age or religion. What brought them together and propelled and sustained their solidarity and companionship was the care of the other, both for the present and the future.

One thinks of other instances, though not parallel that underline prac-tical and mysterious circumstances in which women in challenging circum-stances would define their identity against all odds. "If ever a fool was, he was Judah in Genesis 38. Judah is his own worst enemy. He has not one but two sons who displease the Lord God and thus die at the hand of that God. Judah sends away a cunning and shrewd woman who will return to unravel him."[21] At some level, both the daughters of Lot and Tamar in their particular ways in seeing their futures evaporate decide to take the initiative, and in each case perhaps one might argue, dubious and questionable. In both instances, God is the architect of the death of the husbands and prospective husbands and as such is integral to the matter at hand. Yet textually there is no evidence of further involvement or provision. Thus, in both instances when the future appears barren, the women take the radical action.

The idea of "foreignness" is certainly an underlying factor, clearly with respect to Moab. But particularly as foreignness centers around Nao-mi in Moab; Ruth in Judah; Boaz's hospitality; and the marriage between Boaz and Ruth. In every instance here, the conventions are cast aside, and foreignness is allowed to merge into an accepting community. Such an ideal is possible. In some respects, Naomi's benedictory note to her daugh-ters-in-law to return to their mothers' house reflects a deep kindness and hope for the future. This is significant in that Naomi's words are focused on the future and there is little concern for *her* present. This of course has a quality of urgency to it. Ruth's response might very well be construed as an expression of that which is both necessary and immediate. The several

20. Sakenfeld, *Ruth*, 12.
21. Jackson, p. 40.

exchanges between Naomi, Ruth and Orpah underline and illustrate the complexity and inherent challenges in the relationship and the quest for a future. What is immediately apparent is the fact that while Naomi's exhortation matters in itself, it will preempt further conversations. Naomi's words cannot be placed in the category, "I have spoken; thus, it is!" Even if, as is the case with Orpah, Naomi's exhortation is in fact followed, it is on Orpah's terms and with her voice that it is. All of the women have a voice. No one is silenced. Howsoever we view the discussion between Naomi and her daughters-in-law, we know clearly that they both made choices, on the heels of the fact that Naomi also made a choice to return to Judah. The point is that each woman makes a choice.

Can one ever impose a gift on another? The very premise here seems counter intuitive, being that the language of *imposition* and *gift* is said side by side. Yet, in a way here we have the dramatic announcement by Ruth that she will relinquish the three essential components of her identity and accompany Naomi. Clearly, Ruth chose not to return to her mother's home. Did Naomi in fact see her as an additional burden to take with her, particularly since Ruth was a foreigner, a Moabite? What we do know is that Ruth's decision is indelibly connected to Naomi, and Naomi has no say in the matter. The scenario would in fact end well, but Ruth's decision should not be taken simply as a given. On the other hand, Ruth's decision must be seen for what it is, her decision, not Naomi's and she is certainly not coerced into "serving" her mother-in-law.

> In some Christian circles, both Western and in other parts of the Globe, Ruth's commitment to Naomi is used to exhort all young women to sacrifice everything for their mothers-in-law. Against this use of the story, the larger context should be remembered.
>
> Ruth makes a choice; Naomi does not expect it, indeed discourages it; and the choice is made not in the normal course of events in married life, but in the context of unmitigated family disaster that calls for unusual decisions.[22]

And the initiative of grace, to *take heart* here for both Naomi and Ruth is not an invitation for contemporary society to seize upon it and leverage it for abusive and even subjugating reasons. One of the expressions that we find in Naomi is her response to the tragedies in her life. She is angry; she grieves, and she believes that God is in control. She embraces the truth of her circumstances and is able to hold together both her honest reflection of her pain, together with her unflinching faith. Never does Naomi choose between the two. Naomi sets the stage for one who believes

---

22. Sakenfeld, *Ruth*, 34.

and thus is able to complain freely to God about her calamity. At the same time knowing that she receives goodness and blessings, expresses thanks and gratitude to God. Naomi's complain is not an expression of the loss of faith, but rather that of a faithful person who knows God, and thus is free and able to believe, and simultaneously complain and grieve. She reminds us in the most astonishingly straightforward way that the broken heart of an individual who believes in God cannot be hidden behind clichés, and rhetorical platitudes. Rather, as Naomi expresses, grief and anger are indelibly associated with belief in God.

How does one define worth? What makes one worthy? Or for that matter what makes one noble? Boaz is described as *gibbôr hayil*, often translated as "a prominent rich man," though the more accurate translation is, "a worthy man; a man of power." Later Boaz describes Ruth as *'eshet hayil*, "a worthy woman." What Boaz does is to collapse any socio-economic boundary between him and Ruth and establishes "worthy" as a quality that transcends wealth, and instead points to character. Of note here is the fact that the recognition and assertion that one is worthy and have power typically comes from another source. Any such acclamation from oneself rings shallow and self-promoting. Boaz is described as such by the one who is telling the story. What Boaz does in turn is to recognize the grace and character of Ruth as a widow, childless in a foreign land, and who in large part is responsible for the well-being and survival of her mother-in-law. While it is the case that for most of us, that what makes us worthy of simply being human is perhaps not something that necessarily consumes us on an ongoing basis, as we have a sense of self reflection on what defines us. Whether it is wealth or social status or power, none in itself is by definition an inherent basis for deficiency, but what happens when such factors come to define a person's worth? And if this is the case then what happens when these qualities are lost or taken away?

Thus, when President Trump lauds himself as powerful and great and as "the least racist person in the world" after having repeatedly made racist comments and actions and defines his worth primarily through his wealth and power, he would not be a *gibbôr hayil*. Moreover, the manner in which he ridicules others who may be a challenge to him, makes it clear that he is not a *gibbôr hayil*. What President Trump has failed to recognize and acknowledge is that his self-assessment bears little conformity to his actions. The searing words of Louis Bourdaloue, the Jesuit preacher and professor cannot be more relevant today.

> When ambition has set up ideals of its own, in order to attain its ends, what duties does it not outrage, what feelings of

humanity does it not stifle? What laws of honesty, equity and fidelity does it not subvert? A conscience may remain, but, corrupted as it now is by ambition, what damnable intrigues will it not hatch, what trickery, what treason will it not resort to, to obtain its object?[23]

Christopher Lasch in his influential study on the culture of narcissism has argued:

> Because the narcissist has so few inner resources, he looks to others to validate his sense of self. He needs to be admired for his beauty, charm, celebrity, or power—attributes that usually fade with time. Unable to achieve satisfying sublimations in the form of love and work, he finds that he has little to sustain him when youth passes him by. He takes no interest in the future and does nothing to provide himself with the traditional consolations of old age, the most important of which is the belief that future generations will in some sense carry on his life's work.[24]

In this regard, the confidence and grace of Boaz would be for the president a learning platform. Worth and power are predicated on the qualities that Ruth embody and ones that Boaz recognized in the other, without a modicum of self-promotion. In 2:20, it is unclear whose kindness (*hesed*) is being referred to. Is it Boaz or God? In fact, that ambiguity provides an opportunity to imagine that the *hesed* could be generated by God through Boaz. That is to say, to frame this scenario in a more universal way, God works through human beings. Thus, the act of kindness, is expressed in a variety of ways. Divine providence and human action form the template, and the interconnectedness means that it is inseparable. "In God's providence Ruth came to Boaz's field, but it is Boaz who looks kindly upon Ruth in her need. Divine loyalty takes shape in the community and in individual lives through human actions."[25] One of the further issues that has universal implications is the fact that despite the extraordinary calamities that both Naomi and Ruth face, the ensuing acts of loyalty and kindness underline the significance of *taking heart*. Of course, these are exactly the indescribable circumstances of life that make *taking heart* so very difficult, yet precisely these are the times when one must.

Even as the formal recognition of "fullness" is gradually returning to Naomi, it also reflects the importance of present and ongoing needs. What

---

23. Bourdaloue [1632–1704] Sermons.

24. Lasch, *Culture of Narcissism*, 210 .

25. Sakenfeld, *Ruth,* 48.

is important to note is the fact that the encounter between Ruth and Boaz at the threshing floor was meant to shape and determine the fullness of the future. That is to say these expressions of "fullness" are not exclusive of each other but are intertwined. Of course, it would be far too simplistic to imagine that even as the women do *take heart* and forge a present and future of fullness that would be the end of the story. Indeed, as *Ruth* 4 makes clear, Ruth's future will be inextricably tied to, and be dependent on Boaz. Yet, it is equally clear that their future is forged out of community constraints and expectations. A further significance in this story is that of a comparison of Ruth to Rachel and Leah. The immediate inference might suggest the number of children between them, but perhaps more likely it is the qualitative and profound notion of Ruth carrying on the lineage that makes the comparison. Moreover, in this regard, being compared to these ancestral women, reminds us of the fact that Jacob was sent to Laban's house so that Jacob would not have to marry a non-Israelite. Here, the drama and irony could not be more striking as Ruth the Moabite will continue to live.

9

The Gravity of Grace

"Truth stumbles in the Public Square." (Isa 59:4b)

"And of all kinds of aloneness, moral aloneness is the most terrible." —Balzac

"The moral mind is inherently, necessarily, egalitarian. This is what Abraham Lincoln means when he said, 'If slavery is not wrong, nothing is wrong.'" —Mendelson, pp. 45–47

What do biblical concepts such as "peace" and "equality" and "almsgiving" tell us about God? We know that these terms are ubiquitous in social and political circles and often their importance and application are viewed from these perspectives. As important as this is, it is neither exhaustive nor necessarily the principal platform for interpretation. There is also common and established idea that for some doing charity comes with a *quid pro quo* mentality. This is frequently expressed in language of what is required for entrance into heaven.

> Therefore, O king, may my counsel be acceptable to you: atone
> for your sins with righteousness, and your iniquities with mercy
> to the oppressed, so that your prosperity may be prolonged.
> (Dan 4:27)

In this text, King Nebuchadnezzar is told that in order for him to be redeemed, he needed to do *charity* for the poor. This is the notion expressed in the Lord's prayer: "Forgive our debts as we forgive our debtors" which is the more accurate translation of the Greek, than the more common "trespasses." "It is troubling that assisting the poor seems to be motivated by blatant self-interest. More than one person has wondered whether these texts do not lead inexorably to the rhetoric of this so-called "Prosperity Gospel" which preys on the gullible . . . Charity, in short, is not just a good deed *but a declaration of belief about the world God created.*[1] It is precisely this notion that appears so prevalent in a variety of expressions today that underlines the core meaning of *charity*. As Anderson notes, some Christian religious leaders have preyed on the poor and unsuspecting under the guise of leading them to great wealth as an end result of their faith and beliefs. This particular iteration of preying on others is especially egregious in that religion is used and abused among the faithful, where religious leaders use their positions of power to convince believers of that which has no biblical basis. But this idea of charity is not only found in religious contexts. "An expanding empire always outran its resources . . . And despite its lofty talk about justice for the poor, prosperity had to be confined to the elite . . . Originality was not encouraged, because any new idea that required too great an economic outlay would not be implemented and this frustration could cause social unrest."[2]

Even though Armstrong is speaking of a pre-modern situation, the idea remains resonant as they were generations ago. One of the significant challenges that we face in our society, and one that is routinely overlooked or diminished is the confusion between that which is personal and that which is private. Thus, relationships with God are frequently classified as "private" which is to suggest that no one, no outsider is allowed to enter that particular world. It is to suggest a "closed off" from community relationship and one that functions without the need of community of others. The challenge here is that religion by definition is not to be privatized. In distinction, a personal relationship with God does not by necessity cast aside community. Indeed, the most profound definition of personal is notably in the context of community.

Of course, beyond religion, and religious conviction and allegiance, the issue of private versus personal allows for a not-so-distant ownership of resources with distinct and unmistakable socio-economic quality. Thus, in the United States, for example to privatize social security is to make clear that there is no communal care or responsibility and ownership, by its nature perhaps an indelible connection with greed. And what this invariably leads to is the ownership and even hoarding of resources. Moreover, it is the nature of greed, as a quality of character and being, is to accumulate for private consumption invariably at all costs. With this insatiable mentality, the notion of personal, communal, neighborly will become disposable and cast aside. The language might still be a part of the lexicon, but the practice will be absent or at least secondary. Far too many who espouse communal and neighborly

1. Anderson, *Charity*, 3–4.
2. Armstrong, *Fields*, 39.

principles predicated on biblical or broadly construed religious principles, in fact have a marked disconnect between theory and practice.

In December 2018, Donald Trump and his family agreed to dissolve the Trump Foundation amidst allegations that the Foundation, which was designed to help others, was being used for personal gain. Such deliberate and unabashed actions not only gave the public a misguided impression of charity, but further perpetuated President Trump's self-promotion.

> Treasures gained by wickedness do not profit,
>
> but almsgiving delivers from death.[3]

Proverbs 10:2 is dramatic in its straightforward simplicity. "The treasuries of wickedness make/provide no benefit, but *almsgiving* delivers from death." There's nothing easy or necessarily painless about "doing charity." At its most elemental level, it involves a personal encounter and engagement with the poor and indigent. Mercy is not to be executed by deputy, nor for that matter should it be administered in the abstract. Individual and communal commitments and engagements are not mutually exclusive. The concept of *neighborhood* as a communal idea has expanded into a global *neighborhood,* and the manner in which *alms* and *charity* are attended to, and understood, has expanded as well.

> As any Jew or student of biblical languages will know, the word for commandment in Hebrew is *mitsva.* During the biblical period the meaning of this word was centered on the idea that God had given a set of rules—whether it concerned matters of ritual purity, kosher regulations, or instructions regarding ethics and morals—could be identified as a *mitsva.* In post biblical Jewish texts however, the term undergoes a radical transformation. It develops the secondary meaning of "charity." Thus, the well-known expression bar mitzvah whose primary meaning is 'one obligated to keep the Commandments' could also mean 'a generous person.'[4]

Credo, both in its etymology and its derivatives serves as one appropriate platform for understanding and acting on what it means to embrace and love charity. So, we begin with the idea of "heart" to "belief" and to *creditum,* "a loan." To continue, what is significant here as we explore is what it means to care for the other. Etymologically the Greek *eleos* gives rise to the Latin *elemosina* and through several derivatives, we arrive at the English *alms.* "As such a loan is not just a good thing to do, it is *merit* worthy-that

3. Prov 10:2.

4. Anderson, *Charity*, 16.

is, it improves one's standing with God."[5] In this regard, we may point to
the linguistic connection between *Glaube, glaubige, glaubiger,* terms that
underline both faith and action.[6]

First, and foremost, there is evidence that it has tangible economic implications. To grant a loan, language that has as much theological as it does
economic implications, is not merely a matter of personal inclination or
societal convenience. For example, *creditum* might very well mean a matter
of life and death, and a loan might ensure the planting of a crop, etc. The
importance of this term is seen in the fact that it is not predicated on the
confession of what one believes even when/if such confession is generated
from the heart as the etymology indicates.

Certainly, many who have power and wealth in society view the bor-
rowing of money as a platform for growing wealth, and not for sustenance
or even survival. The divide is further accentuated when those who are
desperately in need of a loan are told they are not qualified, and the irony
about the fundamental nature of credit as a means of survival is lost. Or
one thinks of student loans where often students struggle to repay their
loans, not because they choose to default, but rather because of the interest accrued in addition to the capital. What we know with certainty is
that *creditum* is employed almost exclusively for economic reasons, and
frequently with unscrupulous intent or overarching greed. In the current
investigation of Donald Trump's financial dealings, there are widespread
allegations of financial undertaking that have been predicated on false
information. Allegedly, loans were forfeited and the cycle of loaning for
self-promotion and accumulation continues.

The core idea of the term *creditum* compels us to grant loans born out
of our beliefs and driven by what lies within our hearts. "The person who
borrows money does so in the expectation that in the future he will secure
the means to repay his creditor. Thus, the good path is the one that allows
a person to see into the future."[7] The importance of Anderson's perspective
cannot be underestimated. That is to say, there is a fundamental belief in
the future, though not merely in the sense of a particular timeline for the
repayment of loan, but rather the belief that the present is penultimate, and
the reality and circumstances of the present are not the last word. The hope
therefore of a future to repay points to a future with the distinct possibility
for transformation and newness. Moreover, it is a reminder that God is a
God of the new and re-creation. Regardless of who the lender/loaner is,

5. Anderson, p. 43.

6. See, Anderson, *Charity,* 52.

7. Anderson, *Charity,* 37.

there is undoubtedly a belief that the loan will be repaid in the future. Moreover, such a belief is not always predicated on certainty; indeed, more often than not, such belief is predicated on the future; and for those who believe in God, the future is shaped and created by God.

[1] Then Tobias answered his father Tobit, "I will do everything that you have commanded me, father; [2] but how can I obtain the money from him, since he does not know me and I do not know him? What evidence am I to give him so that he will recognize and trust me, and give me the money? Also, I do not know the roads to Media, or how to get there." [3] Then Tobit answered his son Tobias, "He gave me his bond and I gave him my bond. I divided his in two; we each took one part, and I put one with the money. And now twenty years have passed since I left this money in trust. So now, my son, find yourself a trustworthy man to go with you, and we will pay him wages until you return. But get back the money from Gabael."

[4] So Tobias went out to look for a man to go with him to Media, someone who was acquainted with the way. He went out and found the angel Raphael standing in front of him; but he did not perceive that he was an angel of God. [5] Tobias said to him, "Where do you come from, young man?" "From your kindred, the Israelites," he replied, "and I have come here to work." Then Tobias said to him, "Do you know the way to go to Media?" [6] "Yes," he replied, "I have been there many times; I am acquainted with it and know all the roads. I have often traveled to Media, and would stay with our kinsman Gabael who lives in Rages of Media. It is a journey of two days from Ecbatana to Rages; for it lies in a mountainous area, while Ecbatana is in the middle of the plain." [7] Then Tobias said to him, "Wait for me, young man, until I go in and tell my father; for I do need you to travel with me, and I will pay you your wages." [8] He replied, "All right, I will wait; but do not take too long."

[9] So Tobias went in to tell his father Tobit and said to him, "I have just found a man who is one of our own Israelite kindred!" He replied, "Call the man in, my son, so that I may learn about his family and to what tribe he belongs, and whether he is trustworthy enough to go with you."

[10] Then Tobias went out and called him, and said, "Young man, my father is calling for you." So he went in to him, and Tobit greeted him first. He replied, "Joyous greetings to you!" But Tobit retorted, "What joy is left for me any more? I am a man without eyesight; I cannot see the light of heaven, but I lie in darkness like the dead who no longer see the light. Although

still alive, I am among the dead. I hear people but I cannot see them." But the young man said, "Take courage; the time is near for God to heal you; take courage." Then Tobit said to him, "My son Tobias wishes to go to Media. Can you accompany him and guide him? I will pay your wages, brother." He answered, "I can go with him and I know all the roads, for I have often gone to Media and have crossed all its plains, and I am familiar with its mountains and all of its roads." ¹¹ Then Tobit said to him, "Brother, of what family are you and from what tribe? Tell me, brother." ¹² He replied, "Why do you need to know my tribe?" But Tobit said, "I want to be sure, brother, whose son you are and what your name is." ¹³ He replied, "I am Azariah, the son of the great Hananiah, one of your relatives." ¹⁴ Then Tobit said to him, "Welcome! God save you, brother. Do not feel bitter toward me, brother, because I wanted to be sure about your ancestry. It turns out that you are a kinsman, and of good and noble lineage. For I knew Hananiah and Nathan, the two sons of Shemeliah, and they used to go with me to Jerusalem and worshiped with me there, and were not led astray. Your kindred are good people; you come of good stock. Hearty welcome!"

¹⁵ Then he added, "I will pay you a drachma a day as wages, as well as expenses for yourself and my son. So go with my son, ¹⁶ and I will add something to your wages." Raphael answered, "I will go with him; so do not fear. We shall leave in good health and return to you in good health, because the way is safe." ¹⁷ So Tobit said to him, "Blessings be upon you, brother." Then he called his son and said to him, "Son, prepare supplies for the journey and set out with your brother. May God in heaven bring you safely there and return you in good health to me; and may his angel, my son, accompany you both for your safety."

Before he went out to start his journey, he kissed his father and mother. Tobit then said to him, "Have a safe journey."

¹⁸ But his mother[p] began to weep, and said to Tobit, "Why is it that you have sent my child away? Is he not the staff of our hand as he goes in and out before us? ¹⁹ Do not heap money upon money, but let it be a ransom for our child. ²⁰ For the life that is given to us by the Lord is enough for us." ²¹ Tobit said to her, "Do not worry; our child will leave in good health and return to us in good health. Your eyes will see him on the day when he returns to you in good health. Say no more! Do not fear for them, my sister. ²² For a good angel will accompany him; his journey will be successful, and he will come back in good health."

¹ So she stopped weeping. The young man went out and the angel went with him; ² and the dog came out with him and went

along with them. So they both journeyed along, and when the first night overtook them they camped by the Tigris river. ³ Then the young man went down to wash his feet in the Tigris river. Suddenly a large fish leaped up from the water and tried to swallow the young man's foot, and he cried out. ⁴ But the angel said to the young man, "Catch hold of the fish and hang on to it!" So the young man grasped the fish and drew it up on the land. ⁵ Then the angel said to him, "Cut open the fish and take out its gall, heart, and liver. Keep them with you, but throw away the intestines. For its gall, heart, and liver are useful as medicine." ⁶ So after cutting open the fish the young man gathered together the gall, heart, and liver; then he roasted and ate some of the fish, and kept some to be salted.

The two continued on their way together until they were near Media.[r] ⁷ Then the young man questioned the angel and said to him, "Brother Azariah, what medicinal value is there in the fish's heart and liver, and in the gall?" ⁸ He replied, "As for the fish's heart and liver, you must burn them to make a smoke in the presence of a man or woman afflicted by a demon or evil spirit, and every affliction will flee away and never remain with that person any longer. ⁹ And as for the gall, anoint a person's eyes where white films have appeared on them; blow upon them, upon the white films, and the eyes will be healed." ¹⁰ When he entered Media and already was approaching Ecbatana, ¹¹ Raphael said to the young man, "Brother Tobias." "Here I am," he answered. Then Raphael said to him, "We must stay this night in the home of Raguel. He is your relative, and he has a daughter named Sarah. ¹² He has no male heir and no daughter except Sarah only, and you, as next of kin to her, have before all other men a hereditary claim on her.

Also it is right for you to inherit her father's possessions. Moreover, the girl is sensible, brave, and very beautiful, and her father is a good man." ¹³ He continued, "You have every right to take her in marriage. So listen to me, brother; tonight I will speak to her father about the girl, so that we may take her to be your bride. When we return from Rages we will celebrate her marriage. For I know that Raguel can by no means keep her from you or promise her to another man without incurring the penalty of death according to the decree of the book of Moses. Indeed he knows that you, rather than any other man, are entitled to marry his daughter. So now listen to me, brother, and tonight we shall speak concerning the girl and arrange her engagement to you. And when we return from Rages we will take her and bring her back with us to your house."

¹⁴ Then Tobias said in answer to Raphael, "Brother Azariah, I have heard that she already has been married to seven husbands and that they died in the bridal chamber. On the night when they went in to her, they would die. I have heard people saying that it was a demon that killed them.

¹⁵ It does not harm her, but it kills anyone who desires to approach her. So now, since I am the only son my father has, I am afraid that I may die and bring my father's and mother's life down to their grave, grieving for me—and they have no other son to bury them."

¹⁶ But Raphael said to him, "Do you not remember your father's orders when he commanded you to take a wife from your father's house? Now listen to me, brother, and say no more about this demon. Take her. I know that this very night she will be given to you in marriage. ¹⁷ When you enter the bridal chamber, take some of the fish's liver and heart, and put them on the embers of the incense. An odor will be given off; ¹⁸ the demon will smell it and flee, and will never be seen near her any more. Now when you are about to go to bed with her, both of you must first stand up and pray, imploring the Lord of heaven that mercy and safety may be granted to you.

Do not be afraid, for she was set apart for you before the world was made. You will save her, and she will go with you. I presume that you will have children by her, and they will be as brothers to you. Now say no more!" When Tobias heard the words of Raphael and learned that she was his kinswoman, related through his father's lineage, he loved her very much, and his heart was drawn to her.[8]

One might justifiably be encouraged to *take heart* in the context of the loss of a child, or even the prospects of losing a child. Thus, the biblical stories of the death of David and Bathsheba's first child; the "death" of Joseph and the prospects of losing Benjamin (Genesis 37); the story of Tobias being sent by his father Tobit to Medea (cf. Tob 6:14–15), among others come to mind. As was the case in the Ancient Near East, and still is the case today in some societies and cultures, though in a fashion less publicly proclaimed, is the idea that a son is to carry on the family name.

I cannot say categorically, but arguably one of the most difficult, and painful moments one might face in life is the death of a child, regardless of the child's age. Can one *take heart* after such a moment, when that inevitable quality of broken-heartedness and hopelessness sets in? Yet, these are precisely the moments that *taking heart* finds its most profound

8. Tobit, 5–6.

expression. There is a cautionary note here as well in that no one is in a position to classify, let alone marginalize the pain and suffering by simply saying, *take heart*, or *it's ok* etc. as platitudes, even well-intentioned ones. To *take heart* in such instances is to imagine a future that at the moment seems unimaginable. It is to believe beyond what every iota of logic dictates. Thus, platitudes are not only not helpful, because they seek to collapse hope from an unimaginable future into one that they can control, but ultimately platitudes may be destructive.

Even though it is possible that we may know what will occur, the journey of "how" remains, and while we may even know of the outcome, in the case of Tobit, we journey together, we witness the journey. It is the belief in the possibility that despite the challenges that seem formidable and intractable, Tobit, nonetheless takes a step. Despite Tobit's mother's rhetorical "a good angel will accompany" this undertaking is still a risky and uncertain venture. With Tobias's conversation with his father-in-law Raguel, we are again reminded that the new life that Tobit seeks is not altogether straightforward.

> Antigone's tragedy shares much in common with the stories of Tobit and Sarah . . . Her concern for the dead and the flagrant disregard of the royal edict against burial precisely mirror that of Tobit . . . [Antigone] shares with both Tobit and Sarah a preference for death over joyless life . . . For Antigone and her family, there is no happy ending, no alternative to dying. The gods she might have invoked have already turned a deaf ear to her lament, proving to be without justice or mercy. They are strangely silent throughout the drama, wholly absent from the lives of a suffering humanity . . . Antigone and Tobit part ways for in the book of Tobit we meet a God who is intimately present within the human community and consummately active in the lives of those who suffer.[9]

This idea however, of the known presence of God intimately involved in the lives of the people while present in Tobit does not necessarily have universal claim and is not a pervasive biblical theme. The fact is, in contemporary society, in a variety of contexts, there is a persistent questioning of God's absence and God's silence. "In fact, no biblical theology offers a satisfactory explanation of the origin of, or reason for, individual suffering . . . Yet, though they enter into exile together, in exile they experience isolation,

9. Portier-Young, "Alleviation of Suffering," 35–36.

for they are separated from their homeland and the people left behind, as well as from native people among whom they now reside."[10]

Tobit's compassion and care for others, both the living and the dead, expresses the sacred dignity of those who have been discarded by society. He understands that even the dead cry out for respect. As such, Tobit epitomizes the ideal of one who seeks to live his/her beliefs rooted in God. Yet, there is a quality in Tobit that refuses the help and care from those who are his family and his community. There are two significant issues of note here. First, the very noble quality for which Tobit distinguishes himself, he prevents others from doing. The act of actually caring for others is being taken away, and as such those who seek to live out their beliefs as Tobit does, are prevented from doing so, and are not afforded the requisite freedom. Second, in isolating himself from those closest to him, who might be the very ones to uphold and comfort him, Tobit's actions might suggest that he has no need of community and family. His actions in this regard are counter to his personal commitment to helping others and preserving the sacredness of life, including the burial of the dead. Is Tobit's independence a sign of strength, and potential care afforded him an expression of his weakness? He even goes as far as to accuse his wife Anna of theft and dishonesty, and questions her integrity, all of which are baseness. As Portier-Young states, "Though he would 'suffer' with others, he would not allow others to suffer with him."[11] In this regard, he adopts something of a selfish, perhaps fearful quality.

We are left to wonder what is the motivation or guiding principle behind Tobit's actions? It is not merely skepticism, but a serious concern. There seems to be no joy in Tobit even as he expresses compassion for others. So, while he is intentional and from all indications genuine in his care for others, particularly the abandoned dead, he ultimately prefers to be isolated, and function solitarily. And so instead of joy, he typically chooses isolation in grief. (2:5) Moreover one wonders whether Tobit is a particularly desirable model for how one should live and respond to one's community, family and world. A rejection of family and friends is an abandonment of self. Thus, the very thing that he does for the other, to ensure that they are not abandoned, he declines and rejects for himself.

> In addition, his extended family grieves for him and lends sympathy in his time of misfortune. (2:10) Finally, when he has exhausted all the other resources, Anna his wife, jeopardizes her honor and relinquishes a life of relative comfort to support Tobit by her handiwork . . . We see then that the greatest

10. Portier-Young, "Alleviation of Suffering," 37–38.
11. Portier-Young, "Alleviation of Suffering," 39.

cause of Tobit's suffering is his inability correctly to perceive, and to appreciate the extent of his connectedness in this human community.[12]

It is precisely the issue of Tobit's incapacity to know the extent of his own connectedness with other humans. This is a universal notion and transcends time. President Trump has repeatedly boasted of his independence in accumulating his wealth, and the extent of his wealth exaggerated by some account. This incapacity for the truth removes the essential human connection and relationship. Tobit, who despite his shortcomings in this regard has well defined quality of care and redemption, in sharp contrast to President Trump who has a history of self-promotion, not infrequently using others for self-accolade and adulation. The lack of one's capacity for the recognition of human connectedness and what this means for the essential value of dependence and the true nature of one's worth, is ultimately devastating.

This is clearly Tobit's decision, and he is hopeful, but this hope must also reckon with the depth of the grief of Tobias's mother. Anderson emphasizes the risk that Tobit takes. The future certainly seems to justify Tobit's risk and this parallels Jacob's decision in sending Benjamin to meet Joseph. Here too all works out well and the future which Jacob imagined would have taken him to Sheol as an expression of an incomplete life as Anderson notes[13] is fortuitously avoided. The risk once again pays off. But of course, it is not always this way, and without quantifying the issue, it is more often the case that grief is not abated or that risk pays off. Instead, grief becomes an integral part of the journey's landscape. "Yet, it is precisely the *risk* that Tobit takes that leads not only to the return of the money he had left on the deposit but to the restoration of his sight, the marriage of his son, the acquisition of the enormous inheritance and eventually the birth of seven grandchildren."[14]

Risk is significant, and one might argue that unless one *takes heart* in a hope for a future that then moves beyond the present reality, it is a resignation that the present will always be the way life is, unchangeable and without hope. Yet, the act of taking a risk, even a calculated risk is not in itself a guarantee. It might indeed lead to nothingness, but one may never know. All that Tobit hoped for and what Jacob could not have imagined and indeed feared, eventuated. What is important is the belief that one must take a risk, and imagine beyond the present, and therein lies the

12. Portier-Young, "Alleviation of Suffering," 41.

13. Anderson, *Charity*, 80.

14. Anderson, *Charity*, 81.

quality of hope beyond despair. "When Tobit prepares to send his son on a fateful journey, he is well aware of the great risk he is taking. Life has not offered him reasons to remain confident in the promises of God. Though scripture had promised that "alms giving delivers from death," it seemed for Tobit that the reverse was true: works of charity brought one to the threshold of death itself."[15]

It is striking that for some religious persons, some Christians in particular, the issue of human suffering, certainly personal human suffering invariably leads to the question as to why God is allowing/doing this. Or where is God in the midst of such suffering? Yet, when do we hear such sentiments in the suffering of animals? Are they not part of God's creation as well? Why would God not stop the wanton slaughtering of animals for the sake of skins, furs and ivories? Or for that matter, do we lament to God for the hurting and destruction of the environment? In reality we speak principally of humans, and the rest is secondary. But even here one is compelled to define "human." On May 14, 2019, the Alabama legislature passed the most restrictive abortion law in the United States. On May 15, 2019, Alabama Governor Kay Ivey on signing the Bill declared, "[T]his legislation stands as a powerful testament to Alabamians deeply held belief that every life is precious and that *every life* (my italics) is a sacred gift from God." However, to have this statement be construed in the most gracious way, still leads to the conclusion of how very disingenuous it is. If there is a principled position of every life being sacred, then the governor and the legislature will have legislations and systemic action to ensure the respect and goodness of all life, but this is conspicuously absent. Indeed, Alabama among other States actively undermine the idea that *all life* is sacred. There is, of course a narrowly construed anthropomorphic idea of creation, and with it comes the idea that finally God is only interested in, and concerned about humans, and for some, concerned only about particular types of human beings. "Faith, [God] said is not a call to escape the world but to embrace it. Creation is not an elaborate testing ground, but an invitation to join in the work of restoration. God created the world, but he did not finish it. He left it to us . . . Think of it. He left it to us to finish the work of creation."[16]

We could say that what fostered trust was something more like an adherence to the prevailing outrages against that truth in current political practice. Or to take a slightly different instance, one thinks of this scenario portrayed in Ibsen's *The Wild Duck*, an 'idealistic" and morally absolute character judges that it is his duty to expose skeletons in the family

15. Anderson, *Charity*, 84.
16. Cuomo, "Who is God," 358.

cupboard, with devastatingly destructive results. Is Ibsen's Gregers Werle a person whose speech commands *trust*? Surely not. His truthfulness is pursued without attention to the actual feelings and needs of those around . . . The problem with Ibsen's Gregers is that he has frighteningly simplistic idea of the automatically liberating effect of truthfulness wholly uninformed by any sense of what can be heard by others and how it is heard.[17]

Arguably in sharp relief to Gregers Werle is Dr. Stockman in Ibsen's *Enemy of the People*. Despite the personal and systemic challenges that he faced, Dr. Stockman spoke truth to power regarding contaminated water. While initially he might have been perceived more in a nuisance category, his relentless pursuit made a target of such ridicule that his life, and that of his family are in danger. He has become an enemy of the people. One is not surprised that this play has been re-cast in a variety of global settings, where the themes have been directed to the particular issues in these societies.

In the context of the Donald Trump presidency, the issues of the environment and the moral responsibilities of the average person are being voiced and those who do so may be characterized and viewed as enemies of the State. It is precisely this situation in the current political environment in the United States that has propelled an investigation in the President's abuse of power and his obstruction of Congress that has led to inexorably to his impeachment. Now surprisingly the initial whistleblower regarding the Ukraine scandal and others who have corroborated his/her narrative have faced a relentless barrage of vilification and denigration by the President and his surrogates. This has been the case as well with the media, which at every turn has been classified as *fake* and indeed as enemy of the people. The ongoing aspersions have had a debilitating and dangerous effect on reporting and free speech.

Both the causal and teleological arguments surrounding the problem of suffering are inadequate in so far as they focus on who brought it on and why. There is the emphasis on "purpose" or why such suffering was necessary; here the focus is on the future.

> [N]o matter how good a purpose might it be, we must undergo suffering as a means to that purpose isn't a merely cruel imposition? . . . The teleological view of suffering produces a utopian illusion which is likely to transform the present suffering to an investment for compensation in the future. Thus people are falsely encouraged to endure the present suffering simply with hope for salvation in the future . . . This view is . . . exploited by

17. Williams, *The Edge*, 51.

the oppressor to mesmerize the oppressed with utopian false consciousness.[18]

[8] But when Elisha the man of God heard that the king of Israel had torn his clothes, he sent a message to the king, "Why have you torn your clothes? Let him come to me, that he may learn that there is a prophet in Israel." [9] So Naaman came with his horses and chariots, and halted at the entrance of Elisha's house. [10] Elisha sent a messenger to him, saying, "Go, wash in the Jordan seven times, and your flesh shall be restored and you shall be clean." [11] But Naaman became angry and went away, saying, "I thought that for me he would surely come out, and stand and call on the name of the LORD his God, and would wave his hand over the spot, and cure the leprosy![f] [12] Are not Abana and Pharpar, the rivers of Damascus, better than all the waters of Israel? Could I not wash in them, and be clean?" He turned and went away in a rage. [13] But his servants approached and said to him, "Father, if the prophet had commanded you to do something difficult, would you not have done it? How much more, when all he said to you was, 'Wash, and be clean'?" [14] So he went down and immersed himself seven times in the Jordan, according to the word of the man of God; his flesh was restored like the flesh of a young boy, and he was clean.[19]

Thus, for example, what Elisha does is to restore for the General the essential opportunity to be a member of the community. Healing of leprosy will do that. With leprosy, the king could not lean on him, and no chance of a relationship with the people. Indeed, if this act of healing can bring about peace between Israel and Syria, all the better given the ongoing enmity between these countries. Perhaps for Elisha, he has determined that these possibilities for the common good is more important than either a fee or a condemnation of the General for his *Rimmon* allegiance.

> Elisha dismisses the General with shalom because he knows that leprosy makes any contribution to the common good impossible, and he has contributed mightily to the common good by overcoming this dread disability . . . We dare to enact shalom and then move on to the next chance of performing shalom again, not lingering over the betrayal and ingratitude that seems to come with it.[20]

18. Chung, "Conflicting Readings," 10.

19. 2 Kgs 5:8–14.

20. Brueggemann, "Perpetual Shalom," 33.

While in this case, the disease is literally leprosy, a physical contagion, the term has taken on a figurative manifestation. Lepers are understood to be such that they are set apart from others and consequently others distance themselves. Two issues of contemporary relevance are of note here. First, as a metaphor that which is devastating at its core, it might have the same level of contagious fear attached to it. One sees evangelical leaders such as the Reverend Franklin Graham aligning themselves with President Trump in a manner that belies every evangelical or moral quality. And this is not merely an occasional or a momentary quality, but ongoing. So, the question that must be asked in light of the Elisha-Naaman episode, is *why*. What is to be gained? What we see with Gehazi and Naaman is the quest to profit from that which must be held sacred, and certainly in the case of Gehazi, it is a gift that does not belong to him, and thus cannot be commercialized as a private transaction. It is apparent that many evangelical leaders such as Franklin Graham and Robert Jefress have fixated their theological gaze on constitutive social issues, namely abortion and the so-called *prolife* agenda, and the naming of Supreme Court justices who would align themselves with such an ideology. For this, evangelical leaders have sacrificed qualities that overtly run counter to fundamental precepts.

As President Trump continues to undo policies from previous administrations, and institute new policies that reflect an agenda of avarice and inhumanity, the evangelical leaders have remained conspicuously silent, holding tight to their personal benefits. They are callously willing to abandon their grounding and support a morally unmoored president for their own gain. The undeniable fact is, to use one's vocational position where one acts on behalf of a people or on presenting God for one's personal gain, is not only forbidden, but abusive. Indeed, Article I of the United States constitution establishes that the office of President cannot be used for *profit* not *accept presents*. In these evangelical leaders, Gehazi is alive. Second, as Walter Brueggemann suggests in "Perpetual Shalom," it would be easy and tempting to linger over betrayal or destructive behavior that have consequences that are far reaching to community, nation and world. However, it might take courage to heal, to restore, when there is a natural compulsion to treat betrayal as the final word. As we may learn from Elisha and Naaman, despite the latter's initial elevated sense of self-importance, it is healing that has the possibility of restoration. It should be noted that healing may not dissolve all differences but may become a path to restoration.

In the case of Naaman the General, sometimes doing the "right" thing especially when you are certain you know what it is, still takes courage and risk, and the General chooses otherwise. He recognizes the power of YHWH; he is physically healed and restored, but his courage stops at the

Jordan. One of the challenges one has with the Empire, and there are likely many, is the fact that sometimes someone within the Empire who is in a position of power, faces a new and counter to imperial understanding. For example, Joseph lives into his position and the worldview of Pharaoh. And like Pharaoh, Joseph weaponizes food.

> They said, "You have saved our lives; may it please my lord, we will be slaves to Pharaoh.[21]

As Gen 47:25 notes, we, like the ancient Hebrews might very well arrive at a point where we are so grateful to be alive despite the fact that we have lost everything, including that which is necessary for all of life. As opposed to Joseph, Daniel's response is notably emphatic and unequivocal.

> Daniel's response is not to accommodate the empire, but to insist on the non negotiable character of life in God's world. His promise is that the empire has sinned and that appropriate action must be taken for atonement of sin. The empire is answerable . . . "You showed no mercy." This is the word we heard on the lips of Daniel. The empire was expected to be merciful even to those who were vulnerable and subject to imperial domination.[22]

The importance of memory is such that it was essential for the Hebrews then and the people today to have a memory of what it means to be in slavery both literally and figuratively. As difficult as it might for some to say or hear, the reality is that there are many ideas/issues/words, etc. that are really Christlike. For Christians, this is the gauge; this is the platform from which to think and act, regardless of the issue. Thus, while it might be easy and even popular among many Christians to say as a matter of course, "according to the Bible," or "well I follow the Bible" etc., the fact remains that reading the text without reflection, introspection only expresses a naiveté or more uncharitably put, dishonesty. It is necessary now, and indeed always has been for the Church to ensure that the distinction between the narrative of the State and that of the Church is clearly delineated and lived out. The collapsing of the distinction whereby the Church and the biblical texts have been usurped to reflect a particular political ideology marks a dangerous and perilous path.

Perhaps even worst is the fact that the use of the Bible and the ability to cite particular texts or general references has become no more than a façade behind which personal ideological agendas are hidden, and it is arguably

---

21. Gen 47:25.
22. Brueggemann, "Perpetual Shalom," 30.

the most egregious abuse of the Bible. The right words are betrayed by spurious and disingenuous actions.

Can one abandon oneself? When we think of Ps 22, it would make sense for the psalmist to utter the words, "my God, my God why have you forsaken me?" but in the mouth of Jesus, these words take on a different level of significance, and invite a different rendering such as "my God, my God why have you abandoned yourself?" The significance of this is the abandonment of divine self as both taking the place of human beings, but equally important, the remarkable identifying with the pain of human beings. One cannot take such "identification" and make it universal, since not everyone will find such identification enough of a balm to take away the pain. To use a well-known example, it would not suffice in general to provide such an explanation with regard to the Holocaust and those who suffered and were killed there. Thus, while this might provide an intellectual or even spiritual explanation for some, it still remains the case that for many, the large very existential questions remain, namely, why would God not act? Where is God?

In seeking answers for the various issues in our world, some of which seem either incomprehensible or insurmountable, who do we look to; who should we seek. Mario Cuomo in a striking moment of reflection looks to an understanding of God.

> If the answer could not be compelled by our intellect, we are
> pleased for an answer that at least, we could *choose* to believe
> without contradicting that intellect. It had to be more than just a
> God of prohibition. More than a God of guilt and punishment. It
> had to be more than John Calvin's chilling conclusion that God
> loves Jacob but hates Esau . . . It must be a God like the one that
> was promised in the ancient books: a God of mercy, a God of
> peace, a God of hope. In the end, to make any sense, it must be a
> God of love . . . We are presented with a choice. Either we swim
> with the tide and accept the notion that the best way to improve
> the world is for the government to help the fortunate and then
> hope that personal charity will induce them to take care of the
> rest of us. Or we resist, by affirming that as we hear God, He
> tells us it is our moral obligation to be our brother's keeper, all
> of us, as a people, as a government; that our responsibility to our
> brothers and sisters is greater than any one of us, and it doesn't
> end when they are out of the individual reach of our hand, or
> our charity, or our love. Believing that we have an obligation to
> love is not a comfortable position to be in. It can haunt us. It can
> nag us in moments of happiness and personal success . . . It can

accuse us from the faces of the starving, the disposed and the wounded, faces that stare back at us.[23]

Some of these calamitous issues would include arguably the most devastating of all, war and the devastating lack of presidential leadership during the Covid 19 pandemic resulting in the now 900,000 deaths or as noted before, the caging of children. There is certainly the temptation by individuals to retaliate against others when war is declared. The reality is complex, as it is not only a national matter or a community matter, but also that of a family and the individual. We witnessed the indefensible actions on the part of some individuals who saw the terror of 9/11 as an invitation to attack others who they viewed as responsible, on the basis of their race, ethnicity and religion. In such destructive moments, Rowan Williams wisely reflects.

> Public good is what is natural to human beings, the context in which they may exercise their freedom to realize the image of God . . . The private person must never use the violence that the ruler can rightly use, as a private person has the right of redress by legal due process . . . The point is that coercion is simply not to be justified unless it is answerable to a clear account of common human good.[24]

Certainly, one of the essential aspects of being in relationship within the nation, community and family has to do with wealth. When one reflects on the root meaning of οἶκος (household), and the manner in which the word has spawned English terms such as *economics* and *ecumenical*, we are led with some certainty to the conclusion that family and community have an integral connection with finances and the economics of livelihood.

> Money is a metaphor like other things: our money transactions like our family connections and our farming and fishing labors, bring our features of our human condition that, rightly understood, tells us something of how we might see our relation to God . . . Being a human self is learning how to ask critical questions of your own habits and compulsions so as to adjust how you act in the light of a model of human behavior, both individual and collective, that represents some fundamental truth about what humanity is for.[25]

In other words, the household is literally and simply a place of belonging, where there is necessary and welcome interdependency, where everyone is

23. Cuomo, "Who Is God," 357–58.
24. Williams, *War*, 15.
25. Williams, *Theology*, 607.

integral to the life of the other. This idea belies the sometimes commonly held notion that one achieves one's identity and worth independently. Even the common thief cannot succeed without the reality of those from whom he steals. Indeed, one cannot live without the economy of sustenance and security.

> A working household is an environment in which vulnerable people are nurtured and allowed to grow up (children) or wind down (the elderly); it is a background against which active people can go out to labor in various ways to reinforce the security of the household . . . The model of human existence that is taken for granted is one in which each person is both needy and needed, both dependent on others, and endowed with gifts for others. And while this is not on the whole presented as a general social program, it is manifestly what the biblical writers see as the optimal shape of human life, life in which purposes of God are made plain . . . To separate our destiny from that of the poor of the world, or from the rejected or disabled in our own context, is to compromise that destiny and to invite a life that is less than whole for ourselves.[26]

In Williams's idea, the household as the Greeks suggest is not narrowly defined as a physical household, but as the English derivative *ecumenical* implies a wider household. Indeed, it may be national or international. What is significant in Williams's perspective is not only the centrality of the biblical mandate, but the notion that when individuals of a society disregard and neglect those on the edge of society, the poor and the destitute, those who seek refuge, it is a diminishing of oneself. It is, as Williams says, a compromising of one's destiny.

Language, as Rowan Williams has suggested,[27] is a very useful metaphor for understanding our responsibility to teach others and the need to be aware constantly of the importance of community. Herein lies the idea of connectedness and neighborliness. Our lives are interwoven, and thus, when we seek to separate, we unravel the fabric of our existence. Language, by definition is relational. We are taught; we inherit; we communicate, and this finally is the core value of language; it is not to be used to self-inflict.

> It is simply and literally impossible for us to learn and use language without acknowledging dependence; aspirations to an isolated life in this context are straightforwardly meaningless. No word or phrase is simply a possession; it is there to pass on,

26. Williams, *Theology*, 609–11.
27. Williams, *Theology*, 611.

to use in the creation of a shared reality . . . the silence of cliché and cynicism is the dialogical mirror image that comes on the far side of the most creative speech. The silence of cliché is what happens when there seems no point in listening for the new, and no energy for active response to what is said . . . Silence of cliché is a most appropriate and striking phrase as we reflect on those issues which historically have been guarded by a protective silence. In other words what silence of cliché does is to maintain the convention and the status quo. With regard to the biblical text, this is a silencing of the text—when we assume that no new or particularly challenging questions may be asked.[28]

All of which is to underline the core "relational" quality notably in the very act of teaching an infant to speak, in the context of communicating, of relating one to the other.

28. Williams, *Theology*, 612.

10

Grieving Trauma and Resouling

"Grace, the strange gift of becoming a native speaker of the language proper to humankind, the language of being a creature, . . . rightly provokes both bafflement and gratitude."
—Rowan Williams

If I were alone in the world, I would have the right to choose despair, solitude and self-fulfillment. But I am not alone."
—Elie Wiesel

"There is no cure for grief which time does not lessen and soften." —Cicero

W hat does it mean for God to promise a *homecoming* as God does even as God sends a people into exile? After such a devastating indictment, what does the future hold? What happens when the actual *home, temple, land* are all destroyed and taken away? The land which was promised into perpetuity to the ancestors and to descendants, is now practically deserted and desolate, laid waste. So what does it mean to come home gain? Can *home* ever be the same again, given what the prophet and God mandated for the people to do/be in exile, including a particular level of assimilation and immersion, planting trees, getting married, and then being uprooted again. What of the possibility and indeed probability of change, including language and religious heritage, covenant, the distant possibility that the very covenant relationship meant to nourish, will now be undermined? What happens when the fundamentals of identity have been lost or irreparably altered? What does it mean not only to be in exile, but also to exile one's grief? Perhaps the pain of exile is such that one's grief is in exile as well.

There is a conspicuous absence of trauma as an idea in the Bible, even though there are countless examples of biblical characters who are traumatized. We must at least wonder why this is the case. Why is there no reference to the trauma of Sarah at the binding/sacrifice of Isaac, or the trauma of Abraham at such an extraordinary divine request?

> This is the tragic irony of trauma: it not only prevents the trau-
> matized person from being able to do what they want most, it
> makes them the vehicle of the harm and blinds them from seeing
> the harm they do. Who could bear to recognize such a fate?[1]

What we have come to know is that there are existential consequences to the intentional or unintentional burying of one's traumatic experience, believing that somehow mysteriously, it will disappear into the recesses of one's consciousness. Trauma has the distinct possibility of giving the impression that there is little hope beyond the present traumatic reality, and not only are those who are directly involved in whatever scenario, circumstance or suffering, but those who are a circle of friends and family, and indeed generations to follow. Given what the Babylonian exiles were told and what needed to be done for their life and survival, one can safely surmise that generations born in Babylon will wonder. If silence persists, the hiddenness of what occurred will undoubtedly lead to trauma.

> Though we do not hear Abraham's response to God's request, we
> can imagine that the request horrified and shocked Abraham,
> and that his trauma precluded clear-sighted action. His trauma
> then led to Isaac's and Sarah's which then led to Esau, and Jacob's
> and Joseph's, brother turning against brother, the fathers unable
> to see both literally and figuratively. The word trauma does not
> appear in the Bible. But the moment man shows himself capable
> of killing, from Cain and Abel to Abraham and Isaac, to Joseph
> and his brothers, trauma follows trauma . . . [2]

When we think and reflect on 9/11, it is striking that the names and titles that we recall and have ascribed to the event have to do primarily with structure and time, and very little indirect reference to the almost three thousand persons killed. We want and need to remember 9/11, but what is it about 9/11 that we want to remember? The *Twin Towers*, yes; but that of the people? What of the ripple effects of the trauma? What of the suffering and trauma of those left behind and a new generation? Some of us may feel a sense of affront to be told this in all of its naked truth, but in truth these are our consistent vocabulary and terms; these are the images that we most notably hold to, structure and date.

---

1. Levenson, "Cracking Open the Silence," 304.
2. Levenson, "Cracking Open the Silence," 304.

To be sure, we talk about the desolate land, the destruction of the Temple, the houses that are no longer homes, while the people are spoken of in general, the exiles. Yet, what of the people, the tortured, the traumatized individuals all together spoken of as a collective entity? What of the exiles, persons who have believed in the covenant God, and who being somewhat culpable and responsible cannot fathom the depth of the punishment? What of the people with an outward appearance that belies the internal turmoil and trauma? "The CEO and the cleaner, black, yellow, brown and white, the Christian, the Jew, the atheist, the Muslim, the citizen and the migrant, the rich and the poor. Fragments mingled in the ash and the dust. In death, we are all brothers and sisters, and lovers and friends. It is only the living who hate."[3]

"We may consider biblical texts as a sort of controlled substance because they also have the potential to do both harm and good."[4] Frechette's idea of biblical texts as "controlled substance" is useful, but as a metaphor, as with all metaphors and analogues, there are limitations. The narrative as "controlled substance" is not at the control of those being punished. The subject and architect of the narrative is the one who determines both harm and balm. The challenge of the metaphor is that the destructive aspects of the "controlled substance" is not brought about by the recipients, but the people are being "overdosed" by the one who dispenses the "controlled substance."

Certainly, the risk of being traumatized is intensified by prior experiences of pain and punishment. In the case of God and Israel, the experience of the Babylonian exile and preceding experiences will certainly intensify the traumatic quotient, in repeated moments of punishment coupled with language of promise and homecoming. "While isolated traumatic events may occur in almost any context, repeated traumatic events occur only when victims are unable to flee from others who inflict harm."[5]

If indeed we are to face the distinct likelihood of trauma resulting from divine punishment, particularly recurring instances as such, then it must be reckoned that there may be a change/loss of belief in the one who brings about the pain and punishment. Frechette has suggested that "after collective trauma, new social bonds and collective identity can emerge, even though these may differ markedly from what preceded the traumatic events."[6] Certainly there is truth to Frechette's intimations, and likely widespread in its veracity. The truth of this for the exiles however is the distinct possibility

3. Beattie, "Fragments" 675.

4. Frechette, "Controlled Substance," 21.

5. Frechette, "Controlled Substance," 23.

6. Frechette, "Controlled Substance," 27.

that a community has established new and radically different allegiance and loyalty. Indeed, in the case of these Babylonian exiles, such reconstruction is mandated by God and predicated on actions that may be construed as adding a new level of trauma. One may argue that the divine mandate makes a calculated assessment of the exiles' loyalty. In the midst of reconstructing their identity for a generation, where it is nothing less than pouring "salt in the wound" the exiles will nonetheless "return" to YHWH with all of the depth of meaning of the Hebrew concept of "return." The conflicting, confusing and challenging reality is that the opportunity for the exiles' response to the trauma is not shaped by themselves, but by God, the one who has brought them into this existential crisis moment.

It is the case that on occasions those who are suffering may not have the option or freedom to respond otherwise. Their response is dictated by God, the architect of the punishment. "When damage to survivors' belief system has eroded their confidence in their own prescriptions of reality, including their sense of right and wrong, the listeners can serve as a compass for interpreting the traumatic events."[7] So who will be the listeners? Generation after generation, listeners emerge, and the narrative of punishment and pain cannot be left without voice.

Often it is the case that "safety" is neither easy nor possible for the traumatized. This is something of a challenge in Ps 137. How might people find a sense of belonging and safety when they are exiles in a foreign land? Certainly, as the psalmist expressed, this seems to be the reality. Perhaps, honest, heartfelt expression is one very important way to face guilt and trauma. Among the many questions that must be asked, we must assuredly wonder where punishment for "sin" ends and terror of an unknown and even uncharted magnitude begins. It is neither an easy nor a particularly welcomed question, but in the face of trauma, it strikes me that few, if any question is outside the bounds. Moreover, we are not only examining existential issues such as trauma and trust and restoration, but as we reflect on the divine mandate and divine promises uttered through Jeremiah, can one realistically argue, let alone imagine, that the people can return to the way things were? Often, such is the underlying text of homecoming. Indeed, reflecting on the Babylonian exile, it seemed for a while that the relationship with God might have been irreparable.

Even as Jeremiah is outlining the painful, but necessary qualities for life and survival (Jer 29), he is simultaneously expressing his own anger with God about his suffering. In so doing, as Frechette notes, "his rage echoes

---

7. Frechette, "Controlled Substance," 28.

and validate theirs."[8] The fact is, Jeremiah knows the utterly disproportionate level of suffering. His trauma is inseparable from theirs, and perhaps
even moreso, as he is the bearer of the news. It is a complex issue as the
people are exiled for "their own good"; that is, a lesson to be learned; a
point to be made. So, God weeps for the people that God is made to suffer,
bringing unspeakable terror upon them. As Frechette correctly notes, "the
prophet's attribution of suffering to divine punishment neither indicates nor
precludes the presence of trauma."[9] That is to say trauma is not predicated
on whatever justification is attributed to the punishment. The silence of
God in the aftermath of severe trauma and tragedy is evident. However, we
must note the silence of God is in the midst of trauma, and necessarily only
an aftermath, though that may be true as well. Is God not aware that the
nature and extent of the punishment will bring trauma? It is not equating
punishment with trauma, but it is the case that some kinds of punishment
inherently are predisposed to bring about trauma. (See, e.g., Jer 11:18–12;
15:10–21; 17:14–19; 18:18–23; 20:7–13; 14–18.)

> She weeps bitterly in the night,
>
>> with tears on her cheeks;
>
> among all her lovers
>
>> she has no one to comfort her;
>
> all her friends have dealt treacherously with her,
>
>> they have become her enemies.[10]

> I called to my lovers
>
>> but they deceived me;
>
> my priests and elders perished in the city
>
>> while seeking food to revive their strength.[11]

These texts indicate that the people sought out "friends" and "lovers" ('ahav)
in both instances. The reason for this association is that of starvation, and
the people in part are punished for this, and as we see in Lam 2:5 below,
YHWH is now like the enemy. What would/might a person do in the face
of starvation, and the logical prospects of death: the one who promised to
provide, has not. Where does punishment end and abuse begin?

---

8. Frechette, "Controlled Substance," 30.
9. Frechette, "Controlled Substance," 30.
10. Lam 1:2
11. Lam 1:19.

The LORD has become like an enemy;

    he has destroyed Israel.

He has destroyed all its palaces,

    laid in ruins its strongholds,

and multiplied in daughter Judah

    mourning and lamentation.[12]

The young and the old are lying

    on the ground in the streets;

my young women and my young men

    have fallen by the sword;

in the day of your anger you have killed them,

    slaughtering without mercy.[13]

Can these be justified? "[P]erceiving God's simultaneous presence and silence in the midst of profound suffering is tortuous."[14]

There are two ways in which God perhaps shows respect for Daughter Zion by keeping silent. First, it shows that God is a good listener. There is no clear indication in the text that Daughter Zion wants God to respond to her plight in an audible fashion . . . Daughter Zion certainly shows a desire for her own restoration and the annihilation of other nations, but she never actually asks for God to speak.[15]

Yet, God is the one who placed the people in this devastating position and there was no discussion, and it is God, and only God who made that determination. The fact that God remains silent seems to be particularly indicting. Is God seeing and knowing the depth of suffering, waiting for the people to ask? "There are some scenes that are too horrifying for God to be associated with them, and so God's presence, actions and even the divine name itself is totally missing from them."[16] This idea is particularly challenging and troublesome, precisely because one is left to wonder if God would not

12. Lam 2:5.

13. Lam 2:21.

14. Harris, Maldolfo, "The Silent God," 137.

15. Harris, Maldolfo, "The Silent God," 141.

16. Harris, Maldolfo, "The Silent God," 142.

enter into such situations, then when? Moreover, such an argument, taken to a logical conclusion could mean that God would not intervene, and indeed even if God is present, God would remain silent in the face of the Holocaust. Moreover, for Christians, if ultimately God would be involved with the crucifixion of Jesus Christ, what could be more horrifying?

One of the realities post 9/11, is the relentless hold to an ideology that insisted on the quality of exceptionalism, chosenness. "As with ancient Israel, moreover, that ideology of US exceptionalism has brought with it a sense of entitlement and privilege and a distorted sense of reality that continues to prevent us from seeing clearly how it is in the world of economic and political power over which God governs."[17] US exceptionalism expands at certain defining moments where there are actual or perceived threats, and such moments become enveloped further in the fears that is often embedded in the concept of exceptionalism. This has become a principal focus of the Trump Administration, and in its wake various groups have become targets who are perceived to be threats to this exceptionalism.

> One can only conclude that exceptionalism eventually morphs into a self-serving policy of brutality that is justified with religious fervor, for chosenness becomes an excuse for self-assertion that in the end nourishes a violent society . . . The matter of exceptionalism in our society has now morphed into a broad and deep *militarism* that pervades our society. The ideological insistence is evident everywhere among us, not least in the urge to have U.S. flags in our places of worship . . . The notion of U.S. exceptionalism has now morphed into *an oligarchy* in which power and money flow to a very few persons in our society . . . The ideology of exceptionalism continues to have a *racist component.*[18]

When there is an embedded quality of exceptionalism in a nation or community, together with power, wealth and a sense of entitlement as an inheritance based on these ancestral qualities, it is very difficult not to imagine invincibility. That is to say, there is the sense of disbelief leading to denial that the future of such station in life could unravel. And yet, history has shown that it does.

If one wants to know God, love God, be devoted to God, then caring for the other is the most profound way in which to do so. To put it simply, one cannot love God without love of the other. The prophets in ancient Israel and the prophetic task, then and now, have been and continue to be

17. Brueggemann, *Reality, Grief,* 24.
18. Brueggemann, *Reality, Grief,* 27–31.

the manner in which the system, ideology, politics of the status quo, are challenged. A principal theme is the manner in which a people, a nation sets itself apart, though in actual reality, it is not the entire nation but those in positions and places of power who believe in their sense of entitlement, often at the expense of others. It is perhaps a natural impulse to believe that one's ideology predicated on exceptionalism will always be the way it is, and this invariably leads to arrogance and entitlement. On the other hand, the other who is the neighbor, the one without essential resources might equally imagine that without the prospect of change, life and society will remain the way it is, and thus, the divide widens.

The conventional wisdom/interpretation of doing justice and righteousness and showing mercy and compassion to the other is often understood to be born out of one's faith in God. Yet, in both the Hebrew Bible and New Testament we have the clear articulation of the indelible and inseparable relationship, where there cannot be an unraveling.

> [6] Is not this the fast that I choose:
>
> to loose the bonds of injustice,
>
>> to undo the thongs of the yoke,
>
> to let the oppressed go free,
>
>> and to break every yoke?
>
> [7] Is it not to share your bread with the hungry,
>
>> and bring the homeless poor into your house;
>
> when you see the naked, to cover them,
>
>> and not to hide yourself from your own kin?[19]

Thus, in Isa 58:6–7, the prophet is clear that fasting, as a theological expression of one's belief must be inextricably woven into justice and freedom for the oppressed; feeding the hungry, sheltering the homeless, clothing the naked. Such is the connection, one with the other.

> For from the least to the greatest of them,
>
>> everyone is greedy for unjust gain;
>
> and from prophet to priest,
>
>> everyone deals falsely.
>
> [14] They have treated the wound of my people carelessly,
>
>> saying, "Peace, peace,"
>
>> when there is no peace.

19. Isa 58:6–7.

[15] They acted shamefully,

they committed abomination;

yet they were not ashamed,

they did not know how to blush.

Therefore they shall fall among those who fall;

at the time that I punish them,

they shall be overthrown, says the LORD.[20]

This text establishes an inseparable connection between liturgical practice/speech and the practical reality of neighborly relationship. The indictment here is broad and sweeping from the least to the greatest, including the religious establishment. Meanwhile, they are generated by greed; the ones who need their attention and care are neglected, and not infrequently consoled with "peace, peace" or "trust in the Lord," or "Jesus loves you." The particular problem with such statements is the fact that while they may be used to comfort, they are also used in a cynical way where they serve the function of silencing, and as a duplicitous and insidious band aid. It becomes a readily accessible cliché. But to proclaim, *shalom, shalom* when there is *no shalom* it is "peacemongering" and it takes a particularly shameless person to do so.

The fundamental issue is that there is no shame; no sense of how disgraceful their behavior is. How will the people then believe when the pronouncement of "shalom" is in fact truly shalom? The shameful use of virtue-laden words which then have the unrestricted potential to plant seeds of doubt, and thus in the process destroy faith and trust. What this does as well is to demonstrate a quality of self-indulgence and focus only on the present with a wanton disregard for the future. There is always in these prophetic moments a *therefore* for those who exploit and wound, and a *yet* for those who are cast to the side encased in platitudes and language of baseless assurance. As destructive as they are, they are not the last word, nor are they an indication of a barren end.

Not only is the general leadership of the community taken to task for the divisiveness that they have created and sustained; they have ensured that the people are led to believe that they have no hope in this life. In fact, the repetition of empty and false assurances, have ensured that whatever hope the people might have, has been systematically eroded. But there is an even more devastating indictment.

20. Jer 6:13–15.

> My hand will be against the prophets who see false visions and utter lying divination. Because in truth, because they have misled my people, saying, 'Peace', when there is not peace, and because, when the people build a wall, these prophets smear whitewash on it. (Ezek 13:9–10)

> The people build a wall of denial, a façade of policy. But the religious leaders do the whitewash. They provide the slogans and the mantras and link the whole to God in order to provide false assurances that cover the illegitimate policies . . . The theological failures of the religious leadership consists in debilitating the character of God.[21]

One of the realities that the proponent of exceptionalism have is the fact that with this sense, they feel compelled to insist on the propriety and efficacy of their theology. However, this does not remove the reality of grief, and while it lingers on, it is buried and sinks deeper.

> To have hope is not a matter of simply repeating a refrain of positive thinking mantras that have no basis in reality. Thus while such platitudes such as "peace, peace" might strike a hopeful chord, if it is untrue, then it is doubly destructive. False hope is not destructive, but has the distinct possibility of undoing whatever hope, dim or otherwise one might contemplate for the future . . . Hananiah, the prophet of Jerusalem exceptionalism, challenges Jeremiah's reading of reality. He is guided by exceptionalism . . . and anticipates a speedy return home. (See Jer 28)[22]

As perhaps is the case with an addiction, such as alcohol or drugs, the reality is not whether it has the potential to destroy. That it is not acknowledged does not mean that it does not exist; it does. However, it is only in acknowledgement can the tide of destruction be stemmed. Analogously, only when the ideologues of exceptionalism are able to "know" grief can there be the potential for healing.

> My anguish, my anguish! I writhe in pain!
>
> Oh, the walls of my heart! My heart is beating wildly;
>
> I cannot keep silent;
>
> for I hear the sound of the trumpet,
>
> the alarm of war.

21. Brueggemann, *Reality, Grief*, 52.
22. Brueggemann, *Reality, Grief*, 55.

[20] Disaster overtakes disaster,

the whole land is laid waste.

Suddenly my tents are destroyed,

my curtains in a moment.[23]

When prophetic grief comes as is the case in Jer 4:19–20, it is not emotional self-indulgence for pity, or any such, but rather there lies deep within his heart a brokenness that is acknowledged, and an outpouring of grief. In a most sustained, unfiltered and undiluted way, *Lamentations* give voice to a community's deepest gut-wrenching grief. With the loss of all that matters; all that was promised by God; and all that gave shape to their identity, the exiles no longer are able to be consumed with such a sense of loss and grief, and thus in the face of considerable vulnerability, they allow the embedded grief flow into words. In a place between utter despair and longing; memory and hope, the exiles express the depth and extent of their grief. They are willing to make themselves even more vulnerable in taking God to task. In light of the Shoah, both during and after, in the lived vision and imagination of the displayed Jews, their homes, land, the community all now broken, and the shards of disintegration, and a death is now seen as a reminder of what was. Perhaps when there was still a voice, it might be heard, but now there is no voice, but only the screaming voice within, full of pain and a landscape of hopelessness, abandonment and divine betrayal. [24]

There is no comfort—in the literal sense of the word; there is no one to give strength in the people's weakness. Such lamentation now flies in the face of well-established truth, often repeated. It is not to doubt the sincerity of the exiles community when they say:

If I forget you, O Jerusalem,

let my right hand wither!

Let my tongue cling to the roof of my mouth,

If I do not remember you,

If I do not set Jerusalem above my highest joy.[25]

Perhaps, as was so often the case in times of struggle and pain, the reality is justified by convincing oneself that "it is not so bad." Of course, the memory of how life was will always be in the forefront of one's consciousness. "I will always remember." But in the case of the exile and the

---

23. Jer 4:19–20.

24. See Lam 1:1–2; 1:9. Cf. 17, 21.

25. Lam 1:5–6.

Shoah, is that always possible, even desirable? Soon indeed the Jerusalem of old will be forgotten and promises once deemed impenetrable and unassailable will be cast aside in wonderment. Between God and humans, all the promises made have disappeared. Given that the identity of a people in general and individuals in particular is shaped by promises, when these promises are forgotten or broken, then what is it that remain, but the painful memory of words void of substance.

So, one is left to wonder then, after the idea that "all will be well," can no longer be the ideology of certitude, so what can the people be certain about? It is not so much a matter of divine absence, but divine silence and the profound sense of abandonment. How can words "do not fear"; "steadfast love"; ever again have the depth of meaning as they once did when all seemed well. Yet, in the midst of a sense of abandonment, those who are abandoned are still appealing to God with the hope that the heart of God might be changed. The very act of appealing is indicative that they have an awareness of God's presence and the divine capacity for reengagement and restoration. But the "why" and the "now what" questions continue unabated. Like Job, the questions are piercing and relentless. In Lam 5:50 the two striking and indicting verbs are *forsaken* and *forgotten*. Can God truly forget? Yet, the people can only voice their pain with such terminal language. It seems as if the people, now abandoned, are the only ones who can remember and have a memory of a time and relationship that seems distant. The 'why' questions in Lam 5:20 are not a matter of overlooking the actions of the people, but the utter bewilderment of the degree of the punishment that is expressed in abandonment and erasing a long-established memory. In Lam 5:21–22, the language of prayer is not so much an insistence but in the tradition of prayer, the request for restoration is couched in the imperative mood. In the midst of the 'whys," there is something of a constancy that God could and would act.

The point here is to have the courage to grieve, perchance even to acknowledge that the road on which you travel cannot be sustained, and so the hope for a different future, one in which there is more than cosmetic change, one where there is a genuine transformation in ideology. The possibility of a new future, perhaps even with new defining pillars is clearly not easy, but *trust and hope*, and *taking heart*, and *fear not* must all enter into the equation. This would be integral to the journey of a new reality, a realization that an old form that might have worked in the past for some, but marginalized others must be relinquished. Loosening certitude and the security of what once was is however enormously difficult, but in such a moment, there is really no alternative.

As a matter of course, the church, and certainly those that employ the Lectionary texts, frequently omit "psalms of lament" and for that matter texts of lamentation. With the argument or perception that they are too difficult to bear or too depressing is to imply that that in worshipping one is not a part of a worshipping community in order to feel sadness, grief, mourn, abandonment or express anger. The point then at some level is to hide the pain of the text and in so doing camouflage *our* pain. "The new context of loss, vulnerability and abandonment amounted to a vindication of prophetic realism against the ideology of exceptionalism and of prophetic grief against denial."[26]

So clearly not only the exiles in Babylon, but the *exiles* at home, where it is no longer a *home,* are to live among the ruins and in the face of these ruins, have an ongoing sharp memory of what was, and the fear that the present might in fact be the future. One of the realities of having such an extraordinary collapse of an ideology that seems invincible is the belief that the "ruins" of all that was previously indestructible might now be the way things will always be. Perhaps then, an important quality in the prophetic tradition is that the present must never be construed as "the way things will always be," or "it is the way things will be in perpetuity." It is certainly not possible to determine the varying levels of pain and distress felt between the exiles in Babylon and those who remained at home. However, there is an equally discernible sense that those who remained at home have the ongoing vivid and practical sight of the devastation and the stark reminder of what was.

> My soul is bereft of peace;
>> I have forgotten what happiness is;
> so I say, "Gone is my glory,
>> and all that I had hope for from the LORD."
> The thought of my affliction and my homelessness
>> is wormwood and gall!
> My soul continually thinks of it
>> and is bowed down within me.[27]

Amos the prophet derides those who have turned justice and righteousness in wormwood and gall. So now, the exiles at home, in their homelessness and affliction are viewed as wormwood and gall. Such is the perception of the divine injustice. What the people had hoped for has perished. Thus,

26. Brueggemann, *Reality, Grief,* 90.
27. Lam 3:17–20.

the voices now ring true to what it means to be in relationship and when that relationship is dashed. The people are in a state of what seems like perpetual liminality. Beck suggests that "sick souls" are more willing to question God regarding their suffering. Perhaps it is the case that we in the USA would refuse to challenge and deny, in large part because there is the fear of being, "sick souls." Thus, the façade of invulnerability continues to shape our identity. Until such time though, illusion and self-deception will prevent the possibility of a renewed and tested faith.[28]

This I submit is exactly what is found in the exilic laments of Israel, the haunting wonder and courage to go deep into the reality of divine infidelity and disregard. In its lament, Israel dares to go to the null point of despair and linger in the abyss of abandonment.[29]

Again, this is not the last word; it is not ultimate, but in order to hear a genuine "new word" about a "new future" the people then, and the community of faith now, must relinquish their hold on exceptionalism and invincibility. The idea of acknowledging a sense of abandonment by God, is not to suggest as some within our society have in post 9/11, that God has abandoned the USA and this abandonment is due to the actions, and even the existence of certain groups such as the ACLU or feminists viewed collectively as a uniform body. The idea is not to weep and complain with a catalog of certain expectations of deliverance. Rather it is to reach deep within ourselves and have the courage to face our fears and wonder about God's silence.

One of the most potent challenges that the exilic community faced is not to have the courage to call God's fidelity into question, but also simultaneously believe that there is a future of goodness, refined, and perhaps unimaginable in comparison to the present. Thus, how does one reconcile a God who will never forget (Isa 49:15) on the one hand, and yet in the depth of despair, and a sense of divine abandonment, that in fact God disregards (Isa 40:27) and has forsaken and forgotten. (Isa 49:15)

> Alas for those who devise wickedness and evil deeds on their
> beds!
> When the morning dawns, they perform it, because it is in
> their power.
> ² They covet fields, and seize them; houses, and take them
> away;
> they oppress householder and house, people and their
> inheritance.[30]

---

28. Beck, *The Authenticity of Faith.*
29. Brueggemann, *Reality, Grief,* 98.
30. Mic 2:1–2.

With this, the words of the prophet Micah ring true, for the greedy lie on their bed and plot for the accumulation of wealth (Micah 2). Nothing is sacred, for even the conspicuous setting aside of Sabbath and New Moon are being abused. One should not be surprised that the quality of greediness created the corresponding issue of anxiety an anxiety that seeks to ensure that greed by its very increasing desire for more at any cost is indeed met at any cost, and not infrequently at the cost of those who are most needful.

> O Lord, you have searched me and known me.
> ² You know when I sit down and when I rise up;
>   you discern my thoughts from far away.
> ³ You search out my path and my lying down,
>   and are acquainted with all my ways.[31]

> ³ After a long time the king of Egypt died. The Israelites groaned under their slavery, and cried out. Out of the slavery their cry for help rose up to God. ²⁴ God heard their groaning, and God remembered his covenant with Abraham, Isaac, and Jacob. ²⁵ God looked upon the Israelites, and God took notice of them.[32]

So, who might speak for the voiceless and those who are trapped in pain and despair? Not only must the suffering raise their voice and lament, but more importantly the ones who are not suffering must question, and raise their voice, and not wait for their personal suffering to become the precipitating factor for raising one's voice. Importantly as well, raising questions and lamenting ultimately are not all that matters. There must be a voice of hope as well. Sometimes one must cry out, lament without necessarily addressing a particular person or being. The pain and suffering and the sense of abandonment must be voiced. Despair and lament do not always need to be addressed with particularity. Brueggemann has noted that in Ps 139:1–3, and Exod 2:23–25, there are cries to no one in particular, and perhaps not even expecting an answer, but the laments must be given voice regardless.[33]

The challenge, perhaps the temptation, is the leap to hope, an ongoing, unbroken line that leaves no space or time for lament, question or genuine denial of a reality. Before a renewal or for there to be peace and a renewed sense of belonging, there will need to be time for a deep soul searching that calls into question qualities of identity and divine promises that seemingly have gone awry or forgotten. The longing for a time gone by, an idealized nostalgic time, not only likely did not exist except in the

---

31. Ps 139:1–3.

32. Exod 2:23–25.

33. Brueggemann, *Reality, Grief*, 102.

imagined recollection. But rather it is shaped by time, and an unconscious filtering of a history that was far more nuanced and complex than the sharp division between good versus evil; or black and white. Yet, it is the case that people then and now must hear and long to hear the profoundly moving and hopeful words.

> Speak tenderly to Jerusalem
>> and cry to her
> that she has served her term,
>> that her penalty is paid,
> that she has received from the LORD's hand
>> double for all her sins.[34]

Can a person, a people, community/nation experience hope without having a sense of genuine despair? Difficult as it is to say, a sort of despair or a hint of despair does not have the same effect. Sometimes there are those who might claim that they were on the brink of despair[35] and with whatever resource were able to retreat from the brink. Perhaps as celebratory as such moments are, it is equally a recognition that the recovery from the brink again generated a false sense of security and power, beyond the hidden, but know reality. Without the possibility of despair, in a time and honest and public way, a society, a people that is deeply invested in ensuring that their invincibility and ideological positions of exceptionalism, will always need to find a scapegoat for its pain and perhaps decline. The idea that despair is frequently perceived as an expression of weakness further underlines the fear of facing despair and the necessity of changing the ideology.

The neighbor in the biblical tradition has a central place of importance and prominence and for the person of faith, the love of neighbor is a non-negotiable mandate. One cannot have a relationship with God without neighborliness. In this regard the *Parable of the Good Samaritan* is instructive. The focus is never on self. For there to be any salvation and redemption of oneself, care for the neighbor is sacrosanct. We are reminded from this parable that neighborliness is integrated into who we are. We are neighbor to the other, and as such each person will by definition be a neighbor, both as subject and as object.

The first step in wondering what to do or say after the exile, while still in a state of despair, is to recognize the currency of exile and despair. It is often difficult to speak of hope in the midst of devastation, even in a

---

34. Isa 40:2.
35. Brueggemann, *Reality, Grief*, 113.

world where nihilism seems to be the norm. Yet, it is precisely those moments when the voice of hope must be spoken and heard. Hope is not *policy driven*, when as in an election campaign a candidate may outline details of a particular policy proposal. But the prophetic word of hope is not about policy that is prescriptive. It is rather a call to imagine a future that stands in contrast to a reality of hopelessness, despair, divisiveness and nihilism. In some respects, moral or religious certitude leaves little if any room for hope, and perhaps in so doing it leaves little, if any room for vision and imagination. In fact, such a posture ensures that dialogue comes to an end and the way life is, presently, is believed to be the way life will always be. Certitude ironically has the effect of silencing one's voice.

> Father of orphans and protector of widows
>> is God in his holy habitation.
> God gives the desolate a home to live in,
>> he leads out the prisoners to prosperity
>> but the rebellious live in a parched land.[36]

This is a text that reminds us that herein lies hope that in the present might seem to be an impossibility. The psalmist does not suggest tomorrow or the next day or the day after; there are no temporal constraints. But rather there is a promise predicated on the power and mercy of God for all, particularly those trapped in a state of powerlessness and bondage.

It is such a statement as "God gives the desolate a home to live in" that grant hope to those who seek shelter and a place to call home after being displaced. Currently the quasi policy in fact underlines and negates the established policy that legitimizes refugee status. Those who are refugees and seek refuge are either turned away or placed into detention camps, often where parents are separated from children. It is important to express grief, pain, anger in constructive ways. In this instance, to remain silent, to hold such emotion within is to do so at the peril of emotional implosion. Simply to keep within and imagine that in a matter of time it will mysteriously dissipate, is to flirt with long term devastation. Indeed Ps 137 in all its brutality is an important example why one must voice what lies within. The important factor here, as in Psalm 137 is not to suggest or even imply action, but rather to voice the depth of their pain; the brutality of language and the images testify to the fact that while this is on the people's minds and hearts, it is finally God who will act. Moreover, this is the counterpoint to those in our society who are far too eager to act violently as an indication of their righteous

---

36. Ps 68:5–6.

indignation or anger at being hurt. The people must have a memory; the memory of their bondage that has come to shape who they are and how they relate to, and care for each other.

One of the necessary realities of being in exile by choice or by coercive circumstances is the *opportunity* for the recasting of how one thinks about *home* and God. Could either/both remain the same, particularly if God is the architect of the exile? "If Jeremiah were writing to the exiles today, what would he say? What would become of his directives and promises, his prophecies and calls to remembrance? The sadness, nostalgia and sense of elusive, even fading memory would outweigh the anger, I suspect."[37] In being forced to leave their home, with a land in desolation and a Temple in ruins, and a community scattered and broken, the exiles are forced by circumstances to orient themselves in terms of community, landlessness, strangers and perhaps most of all, reshaping their understanding of God and how to relate to God. "God was no longer a prisoner of the Temple, but rather set free, to be active and present among God's people."[38] The irony here is that on the return to Jerusalem, the "first order of business," for the remnant community was the rebuilding of the Temple. So what lessons are learned in the "new ways" of thinking about God? What happened with the "new ways of thinking about shalom? Seeking the welfare of the other to ensure your welfare? One of the significant and important points to note here is that the exile established the legitimate reality of the diaspora. "As the experience of 'homeland' fades into the stuff of imagination and history, ties to that ancestral home often becomes more abstract and tenuous. Besides all this, diaspora raises nagging questions of authenticity and . . . otherness in ways that do not prove as problematic for those 'merely' in exile."[39]

If indeed this is the case particularly after decades away, the exiles might have been so reoriented and traumatized that "home" as a place or even an idea might have become a matter of historical reminiscence or perhaps an opportunity for absolute rejection. Unlike what Bundang calls "a trial separation or détente in any difficult relationship."[40]The exile is not a matter only for reflection or contrition. Yes, there is a promise of return after seventy years, but in reality, this might be more of a "forever" moment. Given Jeremiah's admonitions and the fact that all has been taken away from them, *land, community, temple,* it is difficult to imagine that this is a matter of détente.

37. Bundang, *Home as Memory*, 88.

38. Bundang, *Home as Memory*, 92.

39. Bundang, *Home as Memory*, 54.

40. Bundang, *Home as Memory*, 96.

It is ironic in that those who have been exiled are precisely the ones with whom the future lies. On the one hand, one may argue that in sending the people into exile with loss of land and Temple, the cornerstone of their identity, God was not only punishing in the present, but consequentially pledging the future as well. On the other hand, one may argue that God is so confident in the future and in the role that all may play in the execution of the future, that no one is outside of the realm of shaping the future. In other words, neither exile nor bondage is the last word, even though for a while it might appear to be the end. This is not to minimize the anguish of exile and bondage and their devastating effects, but rather to note in tension the present and future. The present will always be penultimate, even though it might appear to be the last word. The only possible way the latter could be true is if one myopically loses sight of the future.

There is no indication that the exiles could, or for that matter à la Jeremiah, should continue as they were or live lives as if nothing has changed. There is even "seeking Babylon's good" in Jeremiah's letter. It is certainly not an appendix to their lives, but a principal requirement. "The reorientation demanded by being away from home, whether in exile or diaspora, physically and metaphorically, afforded them both a freedom from the forms and ideas to which they were so attached and a freedom to imagine and create anew."[41]

If in fact this is the truth then God either took the people for granted, and therefore potentially sacrificed the future of a covenant relationship, or at least as likely, they will establish a new less constrained identity, and granted this does not necessarily mean a *better* identity, but now they have a choice. One might argue that hope and tragedy have to be held together, particularly in light of the author's use of the storm metaphor. Thus, given the havoc wreaked by the storm even with "hope" in the "center" we also must consider the distinct possibility that the devastation is such that only a stronger, more resilient relationship might emerge, that is, a rebuilding on whatever foundation is still intact—or the alternative must be considered as a viable position as well, namely that this is a radical break and the establishing of an entirely new relationship. "The ongoing, relentless tragedy experienced by the community in Jerusalem suggests that Yahweh has acted capriciously, with the punishment meted out far outweighing the crime . . . In the case of the book of Lamentations, then the answer is not either/or, but both/and."[42] "[God] is certainly not cruel, as are all the gods of the ancient Near East, of the Greco-Roman religions, of the modern world. So,

41. Bundang, *Home as Memory*, 98.
42. Middlemas, "The Violent Storm," 94–96.

all considered I'll return to that God, if only because I don't know to whom else I'd go."[43] LaCocque's premise here is that one must have someone to go to. Without even needing to take this to a logical conclusion, it seems the "return" to YHWH is to return to someone terrifying and prone to devastating punishment as the lesser evil. This, however, need not be the only two choices. As a notable example in terms of domestic violence, is this really a life affirming option? On an everyday practical level, this would be an unconscionable to conclude that returning to an environment of violence is the most viable option. "God's omnipotence as an attribute is not in question; what is in question is its practice. The truth enunciated by Job in 42:2 is a truth has been set dialectically aside, or in parenthesis by God. Consequently, we could say that Job is tempting God. He is tempting him to divest of his divesting and return to his omnipotence."[44]

In reading texts, one cannot disconnect the ancient words from the contemporary world, unless one is interested only in historical reminiscences. One must resist the temptation to explain away or even worst, justify all divine action without questions. "How can unpunished evil be explained? And paradoxically, the more power and righteous, the *Parens Patriae* in whom the people believed, the greater the pain and the intellectual confusion."[45] How does one fathom, let alone embrace the notion of "absolute forgiveness"? Is there even such a possibility in the human realm? How does one defend the idea of "forgiveness at all costs"? In fact, even if this were possible, would it not then perpetuate the actions and perhaps even widen the effects of the person's actions. What would be there to stop the negative or destructive behavior?

43. LaCocque, "Job," 32.

44. LaCocque, "Job," 22.

45. Levine, "Justice," 188.

11

Resouling for Wisdom and Compassion

"The person who talks most of his virtue is often the least virtuous." —Jawaharlal Nehru

"As we keep or break the Sabbath day, we nobly save or manly lose the last best hope by which man rises." —Abraham Lincoln

"Our greatest ability as humans is not to change the world, but to change ourselves." —Gandhi

"The reason that Sabbath is a radical discipline is that it is a regular, disciplined, highly visible withdrawal for the acquisitive society of production and consumption that is shaped only by commodity." —Brueggemann, *A Gospel of Hope*, 59

Now Samuel died; and all Israel assembled and mourned for him. They buried him at his home in Ramah. Then David got up and went down to the wilderness of Paran. 2 There was a man in Maon, whose property was in Carmel. The man was very rich; he had three thousand sheep and a thousand goats. He was shearing his sheep in Carmel. 3 Now the name of the man was Nabal, and the name of his wife Abigail. The woman was clever and beautiful, but the man was surly and mean; he was a Calebite. 4 David heard in the wilderness that Nabal was shearing his sheep. 5 So David sent ten young men; and David said to the young men, "Go up to Carmel, and go to Nabal, and greet him in my name. 6 Thus you shall salute him: 'Peace be to you, and peace be to your house, and peace be to all that you have. 7 I hear that you have shearers; now your shepherds have been with us, and we did them no harm, and they missed nothing, all the time they were in Carmel. 8 Ask your young men, and they will tell you. Therefore let my young men find favor in your sight; for we have come on a feast day. Please give whatever you have at hand to your servants and to your son David.'"

[9] When David's young men came, they said all this to Nabal in the name of David; and then they waited. [10] But Nabal answered David's servants, "Who is David? Who is the son of Jesse? There are many servants today who are breaking away from their masters. [11] Shall I take my bread and my water and the meat that I have butchered for my shearers, and give it to men who come from I do not know where?" [12] So David's young men turned away, and came back and told him all this. [13] David said to his men, "Every man strap on his sword!" And every one of them strapped on his sword; David also strapped on his sword; and about four hundred men went up after David, while two hundred remained with the baggage.

[14] But one of the young men told Abigail, Nabal's wife, "David sent messengers out of the wilderness to salute our master; and he shouted insults at them. [15] Yet the men were very good to us, and we suffered no harm, and we never missed anything when we were in the fields, as long as we were with them; [16] they were a wall to us both by night and by day, all the while we were with them keeping the sheep. [17] Now therefore know this and consider what you should do; for evil has been decided against our master and against all his house; he is so ill-natured that no one can speak to him."

[18] Then Abigail hurried and took two hundred loaves, two skins of wine, five sheep ready dressed, five measures of parched grain, one hundred clusters of raisins, and two hundred cakes of figs. She loaded them on donkeys [19] and said to her young men, "Go on ahead of me; I am coming after you." But she did not tell her husband Nabal. [20] As she rode on the donkey and came down under cover of the mountain, David and his men came down toward her; and she met them. [21] Now David had said, "Surely it was in vain that I protected all that this fellow has in the wilderness, so that nothing was missed of all that belonged to him; but he has returned me evil for good. [22] God do so to David[a] and more also, if by morning I leave so much as one male of all who belong to him."

[23] When Abigail saw David, she hurried and alighted from the donkey, and fell before David on her face, bowing to the ground. [24] She fell at his feet and said, "Upon me alone, my lord, be the guilt; please let your servant speak in your ears, and hear the words of your servant. [25] My lord, do not take seriously this ill-natured fellow, Nabal; for as his name is, so is he; Nabal[b] is his name, and folly is with him; but I, your servant, did not see the young men of my lord, whom you sent.

²⁶ "Now then, my lord, as the LORD lives, and as you your-self live, since the LORD has restrained you from bloodguilt and from taking vengeance with your own hand, now let your enemies and those who seek to do evil to my lord be like Nabal. ²⁷ And now let this present that your servant has brought to my lord be given to the young men who follow my lord. ²⁸ Please forgive the trespass of your servant; for the LORD will certainly make my lord a sure house, because my lord is fight-ing the battles of the LORD; and evil shall not be found in you so long as you live. ²⁹ If anyone should rise up to pursue you and to seek your life, the life of my lord shall be bound in the bundle of the living under the care of the LORD your God; but the lives of your enemies he shall sling out as from the hollow of a sling. ³⁰ When the LORD has done to my lord according to all the good that he has spoken concerning you, and has appointed you prince over Israel, ³¹ my lord shall have no cause of grief, or pangs of conscience, for having shed blood without cause or for having saved himself. And when the LORD has dealt well with my lord, then remember your servant." 32 David said to Abigail, "Blessed be the LORD, the God of Israel, who sent you to meet me today! ³³ Blessed be your good sense, and blessed be you, who have kept me today from bloodguilt and from aveng-ing myself by my own hand! ³⁴ For as surely as the LORD the God of Israel lives, who has restrained me from hurting you, unless you had hurried and come to meet me, truly by morning there would not have been left to Nabal so much as one male." ³⁵ Then David received from her hand what she had brought him; he said to her, "Go up to your house in peace; see, I have heeded your voice, and I have granted your petition."

³⁶ Abigail came to Nabal; he was holding a feast in his house, like the feast of a king. Nabal's heart was merry within him, for he was very drunk; so she told him nothing at all until the morning light. ³⁷ In the morning, when the wine had gone out of Nabal, his wife told him these things, and his heart died within him; he became like a stone. ³⁸ About ten days later the LORD struck Nabal, and he died.

³⁹ When David heard that Nabal was dead, he said, "Blessed be the LORD who has judged the case of Nabal's insult to me, and has kept back his servant from evil; the LORD has returned the evildoing of Nabal upon his own head." Then David sent and wooed Abigail, to make her his wife. ⁴⁰ When David's servants came to Abigail at Carmel, they said to her, "David has sent us to you to take you to him as his wife." ⁴¹ She rose and bowed down, with her face to the ground, and said, "Your servant is a slave to

wash the feet of the servants of my lord." [42] Abigail got up hurriedly and rode away on a donkey; her five maids attended her. She went after the messengers of David and became his wife. [43] David also married Ahinoam of Jezreel; both of them became his wives. [44] Saul had given his daughter Michal, David's wife, to Palti son of Laish, who was from Gallim.[1]

F irst Samuel 25 relates the story of a man whose name was Nabal, a vivid personification of the vile traits of a person who essentially denies God, while his wife who is in sharp contrast as the one who is the epitome of wisdom and does not discount God. As we witness from the 1 Samuel 25 narrative, even for Nabal and the Nabals of this world, one must *take heart*.

> Like the partridge hatching what it did not lay,
>> so are all who amass wealth unjustly;
> in mid-life it will leave them,
>> and at their end they will prove to be *fools*.[2]

> *Fools* say in their hearts, "There is no God."
>> They are corrupt, they do abominable deeds;
>> there is no one who does good.[3]

> A *fool* will no longer be called noble,
>> nor a villain said to be honorable.
> [6] For *fools* speak folly,
>> and their minds plot iniquity:
> to practice ungodliness,
>> to utter error concerning the LORD,
> to leave the craving of the hungry unsatisfied,
>> and to deprive the thirsty of drink.[4]

---

1. 1 Samuel 25.
2. Jer 17:11, my italics.
3. Ps 14:1, my italics.
4. Isa 32:5–6, my italics.

Under three things the earth trembles;

under four it cannot bear up:

²² a slave when he becomes king,

and a *fool* when glutted with food.⁵

The one who begets a *fool* gets trouble;

the parent of a *fool* has no joy.⁶

The Hebrew word used for "fool" in these select texts is *nabal*. What we have in these texts is the wide-ranging instances of crude and self-indulgent behavior that constitute being a *nabal*. From abominable deeds; to being unkind and ungodly; to hoard and be gluttonous; to one who has caused his father to lose joy in his life. Certainly, in this last example, a parent's hope for the future in his son is also lost. The *nabal*, in his self-centered arrogance, refuses to acknowledge a higher authority in his life. While staying a step ahead of Saul, David and this makeshift army provided protection for people in the region, including the shepherds of a wealthy rancher named Nabal. David brought hope and heart to a people. When Nabal is first mentioned in 1 Samuel 25, the initial and principal descriptor that defines him is wealth. The central focus of his identity is the extent of his wealth. The four significant factors that have defined him are: wealth, Calebite ancestry, surly demeanor, meanness in his dealings. In fact, one might say that his entire world was defined by his wealth. It is wealth that mattered most to him; it appears that he valued it above the priceless treasure of an intelligent and beautiful wife. And in spite of the great blessing he has been given he had a disagreeable personality.

In the ancient Near East, the time for sheep-shearing was a season of great celebration and thanksgiving and given that David's men had helped to protect Nabal's sheep and shepherds from harm, he thought that Nabal would see fit to reward them with some much-needed provisions. He sent ten young men to Nabal with a request for a reasonable recompense in the form of provision (vv. 4–9). Instead Nabal answered their polite request with a dismissive and arrogant rejection (vv. 10–11) There is clearly hubris and pride that at least in this case reflects the power and the wealth of Nabal. There is disdain in his question. "Who is this David? Who is this son of Jesse? Many servants are breaking away from their masters these days. His point is that no one would situate himself in a position that appears more powerful

5. Prov 30:21–22, my italics.

6. Prov 17:21, my italics.

that his position, and certainly not one to whom he is beholden. Once again, it is Nabal's obsession and greed that define who he is, as is evident also in his response to David's request. For Nabal, the idea of gratitude is not only foreign, but he sees his *goods* as entirely only for himself.

Two biblical statements about a *nabal* are relevant here: Prov17:7 and Isa. 32:6. It is instructive to compare Nabal's reaction with a response that Moses had received from the Pharaoh of Egypt in Exod 5:2: "Who is the LORD, that I should obey him and let Israel go? I do not know the LORD and I will not let Israel go. "The ten young men returned to David and "reported every word" of Nabal's wicked rejoinder (v. 12). David was generally inclined to leave retribution in God's hands (See, 1 Samuel 24), but on this occasion his anger rose to the surface and appeared ready to follow in the footsteps of Abimelech. With four hundred men, David set out for Nabal's estate, vowing to kill Nabal and all of his servants (vv. 13, 21–22).

As it is, David and his men were not the only ones who were upset over Nabal's behavior. Nabal had rejected David's request on the pretense of concern for his own men, but those men knew that he hadn't acted justly or in their best interests. Nabal's actions epitomized the deceit embedded in his character. His workers are painfully aware that while he purports to "protect" them, he is in fact distinctly uncaring in this regard. His attitude that he cannot afford to give away the food set aside for his workers, to David's men underlines the notion that even with the abundance at his disposal, he nonetheless views his world as a place fenced in, a world of scarcity and hoarding. Greed and gluttony are thus not only private and personal, but these qualities also govern the availability of basic sustenance for the public. Neighborliness, and gratitude become instant casualties, and the sometimes hidden character embedded in the name Nabal becomes public.

Yet with Abigail, there is a life changing moment of *take heart*. One of the servants approached Abigail to ask for her help, evidently very aware of Nabal's temperament. (vv. 14–17). In this instance it was Abigail who instantly took the initiative to stave off what most assuredly would have been an unnecessary act of violence. She knows of the arrogance and barbaric nature of her husband, and yet, in fearless fashion acted. Certainly, over the centuries, there were such individual instances of courage and grace. But it is also in countless instances where both nations and individuals have refused to use their voice or act, and in some remarkable moments intentionally fuel the flame of racism and bigotry. In the case of the Trump administration, it is widely acknowledged after a single term in office, very few Republican leaders are willing to challenge the president, most notably in the face of his confirmed election defeat. Instead, breathtaking falsehoods are allowed to go uncontested and the ongoing concession and disavowing of such words and actions have led to a sense of unchecked boldness. Indeed, a majority of Republicans are willing to justify actions and statements that are either illegal or *prima facie* false. The result is that violence is viewed as acceptable.

Abigail apparently agreed that it would be fruitless to confront Nabal over the matter, and this is particularly striking, given all of the potential consequences that could ensue. Instead, she quickly gathered provisions for David's men and set out to make a direct personal appeal to David himself (vv. 18–19). Her point here is not to publicly shame her husband, though that might have happened simply through her public actions. What we also notice is that her actions are immediate, urgent and reflect the need for sustenance for David's men, not something for which she feels compelled to receive permission from her husband. She walks a necessary fine line between responsibility both for the present and the future. She is able to do as a Stateswoman what her husband is naturally incapable of doing. She accepts responsibility for the situation, showing loyalty to her husband while not condoning his actions. At the same time, she distances herself from Nabal's attitude and urges David to reflect on his role and not sink to the level of her husband. We also notice the hiddenness of God at work, for David is made aware that he must not exert the kind of force and violence that perhaps he naturally feels an impulse to do. What Abigail does, is to establish a platform for the manner in which one might seek to resolve such difficult issues with the *Nabals* of the world. It might not be universally applicable, but the pillars for such action are established. Abigail's immediate and urgent interface with David does not only resolve the issue in an ideal manner, but in so doing staves off what most assuredly would have bloodshed of a massive proportions. What her actions clearly demonstrate is a distinct attentiveness to the present crisis, but also a vision for the future that goes beyond the important resolution with David.

Abigail's thoughtful and eloquent appeal presents quite a contrast to Nabal's stubborn outburst, and his arrogant dismissal of David, Abigail recognized David's place in God's plan by him. Recognizing the truth in Abigail's words, he praised both her and God for steering him away from violence and bloodshed. (vv. 32–35) Here we have the clear evidence of self-awareness, and the capacity for self-critique by David who acknowledges his possible violent role in his response to Nabal. It is to be noted that despite Nabal's crude and despicable behavior, Abigail is still his advocate; she still beseeches David for his life. In a not surprising moment, Abigail pleads for Nabal's life while he is lavishing himself, entirely oblivious to the suffering he has caused to David's men by not affording them the basic means of sustenance. While Abigail pleaded for her husband's life, she returned home to find him "very drunk," so she waited until the next morning to tell him what had happened.

The text does not provide any details about Nabal's reaction when Abigail told him what she had done. We know the reason behind Abigail's decision to speak with David, namely one that seeks mercy and redemption. We have a sense that Nabal's pride might have prevented him from acknowledging the goodness and wisdom of Abigail's action. If Nabal was angry or humiliated, there is no textual evidence. We are simply told, "Then in the morning, when Nabal was sober, his wife told him all these things, and his heart failed him and he became like a stone. About ten days later, the LORD struck Nabal and he died." (vv. 37–38) The language, "his heart failed him, and he became like a stone" suggests the hardening of Nabal's heart, which could not be moved with joy or gratitude; the very core of his being once again failed him and shortly thereafter, God struck him. One might even extrapolate from the days of waiting, perhaps for Nabal's change, which he does not, and so he dies at the behest of God.

It is instructive once again to compare the attitudes of Nabal, Abigail, and David. When Abigail presented her case to David, his heart softened, and he accepted her kindness and act of mercy. With his self-reflection he turned away from his plans. On the other hand, when Abigail told the news to Nabal, his heart hardened in some combination of anger, jealousy, and fear. Abigail bowed down in submission to David (v. 24), and David responded by submitting to God. Nabal, however, submitted to no one. One cannot pretend or argue that David is anywhere near perfect, and he will in fact go on to make grave mistakes in his personal and public life. The difference however is that in the case of Nabal, it is the nature of the man. Nabal, like leaders since brings together qualities that make for devastating consequences. President Donald Trump, for example, sees himself as above reproach and does not believe that there is anything for which he should apologize or seek forgiveness. The challenge for the Trump administration, however, is that there is apparently no "Abigail" who has either the will or courage to do the right and noble thing.

Similar to Nabal, the Trump administration has collective and corporate power, and as such, his actions have wide ranging consequential effects. On the weekend of August 3–4, 2019, mass killings in El Paso, Texas, and Dayton, Ohio, once again shocked the nation. Once again, the killing of twenty-two persons in El Paso by a white supremacist has been classified as domestic terrorism. The President reading a script condemned hatred and white supremacy but took no responsibility for his vitriolic rhetoric and incitement of such groups. Indeed, the blame is cast on others and other societal ills. There is no empathy for those who have experienced such brutal violence.

In July 2019, President Trump unleashed a series of tweets that denigrated Representative Elijah Cummings and the city of Baltimore using language of infestation and referring to the city as "living in hell." Shortly after this berating of Representative Cummings and the maligning of the city of Baltimore, Representative Cummings's home was burglarized, and the President took the moment to sarcastically mocking the incident.

In her deeply affecting exploration of moral life, and the lack thereof in the public and political square of American life, Cheryl Mendelson reflects on what she refers to as the moral earnestness of political leaders from the foundation of the United States into the heart of the twentieth century, where such moral earnestness was viewed as natural. She cites an excerpt from a letter written by John Adams to his wife Abigail, regarding the news that Samuel Quincy Adams's house in Boston that had suffered "abominable damage." "Whenever Vanity and Gaiety, a Love of Pomp and dress, Furniture and, Equipage, Buildings, great Company, expensive Diversions, and elegant Entertainments get the better of Principles and Judgments of Men or Women there is no knowing where they will stop, not into what Evils, natural, moral, or political they willed us."[7]

It is very difficult to imagine any person who subscribes to a Religion or have an ethic of moral wellbeing and beneficence who would not have social action and intervention as an integral quality in their lives. Faith and action go together, particularly in matters of justice and peace. Not surprisingly some of the choices that those who embrace an active social justice ethic will arguably go against the more popular current. Particularly in moments of despair and misery, where the life of the *other* becomes *our* life, faith and belief must take flight into action. The temptation that *time will heal all things*, becomes a misplaced and empty cliché, and a pure betrayal of the foundations of faith.

Prior to the Exodus reference to the Sabbath, I am aware of only one other instance where there is an earlier biblical reference to Sabbath, and it is in the Eighth Century prophet Amos 8. One distinctly identifiable quality in the Sabbath texts, whether or not we attend to it, is the idea that the Sabbath stands in sharp distinction to everyday busyness, chaos of life, commerce of life, toil, national imperial edicts. When the Sabbath is only recognized nominally, that is by name, but merges seamlessly in the busyness of everyday life, the productivity that is the fabric of most of our lives, then it is no longer the Sabbath. In Exod 25–31, for seven days in seven speeches, the phrase "God said to Moses" is spoken seven times. But it is the seventh speech in Exod 31:12–17 that is of particular interest to the discussion here.

---

7. As cited by Mendelson, *The Good Life*, 41.

[12] The LORD said to Moses: [13] You yourself are to speak to the Israelites: "You shall keep my *sabbaths*, for this is a sign between me and you throughout your generations, given in order that you may know that I, the LORD, sanctify you. [14] You shall keep the sabbath, because it is holy for you; everyone who profanes (NIV desecrates; KJV, defileth) it shall be put to death; whoever does any work on it shall be cut off from among the people.

[15] Six days shall work be done, but the seventh day is a sabbath of solemn rest, holy to the LORD; whoever does any work on the sabbath day shall be put to death. [16] Therefore the Israelites shall keep the sabbath, observing the sabbath throughout their generations, as a perpetual covenant. [17] It is a sign forever between me and the people of Israel that in six days the LORD made heaven and earth, and on the seventh day he rested, and was *refreshed*."[8]

While the Sabbath is not typically associated with Exodus 31, there are particular reasons why this text has been challenging, and perhaps overlooked in the conversation about the Sabbath. There are three points in this regard. First, in v. 13, the Hebrew term for Sabbath is in the plural. The text speaks of my *Sabbaths*! Here, unambiguously, it is to God that the Sabbath belongs, and so one is left to wonder what to do with this plurality, and particularly when the term Sabbath through the rest of the text is in the singular. The fact that we struggle even with one Sabbath should give us pause with the plurality of Sabbaths. Perhaps it might very well have to do with the year of the Jubilee which is also a Sabbath, the Sabbath year which has a distinctly economic and social orientation. It certainly has a distinct egalitarian quality to it and expresses where our sense of being made a holy people has its origins. In fact, the people then and us now, are reminded that the Sabbath is holy.

Second, twice in these verses, there is the unequivocal statement that anyone who profanes the Sabbath or works on the Sabbath shall be put to death! Maybe this is expressly one of the reasons why this is not a favored biblical reference used to discuss the Sabbath. But there is a larger issue here. It is inconceivable that anyone who reads this text today will say that this text should be taken *literally*. Yet, there has persisted the tendency on the part of some to proclaim that the Bible must be read and interpreted literally. When verses such as this inevitably surfaces, it is explained away, and justified by being applicable only in its time. To be sure, this verse should be interpreted in light of a variety of factors, not least being the context. However, simply to isolate verses that pose challenges as no

8. Exod 31:12–17, my Italics.

longer relevant or applicable, is a fundamentally flawed manner of reading the biblical text. How might we profane the Sabbath? And if this is complicated, what might it mean to speak of execution of one who works on the Sabbath? We can begin to understand the anger of the Pharisees directed at Jesus as his disciples are plucking grain on the Sabbath. The people are to keep, observe and remember the Sabbath into perpetuity. *Remember*, as a significantly active word in this regard is of principal importance. It is more than simply a matter of recall, but it brings freedom and life. One might reflect on this in the context of Ps 121.

> I lift up my eyes to the hills—
>
>> from where will my help come?
>
> ² My help comes from the LORD,
>
>> who made heaven and earth.
>
> ³ He will not let your foot be moved;
>
>> he who *keeps* you will not slumber.
>
> ⁴ He who *keeps* Israel
>
>> will neither slumber nor sleep.
>
> ⁵ The LORD is your *keeper*;
>
>> the LORD is your shade at your right hand.
>
> ⁶ The sun shall not strike you by day,
>
>> nor the moon by night.
>
> ⁷ The LORD will *keep* you from all evil;
>
>> he will *keep* your life.
>
> ⁸ The LORD will *keep* your going out and your coming in
>
>> from this time on and forevermore.⁹

It is no accident that the central recurring theme in this psalm is that of the unflinching divine commitment to *keep*. *Keep* carries all of the overtones of protecting and saving in all circumstances. Third, we are told that God created the universe in six days and on the seventh day God rested, and *God was refreshed*. It is arguably the last term that most reflects what the holiness of the Sabbath entails. What does it mean for God to be *refreshed*; that God needs to be *refreshed*? The Hebrew term translated here, *refreshed* is *nefesh*, a significant and defining term for understanding what it means to be human with a divine quality. 99% of its use in the Hebrew Bible is as a noun. It is certainly not an uncommon word, though it is a complex word to translate, and

---

9. Psalm 121.

the most common translation being *soul*. As one can immediately conclude this would be difficult to understand in this context. What makes it more complicated is the fact that in this instance the word used is a *verb;* used as a verb this word is found three times in the Hebrew Bible, and this is one instance, and it is in reference to God!

God is *refreshed* in large part because we are not sure how else to translate this word in the context. But while the word is difficult to translate, the closest sense of *nefesh* is *soul* or *inner self.* So, it might be that after six days of creation, God is *re-selfed* as Walter Brueggemann has suggested. So, if God needs to be *re-selfed* and humans are created in the image of God, and are told to keep the Sabbath precisely because of this holiness, then humans need to be *re-selfed* every seventh day! There are certainly texts that are very much within our consciousness when it comes to Sabbath. Two in particular comes to mind, the Ten Commandments and the reference at the end of the first Creation account, in Genesis 2. While it is common knowledge that there are two accounts of the Decalogue, there are some who would refuse to even imagine that this is the case and would be indignant if they were told that these versions were not identical. The reality is that there are two versions, and they are not identical! Having said this however, I will explore these texts by conflating them, emphasizing the parts that are unique to each.

> Thus the heavens and the earth were finished, and all their multitude. ² And on the seventh day God finished the work that he had done, and he rested on the seventh day from all the work that he had done. ³ So God blessed the seventh day and hallowed it, because on it God rested from all the work that he had done in creation.[10]

> ² I am the LORD your God, who brought you out of the land of Egypt, out of the house of slavery; ³ you shall have no other gods before me . . . ⁸ Remember the Sabbath day, and keep it holy. ⁹ Six days you shall labor and do all your work. ¹⁰ But the seventh day is a Sabbath to the LORD your God; you shall not do any work—you, your son or your daughter, your male or female slave, your livestock, or the alien resident in your towns. ¹¹ For in six days the LORD made heaven and earth, the sea, and all that is in them, but rested the seventh day; therefore the LORD blessed the Sabbath day and consecrated it.[11]

---

10. Gen 2:1–3.

11. Exod 20:2–3; 8–11.

⁶ I am the LORD your God, who brought you out of the land of Egypt, out of the house of slavery; ⁷ you shall have no other gods before me . . . ¹² Observe the Sabbath day and keep it holy, as the LORD your God commanded you. ¹³ Six days you shall labor and do all your work. ¹⁴ But the seventh day is a Sabbath to the LORD your God; you shall not do any work—you, or your son or your daughter, or your male or female slave, or your ox or your donkey, or any of your livestock, or the resident alien in your towns, so that your male and female slave may rest as well as you.

¹⁵ Remember that you were a slave in the land of Egypt, and the LORD your God brought you out from there with a mighty hand and an outstretched arm; therefore, the LORD your God commanded you to keep the Sabbath day.[12]

As Genesis 1 outlines very clearly, creation has the rhythm of work and rest. Even before the language of *seventh day* is used in Gen 2:1–3, the idea of rest is indelibly embedded. There is the rhythm of ending and beginning, reflection of good, and finally very good. The only way this works is that God rests and reflects. One could say that after every day God is wearied or since creativity takes imagination, God needs rest to re-imagine anew. Perhaps though, it is a rest to create the very sharp distinction between productivity and a sense of selfcare. What might be notable here as well is that the work that is being done is creative work. This is not a God who is anxious; not a God who rushes creation into being; not a God who is hasty. One of the elements that is often overlooked is the fact the God blessed and hallowed the seventh day. Before this, only the humans and the animals were blessed. In the midst all being pronounced very good, the day set apart for rest is made a holy and blessed! The day is infused with blessing, and therefore that there is something uniquely shared with humans and animals.

The Sabbath in both instances is set immediately and straightfor-wardly within the context of slavery in Egypt. Slavery is bondage and productivity; a time of being tethered to those in power positions. One is never enslaved to rest and idle; it is always for productivity. In the scheme of slavery, Sabbath comes as a gift. And thus, one must ask questions that are germane to us. What is it that enslaves us today? To what are we bound? What might it take to get out of such bondage?

One cites Prometheus and his struggle through the punishment by Zeus, being punished for stealing fire and making it available to humans. This might seem to be a self-evidently noble and virtuous thing, but Zeus did not see it that way and Prometheus was made to suffer day after day where death was not even an option. Prometheus, in eternal punishment,

12. Deut 5:6, 12–15.

is chained to a rock in the Caucasus, Kazbek Mountain, where his liver is eaten daily by an eagle, a symbol of Zeus only to be regenerated by night, due to his immortality. Hercules would finally free him. Something of a permanent Sabbath in the sense that he is not yoked to suffering from which he cannot extricate himself. Maybe it is the case that sometimes we might have to free others from their bondage simply because it is the right and proper thing to do without regard for personal benefits. There is no *quid pro quo*; there is no, "what's in it for me."

While one thinks of the Sabbath as fundamentally ceasing work, and it is that to be sure, it is more. Sabbath has a freeing, social, economic and life component to it. And it is not about doing God a favor; it is a gift into perpetuity! Some treat Sabbath as an interruption in one's routine and rhythm. But is it an interruption or a welcome invitation to freedom?

> Hear this, you that trample on the needy,
>
>> and bring to ruin the poor of the land,
>
> ⁵ saying, "When will the new moon be over
>
>> so that we may sell grain;
>
> and the sabbath,
>
>> so that we may offer wheat for sale?
>
> We will make the ephah small and the shekel great,
>
>> and practice deceit with false balances,
>
> ⁶ buying the poor for silver
>
>> and the needy for a pair of sandals,
>
>> and selling the sweepings of the wheat.[13]

This is a pointed example of treating the Sabbath as an interruption to profit making and not as a gift. This text is an essential part of a platform that demonstrates the inseparable connection between Sabbath and socio-economic reality. The wealthy and the merchants cannot wait for the Sabbath to be over in order that transactions might continue, and of course these transactions proceed to the detriment of the poor as the prophet Amos points out. Roman jurists and writers such as Juvenal and Seneca among others saw the keeping of the Sabbath by Jews not as a sacred act, and an essential time of rest and re-creation, but as a sign of laziness and perhaps recalcitrance. On the other hand, in defense of the Sabbath, Philo, the spokesman of the Greek-speaking Jews of Alexandria, says:

---

13. Amos 8:4–6.

[O]n this day we are commanded to abstain from all work, not because the law indicates slackness . . . Its object rather is to give man relaxation from continuous and unending toil and by refreshing their bodies with a regularly calculated system of remissions to send them out renewed to their old activities. For a breathing spell enables not merely ordinary people but athletes also to collect their strength with a stronger force behind them to undertake promptly and patiently each of the task set before them.[14]

Heschel has a notably different perspective: "Here the Sabbath is represented not in the spirit of the Bible but in the Spirit of Aristotle . . ."[15] In a way, it is not surprising that we have inherited this Aristotelian notion of Sabbath. Sabbath cannot only be rest for the sake of work, but *rest for its own sake*. Heschel notes correctly that in the spirit of Aristotle, the idea of Sabbath is not an end in itself but rather a reprieve from work to allow for relaxation that once again energizes for work. This, according to Heschel, makes Sabbath a *means* and not an *end*, and this is antithetical to the biblical notion of Sabbath. "The Sabbath is a day for the sake of Life."[16]

One of the more common misconceptions and practices is the idea that the Sabbath is simply a respite from work. In this way, the Sabbath is being used for the rest of the week. This is exactly the opposite of the biblical intention. The six days are made for the Sabbath, not the Sabbath for the six days. It is both a requirement but one that only comes alive with love, love of Sabbath. We do not love and keep Sabbath for the sake of six days of working, but love for the sake of ove, because we cannot do otherwise. Thus, it is not intended to be a pause but a climax to the rest of the days. It is certainly true that one does not have infinite energy, and so as in the case of all finite resources, one must decide how one's energy will be used and what the principal focus will be on. So, to be sure one must rest from work, purely as a practical matter, but this cannot be understood to be the *raison d'être* for the Sabbath.

In such a context of enormous fearfulness, our propensity is to enormous destructiveness. Grow more strident, more, more fearful, more anxious, more greedy for our way, more despairing, and consequently more, more brutal. The propensity for destructiveness is all around us.[17]

14. Philo, *De Specialibus Legibus*, II 60.
15. Heschel, *The Sabbath*, 14.
16. Heschel, *The Sabbath*, 14.
17. Brueggemann, *A Gospel of Hope*, 17.

We continue to see in the call of Moses that bondage, slavery and perpetual work will not be the last word. We live in a society where there are groups that are very confidently proud to emphasize that they function, and are available 24/7, a notion that has taken on exponential proportions. Certainly, there are instances where such availability is sought and arguably essential for health and wellbeing. Thus, medical or police or firefighters would all be viewed as essential, but this is not an invitation for terminable toil. This might be what the writer of Ecclesiastes calls, *toil*. Inherent in this work availability is that there is no structured time for rest, for Sabbath, but perpetual toil. Part of the idea of having love and law cohere in giving definition to Sabbath is that there will be moments when in fact matters of gravity will take precedence over rest. But this must be the exception to the rule and not the rule. *Love* of Sabbath cannot give way to the *Law* of Sabbath.

> On the sixth day they gathered twice as much food, two omers apiece. When all the leaders of the congregation came and told Moses, [23] he said to them, "This is what the LORD has commanded: 'Tomorrow is a day of solemn rest, a holy Sabbath to the LORD; bake what you want to bake and boil what you want to boil, and all that is left over put aside to be kept until morning.'" [24] So they put it aside until morning, as Moses commanded them; and it did not become foul, and there were no worms in it. [25] Moses said, "Eat it today, for today is a Sabbath to the LORD; today you will not find it in the field. [26] Six days you shall gather it; but on the seventh day, which is a Sabbath, there will be none." [27] On the seventh day some of the people went out to gather, and they found none. [28] The LORD said to Moses, "How long will you refuse to keep my commandments and instructions? [29] See! The LORD has given you the Sabbath, therefore on the sixth day he gives you food for two days; each of you stay where you are; do not leave your place on the seventh day." [30] So the people rested on the seventh day.[18]

What is particularly noteworthy is the emphasis on the centrality Sabbath. It is the one day where there is no gathering of food! God accommodates the people by double provision to be gathered the previous day. It seems that with regard to food, for basic sustenance, there must be rest, let alone when work is purely for economic gain, and frequently at the expense of the least among us. One of the critical and indeed essential components of the Sabbath is the underlying notion that in "rest"

---

18. Exod 16:22–30.

lies a quality of confidence in the future without the frenetic activity that seems to characterize modern life. Maybe, part of the role of the Sabbath might be encapsulated by Lorraine Hansberry's sage observation, "Never be afraid to sit a while and think." Sabbath is the invitation couched in the language of mandate to pause and sit a while and know that God is neither hasty nor frenetic, nor was creation brought into being hastily. In this regard, the keeping of the Sabbath is an act of trust, to believe in tomorrow and the hope that comes with it.

The Exodus version of the Sabbath is predicated on the fact that God rested on the seventh day, and the mandate to the people then and now is to do likewise. On the other hand, the Deuteronomy emphasis is on the ending of the bondage and slavery and deliverance, and thus on freedom, and the essential importance of community and belonging. If one is to be in covenantal relationship, then exploitation of the other cannot be a part of that relationship. Certainly, exploitation is predicated on commercial gains that create economic hardship, and a challenge to daily sustenance for those who can ill afford such a challenge. The Sabbath in large part seeks to ensure that this will not occur by providing a reminder of what it means to be equal as the Creator intended.

> Shall we die before your eyes, both we and our land? Buy us and our land in exchange for food. We with our land will become slaves to Pharaoh; just give us seed, so that we may live and not die, and that the land may not become desolate." [20] So Joseph bought all the land of Egypt for Pharaoh. All the Egyptians sold their fields, because the famine was severe upon them; and the land became Pharaoh's. [21] As for the people, he made slaves of them from one end of Egypt to the other.[19]

Exodus is justifiably and not surprisingly most closely tied to the exodus out of Egypt; the subsequent Passover; the Decalogue. No one is particularly keen to dispute the centrality of these themes, but what is overlooked in the process, notably slavery, is of serious concern here. Can one have time for Sabbath when one's world is defined by fear and enslavement?

Before Exodus can happen and before the Exodus may be celebrated, slavery, and all of the attending factors that brought it about, must be reckoned with. Thus, for example can one speak of homecoming apart from leaving home by choice or by force? In the case of Exodus and the Egyptian Empire, the powerless and poor are not only "dreaming" of scarcity but actually living it. They were not only weak in the face of imperial policy, but one forced into sacrificing the prospects of a future for the meager realities

19. Gen 47:19–21.

of the present. They feel beholden to the Pharaoh simply for such meager existence. They are forced to redefine what constitutes life and living, and for a while slavery becomes the new normal. Ultimately it is about the wielding of power through the control of food, the very basic and necessary means of daily sustenance. It would have been helpful later while in the wilderness and being told by God only to gather manna for daily use, and not for tomorrow, that the Hebrews recall that Pharaoh hoarded, and that was the *modus operandi* of slavery. Hoarding and monopoly is part of the lexicon of imperial abuse and slavery. This is a critical part of Exodus repeatedly overlooked or redacted. What happens when the quest for freedom from bondage, including economic bondage is such that it reaches a point of unavoidable interface with the underlying realization that it cannot continue. What is necessary for the "common good" to occur is for a shared vision of the community where there is no divide on the binary basis of power and powerless, owner and slave. Later, when the erstwhile enslaved Hebrews are journeying through the wilderness, they will begin to revise the memory of their experience, and that in itself is dangerous. What they are promised and given is so out of the ordinary that it seems to be literally incredible. For a while the wisdom from Moses did not appear to suffice. Their time in the wilderness might be captured by the twin ideas of *wondering* and *wandering*. The Decalogue is not designed to be used in order to beat others, as is so often employed. Rather, it could be argued that the Ten Commandments is about is about "common good." It is about relationships, and a call to make new alignments.

> Again he entered the synagogue, and a man was there who had a withered hand. [2] They watched him to see whether he would cure him on the Sabbath, so that they might accuse him. [3] And he said to the man who had the withered hand, "Come forward." [4] Then he said to them, "Is it lawful to do good or to do harm on the Sabbath, to save life or to kill?" But they were silent. [5] He looked around at them with anger; he was grieved at their hardness of heart and said to the man, "Stretch out your hand." He stretched it out, and his hand was restored.[20]

> [27] Then he said to them, "The Sabbath was made for humankind, and not humankind for the Sabbath; [28] so the Son of Man is Lord even of the Sabbath."[21]

20. Mark 3:1–5.

21. Mark 2:27–28.

In two instances in the Gospel of Mark, Jesus makes clear that the approach to the Sabbath is not about the keeping of the law but about life. In the eyes of the "religious folk" on two recorded instances, Jesus does the unthinkable by acting humanly and humanely on the Sabbath. He chose humanity over legal religiosity. It is not that Jesus did not care about the particular commandment, but rather the Sabbath must reflect and fulfill the Exodus ethic of freedom from human bondage. In this regard then, Jesus makes it clear that the Sabbath cannot be turned into another form of bondage. Sabbath invites us to imagine what God intended, and what human response might be. It means to cease exploitation. Brueggemann has observed that in the context of Sabbath rest, both for God and humanity, the necessity is clear as expressed in Exod 23:12; 31:17, in the niphal of *naphash*.[22]

---

22. Brueggemann, *Mandate*, 149.

12

Peace, Bread, and Resouling

"You cannot shake hands with a clenched fist." —Indira Gandhi

"Without peace, all other dreams vanish and are reduced to ashes." —Jawaharlal Nehru

"I am willing to fight for peace. Nothing will end war unless the people themselves refuse to go to war." —Albert Einstein

"We who lived in concentration camps can remember the men who walked through the huts comforting others, giving away their last piece of bread." —Viktor Frankl

"To eat bread without hope is still slowly to starve to death." —Pearl Buck

There is something ubiquitous about the word *shalom* even if it is the case that we have not formally or intentionally thought about it. I am confident that all of us have some idea of what *peace* means to us, and what we associate with it. Perhaps what this does is to invite us to focus on that which we see as central, as the very cornerstone in our lives.

The language of peace is certainly ubiquitous in our common vernacular. So, what do we associate with peace? How do we see peace expressed in our lives, in our community, in our nation, in our world? Peace in all its varied expressions certainly has the potential for us to *take heart*, particularly in times when it seems that our lives in the many and varied contexts are surrounded by, and littered with pain and tribulation, violence and destruction. One can point to the seditious violence and insurrection of January 6, 2021, on the United States Capitol. Here the damage and destruction are incalculable, and many who have incited such violence have also called for unity and peace in the aftermath. But in some instances, with President Trump and some of his supporters, such a call rings hollow. Shalom occurs more than 250 times in the Tanach, in as many as 213 verses. It is found throughout the Bible in a variety of contexts, and is as common a word today as phrases such as "how are you?" For some, peace is finally the absence of, or the ceasing of violence by the "other." This is the peace that many imagine the principal reference to be, that is, the idea of peace that is really *the absence of* . . . But this is not the biblical concept of shalom. It is in fact a *state of being*. Simply repeating the word, *shalom, shalom, shalom* does not in itself bring about meaning and action. To be, and do shalom, is not an indicative; it is not a subjunctive; it is an imperative!

> The LORD bless you and keep you;
>
> The LORD make his face to shine upon you and be gracious to you;
>
> The LORD look upon you with favor and give you shalom.[1]

Bless, keep, shine, grace, favor, peace! That is the Aaronic benediction, and the climax is shalom! This is the benediction, the good word to the people as they scatter into the community and world. There are also texts that on the surface seems to be without an apparent connection with shalom.

> [6] So David sent word to Joab, "Send me Uriah the Hittite." And Joab sent Uriah to David. [7] When Uriah came to him, David asked how Joab and the people *fared*, and how the war was *going*.[2]

David asked Uriah about the *shalom* of Joab, and the *shalom* of the people, and the *shalom* of the war. This exchange with David sharply reminds us how cynical the language of peace might be used, precisely when there seems to be little or no interest in actual peace. For example, how does one understand the *shalom* of a war? David's question about the *shalom* of the various situations and persons, is acutely cynical and unconscionable given his intentions in this narrative. What we know in this regard is the fact shalom can be, and has been misused over the years, both by biblical characters, including God's anointed, and many in religious establishments. Yet, another use of shalom that illustrates the expanse of use and application is in reference to the wellbeing of one's family.

> And he [Joseph] asked of them (his brothers) concerning their shalom, and he said, "is your father shalom."[3]

---

1. Num 6: 24–26.

2. 2 Sam 11:6–7.

3. Gen 43:27.

The NRSV renders it as: "And he inquired about their welfare, and said 'is your father well?'"

> "He has told you, O mortal, what is good;
>> and what does the LORD require of you
> but to do justice, and to love kindness,
>> and to walk humbly with your God?"[4]

At immediate blush this might not strike us as the natural choice for a text on shalom, yet this must be what brings about shalom in our individual lives and the lives of the community and the world. This is what one might call restorative justice. Is it possible to achieve shalom in whatever form it comes without acting justly and seeking reconciliation with each other? And with whom do we need reconciliation? Is it not with those with whom we have a broken relationship, where there is wounding, and the need for healing?

> For from the least to the greatest of them,
>> everyone is greedy for unjust gain;
> and from prophet to priest,
>> everyone deals falsely.
> They have treated the wound of my people carelessly,
>> saying, "*Peace, peace,*"
> when there is not peace.
> They acted shamefully, they committed abominations;
>> yet they were *not ashamed,*
>> they did *not* know how to *blush.*
> Therefore they shall be among those who fall;
>> at the time that I punish them,
> they shall be overthrown,"
>> says the LORD.[5]

At the very center of this text is the unmistakable pronouncement of the leaders, that there is *shalom, shalom, shalom* when in fact there is *no* shalom. By any other name, this is simply deception. Their leaders have deceived the people. Part of the challenge that we have might very well have to do with our language. Shalom hardly has to do with what is absent such as the absence

---

4. Mic 6:8..

5. Jer 6:13–15, my italics.

of war, but more with what is present. Of course, when there is no war, that is significant, and certainly that is shalom in a particular way, but shalom is much broader in scope. Shalom has more to do with that which gives life, harmony, wellbeing, order to life and the world in which we live.

One might say that the absence of shalom is not necessarily the presence of war specifically, but more likely and accurately, chaos. We might think of the existence of a less than peaceful environment of Genesis 1, before there is an ordering out of the chaos; always there will be more to do, but one then builds on shalom. But as we witness in the United States the political issue of shalom is often tied to economic and justice issues, and the connection is inseparable. In reality, one cannot have peace where there is injustice. They are inseparable, and maybe for a while, things might appear peaceful, because of the use of power and force, but finally, neither the abuse of power nor the use of force can bring about lasting shalom; such artificial, and on the surface, calmness cannot be misconstrued for shalom. There must be a marked distinction between *peacemaking* and *peacekeeping* on the one hand, and the very destructive *peacemongering* on the other. Peace at all costs; peace that is coercive at the expense of justice and goodness, and life and harmony, is no peace.

Often it is the case that shalom is in conflict with those who espouse the force of imperial power. Even though it might appear that the *shalom* of dreamers, the *shalom* of the poets, the *shalom* of the ordinary might be subsumed under the force of power, but finally, the imperial forces of the world cannot stop or halt *shalom*. Nothing that imperial force can do will stop shalom. Warmongers will inevitably view war and violence against the other as *the* solution. Do we have the capacity to face the imperial power, whatever or whoever that empire is? Do we have the capacity personally to face those well-established conventions that might stand in the way of shalom in its various manifestations?

> When he came near and saw the city, he wept over it, saying, "If you, even you, had only recognized on this day the things that make for shalom! But now they are hidden from your eyes."[6]

Jesus thus grieves over Jerusalem because he knew that Jerusalem would be destroyed. Of course, he had the courage to say these words about his own city, and we cannot be blind to that which is closest to us and point the finger to others far away or who we might conveniently disconnect from or refer to as the enemy. Jerusalem as a metaphor for all such cities is alive and well today.

6. Luke 19:41–42.

Ah, you who call evil good and good evil,

who put darkness for light and light for darkness,

who put bitter for sweet and sweet for bitter![7]

This is certainly a distortion of a classic and non-negotiable order. Those who say this, know the truth and have intentionally perpetrated the opposite. This is so egregious that for those who do this, the truth has become a casualty. It has not in fact set them free.

[1] Truly God is good to the upright,

to those who are pure in heart.

[2] But as for me, my feet had almost stumbled;

my steps had nearly slipped.

[3] For I was envious of the arrogant;

I saw the prosperity of the wicked.

[4] For they have no pain;

their bodies are sound and sleek.

[5] They are not in trouble as others are;

they are not plagued like other people.

[6] Therefore pride is their necklace;

violence covers them like a garment.

[7] Their eyes swell out with fatness;

their hearts overflow with follies.

[8] They scoff and speak with malice;

loftily they threaten oppression.

[9] They set their mouths against heaven,

and their tongues range over the earth.

[10] Therefore the people turn and praise them,

and find no fault in them.

[11] And they say, "How can God know?

Is there knowledge in the Most High?"

[12] Such are the wicked;

always at ease, they increase in riches.

[13] All in vain I have kept my heart clean and washed my hands

in innocence.

7. Isa 5:20.

¹⁴ For all day long I have been plagued, and am punished every
  morning.

¹⁵ If I had said, "I will talk on in this way,"

  I would have been untrue to the circle of your children.

¹⁶ But when I thought how to understand this,

  it seemed to me a wearisome task,

¹⁷ until I went into the sanctuary of God;

  then I perceived their end.

¹⁸ Truly you set them in slippery places;

  you make them fall to ruin.

¹⁹ How they are destroyed in a moment,

  swept away utterly by terrors!

²⁰ They are like a dream when one awakes;

  on awaking you despise their phantoms.

²¹ When my soul was embittered,

  when I was pricked in heart,

²² I was stupid and ignorant;

  I was like a brute beast toward you.

²³ Nevertheless I am continually with you;

  you hold my right hand.

²⁴ You guide me with your counsel,

  and afterward you will receive me with honor.

²⁵ Whom have I in heaven but you?

  And there is nothing on earth that I desire other than you.

²⁶ My flesh and my heart may fail,

  but God is the strength of my heart and my portion forever.

²⁷ Indeed, those who are far from you will perish;

  you put an end to those who are false to you.

²⁸ But for me it is good to be near God;

  I have made the Lord God my refuge, to tell of all your
  works.[8]

In some respects, this psalm could be the narrative of many of our
lives. It is divided into two parts. The psalmist sees those in the world

---

8. Psalm 73.

who pay lip service to Torah, without heeding the many stipulations and admonitions. This is reminiscent of the people in Jeremiah's time who kept repeating, "The Temple of the LORD" (3x) while neglecting all the essential meaning that went along with Temple and worship life. Indeed, the Psalmist sees those who are superficial and disingenuous as thriving, as being admired; cast as heroes. People begin to admire them; emulate them; idolize them. In the current climate in the United States, there are those who will frequently cite biblical verses, but their actions equally betray the sanctimony of their words. Nothing about the trials and tribulations of the neighbors seem to bother them. Part of what happens here is that the people begin to believe in the manner in which they are held in the eyes of others. This is what the psalmist saw and thought that he could be like that. This is what he wanted, to be admired, to be emulated to be adored. After all, why should he toil for nothing.

But then there is the "until" in v. 18. Occasionally one such word such as "until"; "yet" "though" etc., may very well be the turning point. "Until" changed everything. The Psalmist does not explain what exactly precipitated this change, but there is a clear change here that the lives of those who bask in the limelight of the people's adoration because of their fame (reality shows have expanded exponentially and have, as a consequence, propelled many in the view of an adoring public) and others who may become a magazine "sexiest man alive" because of physical appearance or some such. But before we explore the Psalmist's change, we do become acutely aware of the fact that there is a community longing for a subject of adoration, and repeatedly, and in more insidious ways it leads to idolatry. The Psalmist has come to recognize that self-indulgence and the principal focus on self cannot be the last word and indeed will not endure. The only quasi specific point that the Psalmist makes is that he went to the sanctuary! There is something particularly significant about this in that the Psalmist in the face of substantial and attractive temptations chose otherwise and went to the sanctuary. Perhaps one might say that in the face of commodization, he chose that which is sacred as sanctuary implies.

Bread and Resouling

To weaponize food as is sometimes done is particularly evil and unconscionable. Yet, some in positions of power in society do; the Pharaoh in ancient times comes to mind as a principal example. It is a major enough issue to use war and the military as a platform for power, but to monopolize and weaponize food, a basic sustenance, should generate moral outrage

and an indictment of infinite proportions. Against one's own people adds
a dimension of unique gravity.

> [20] So Joseph bought all the land of Egypt for Pharaoh. All the
> Egyptians sold their fields, because the famine was severe upon
> them; and the land became Pharaoh's. [21] As for the people, he
> made slaves of them from one end of Egypt to the other. [22] Only
> the land of the priests he did not buy; for the priests had a fixed
> allowance from Pharaoh, and lived on the allowance that Pha-
> raoh gave them; therefore they did not sell their land. [23] Then
> Joseph said to the people, "Now that I have this day bought you
> and your land for Pharaoh, here is seed for you; sow the land.
> [24] And at the harvests you shall give one-fifth to Pharaoh, and
> four-fifths shall be your own, as seed for the field and as food for
> yourselves and your households, and as food for your little ones.[9]

Here then there is a change of power control. One may certainly question
the silence/absence of God for a lengthy period of time, and arguably such
questioning has legitimacy. But God arrives and speaks.

> Then the LORD said, "I have observed the misery of my people
> who are in Egypt; I have heard their cry on account of their
> taskmasters. Indeed, I know their sufferings, [8] and I have come
> down to deliver them from the Egyptians, and to bring them up
> out of that land to a good and broad land, a land flowing with
> milk and honey, to the country of the Canaanites, the Hittites,
> the Amorites, the Perizzites, the Hivites, and the Jebusites. [9] The
> cry of the Israelites has now come to me; I have also seen how
> the Egyptians oppress them.[10]

Yet, we are struck by the fact that while YHWH is the one who immediately brings Pharaoh's unfettered violence under divine scrutiny, it is Moses who must act. Human beings are the instruments to lead out of bondage.
This is an unencumbered relationship, a divine-human partnership; this is
the principal manner in which God functions in community.

The divine intent in this text is not to use any violence or deliver/free
only those who subscribe to a particular ideology or allegiance but intended
for all those who are in bondage. It is in the language of incumbency. "Let
my people go." It is not a request or a hope in the subjunctive. When one is
pharaonic, such an imperative might seem to be preposterous. Thus, not surprisingly, Pharaoh's response is one of belligerence. "I have no idea who this

9. Gen 47:20–24.

10. Exod 3:7–9.

YHWH is." Who is he is to make such a demand! When one is accustomed to brute force, such a demand would appear to be ludicrous. True to his history and his wielding of power, Pharaoh is unimpressed. Following this demand, however, YHWH produces a series of plagues that decimate Pharaoh's land, and thus the clash between divine and imperial powers. Either he does so genuinely or not, Pharaoh is forced to relent. So, Pharaoh said, "I will let you go to sacrifice to the LORD your God in the wilderness, provided you do not go very far away. Pray for me" (Exod 8:28).

But as is so often the case, the entrenched power may agree to compromise or relent in the face of another more powerful source, but then proceed to negotiate anything to its advantage. Here is a variation of the theme: "So who all do you want to be free?" Everyone, for there is not negotiation when it comes to enslavement.

> "You all leave; go worship the LORD, but leave behind all your herd and flocks." "NO!" Our livestock also must go with us; not a hoof shall be left behind, for we must choose some of them for the worship of the LORD our God, and we will not know what to use to worship the LORD until we arrive there."[11]

For the Pharaohs of this world, who come in many and varied manifestations, truth is often a casualty at the cost of sustaining that which is unsustainable, and the vision is short sighted, in believing that the power of the present will linger into the future forever! "What counts rather than economic theory or ideology is the *God who hopes* and the *neighbor who needs*. The mission humanly speaking is to enact a workable transformative, connection. Between God's hope and neighbor need."[12]

Generosity and Scarcity

> [30] The apostles gathered around Jesus, and told him all that they had done and taught. [31] He said to them, "Come away to a deserted place all by yourselves and rest a while." For many were coming and going, and they had no leisure even to eat. [32] And they went away in the boat to a deserted place by themselves. [33] Now many saw them going and recognized them, and they hurried there on foot from all the towns and arrived ahead of them. [34] As he went ashore, he saw a great crowd; and he had compassion for them, because they were like sheep without a shepherd; and he began to teach them many things. [35] When

11. Exod 10:26.

12. Brueggemann, *Truth Telling*, 36.

it grew late, his disciples came to him and said, "This is a deserted place, and the hour is now very late; [36] send them away so that they may go into the surrounding country and villages and buy something for themselves to eat." 37 But he answered them, "You give them something to eat." They said to him, "Are we to go and buy two hundred denarii[i] worth of bread, and give it to them to eat?" [38] And he said to them, "How many loaves have you? Go and see." When they had found out, they said, "Five, and two fish." [39] Then he ordered them to get all the people to sit down in groups on the green grass. [40]

So they sat down in groups of hundreds and of fifties. [41] Taking the five loaves and the two fish, he looked up to heaven, and blessed and broke the loaves, and gave them to his disciples to set before the people; and he divided the two fish among them all. [42] And all ate and were filled; 43 and they took up twelve baskets full of broken pieces and of the fish. [44] Those who had eaten the loaves numbered five thousand men.[13]

8 In those days when there was again a great crowd without anything to eat, he called his disciples and said to them, [2] "I have compassion for the crowd, because they have been with me now for three days and have nothing to eat. [3] If I send them away hungry to their homes, they will faint on the way—and some of them have come from a great distance." [4] His disciples replied, "How can one feed these people with bread here in the desert?" [5] He asked them, "How many loaves do you have?" They said, "Seven." [6] Then he ordered the crowd to sit down on the ground; and he took the seven loaves, and after giving thanks he broke them and gave them to his disciples to distribute; and they distributed them to the crowd. [7] They had also a few small fish; and after blessing them, he ordered that these too should be distributed. [8] They ate and were filled; and they took up the broken pieces left over, seven baskets full. [9] Now there were about four thousand people. And he sent them away. [10] And immediately he got into the boat with his disciples and went to the district of Dalmanutha.[14]

In these texts from Mark, we have a quintessential expression of the juxtaposition between generosity and scarcity. The four verbs, *take, bless, break, give*, all suggest freedom and generosity. Indeed, in the midst of what

13. Mark 6:30–44.
14. Mark 8:1–10.

appears to be scarcity, Jesus makes clear that there is abundance and generosity. The disciples are limited on the basis of what they see and in the present. Jesus makes clear that what is, might be multiplied to what could become; this is the platform for shared generosity when to the world it seems that there is scarcity. The reality here is not to minimize the limited food, but rather to imagine what could be done with shared resources. How does one feed thousands with only a couple loaves and fish? On the surface who can fault the disciples for seeking to dismiss the crowds, for it seems to be some place between the improbable and the impossible. Yet, one phrase changes everything, namely *breaking of bread*. In the *breaking of bread*, we have the defining expression of intimate neighborliness and belonging; we have shared community. We should also note that in Mark 6:31, the initial admonition of Jesus to the disciples is twofold: *solitude* and *rest*. There is clearly a conspicuous place for being by oneself away from the crowds, the masses, and the busyness of life, even if the busyness might be about what is central. In this case, this comes in the midst of the preaching and teaching and healing by Jesus. In this case, the *rest* is likely more about sleep than Sabbath, and as such a reminder that rest is more expansive than only a spiritual matter; it is the physical rest as well.

After the *breaking of the bread* episode in Mark 8:1–10, Jesus questions the disciples, and they are able to answer correctly the fact-based questions. But the questions that Jesus asks are not just about the facts. In sharp distinction to many institutions and persons today, the vision of Jesus and what ultimately mattered to him was not driven or shaped by data. Jesus wants them to understand. As if neighborliness is not enough, the people and those of us who are inheritors of this tradition must do what is necessary to sustain the neighbors. The bondage and enslavement cannot be forgotten for they must become the platform for being free.

> [12] If a member of your community, whether a Hebrew man or a Hebrew woman, is sold to you and works for you six years, in the seventh year you shall set that person free. [13] And when you send a male slave out from you a free person, you shall not send him out empty-handed.
>
> [14] Provide liberally out of your flock, your threshing floor, and your wine press, thus giving to him some of the bounty with which the LORD your God has blessed you. [15] Remember that you were a slave in the land of Egypt, and the LORD your God redeemed you; for this reason I lay this command upon you today.[15]

15. Deut 15:12–15.

Rejoice before the LORD your God—you and your sons and your daughters, your male and female slaves, the Levite residents in your towns, as well as the strangers, the orphans, and the widows who are among you—at the place that the LORD your God will choose as a dwelling for his name. [12] Remember that you were a slave in Egypt, and diligently observe these statutes.[16]

[17] You shall not deprive a resident alien or an orphan of justice; you shall not take a widow's garment in pledge. [18] Remember that you were a slave in Egypt and the LORD your God redeemed you from there; therefore, I command you to do this. [19] When you reap your harvest in your field and forget a sheaf in the field, you shall not go back to get it; it shall be left for the alien, the orphan, and the widow, so that the LORD your God may bless you in all your undertakings. [20] When you beat your olive trees, do not strip what is left; it shall be for the alien, the orphan, and the widow. [21] When you gather the grapes of your vineyard, do not glean what is left; it shall be for the alien, the orphan, and the widow. [22] Remember that you were a slave in the land of Egypt; therefore, I am commanding you to do this.[17]

Challenging Greatness

There cannot be any illusion, for this is a challenging and difficult journey. The temptation to return to Egypt is strong and relentless. For the entirety of Donald Trump's presidency and the campaign leading to his 2016 election, he firmly established the slogan, *Make America Great Again*. What has *never* been made clear is the time, the era that is the template for this *greatness*. Surely in every defined era in American history, there has been challenges and pain, generated by self-inflicted wounds, and actions of such horror, in terms of slavery and racism that are beyond words. So, to *Make America Great Again*, one must begin with this question. Martha Nussbaum has astutely noted:

> Our society (like most) has an ugly history of exclusion based on race, gender, sexual orientation, disability, age, and religion. In our current political moment, demands for equality and dignity by previously excluded groups are met, distressingly often, by hate propaganda or even hate crimes.[18]

16. Deut 16:11–12.

17. Deut 24:17–22.

18. Nussbaum, *The Monarch of Fear*, 98.

One may use Solomon's reign as an explanation of the complexity. Solomon's reign is one of power; one perhaps would not call it a "reign of terror" given that the centrality of the reign was the building of the Temple. Yet, were it not for the building of the Temple, surely his actions would be classified as terror. Yet an apologist for Solomon might say, "but he built the Temple!"

> And as Solomon extended his power in the region, he expected and received tributes and payments from others. ²² Solomon's provision for one day was thirty cors of choice flour, and sixty cors of meal, ²³ ten fat oxen, and twenty pasture-fed cattle, one hundred sheep, besides deer, gazelles, roebucks, and fatted fowl.[19]

However, in the midst of the Temple building, cues are taken from Egypt and Pharaoh's approach to enslavement, and the expansive building of the military, where weapons are imported from other nations, including Egypt, as arsenal is built up. One might even say that Solomon's quest for wisdom is in the service of his power. Empire is always about power. It always seems to be about building empire, never to dismantle empire. If the empire is to be built, it is done so at the expense and life of the powerless and oppressed.

> ²⁸ Solomon's import of horses was from Egypt and Kue, and the king's traders received them from Kue at a price. ²⁹ A chariot could be imported from Egypt for six hundred shekels of silver, and a horse for one hundred fifty; so through the king's traders they were exported to all the kings of the Hittites and the kings of Aram.[20]

In a way Solomon designed his own world and the world came to him for wisdom. There is no indication that the prophet Nathan could have imagined that Solomon would be this kind of king.

> When David's time to die drew near, he charged his son Solomon, saying: ² "I am about to go the way of all the earth. Be strong, be courageous, ³ and keep the charge of the LORD your God, walking in his ways and keeping his statutes, his commandments, his ordinances, and his testimonies, as it is written in the law of Moses, so that you may prosper in all that you do and wherever you turn. ⁴ Then the LORD will establish his word that he spoke concerning me: 'If your heirs take heed to their way, to walk before me in faithfulness with all their heart and

19. 1 Kgs 4:21–23.
20. 1 Kgs 10:28–29.

with all their soul, they shall not fail you as successor on the throne of Israel.'[21]

David's advice and admonition to the future king, Solomon, is singularly focused on Torah and what it means to stay in relationship with YHWH and rooted in the traditions of his ancestors. The words are striking and poignant and sharply focused. *Be strong, be courageous,* and keep the charge of the LORD your God, walking in his ways and keeping his statutes, his commandments, his ordinances, and his testimonies, as it is written in the law of Moses, so that you may prosper in all that you do and wherever you turn. In the heart of David this would be what would define the Kingship of Solomon. Indeed, David is also looking at those who will succeed Solomon, and so indeed he has a vision of the distant future, even as he is on his death-bed. There is no sense of "working" with the enemy, but rather, in all its straightforward simplicity, it is to *keep Torah.* Solomon not only kills the enemy, but for good measure he also kills Adonijah, brother and challenger. It is not that Adonijah is noble or any such, for he is in fact an unscrupulous person, but it is Solomon's ruthless execution that stands out. What is the message that confronts the legacy? It is a legacy of "wisdom," insatiable "wealth," imperial and unscrupulous "power."

> [26] The king said to the priest Abiathar, "Go to Anathoth, to your estate; for you deserve death. But I will not at this time put you to death, because you carried the ark of the Lord GOD before my father David, and because you shared in all the hardships my father endured." [27] So Solomon banished Abiathar from being priest to the LORD, thus fulfilling the word of the LORD that he had spoken concerning the house of Eli in Shiloh.[22]

This is what happens when there is a hint of challenging those in power, and those who are determined to keep and consolidate that power. Even if one is a priest as is the case with Abiathar who does the challenging, one's life may be spared but he is still exiled. Solomon will not be challenged. Even though this banishment is encapsulated in a brief form, it is intended to have wide-ranging and extensive repercussions. So, for example, Abiathar is banished to his hometown of Anathoth (1 Kgs 2:26). We know from the story, Abiathar did not simply disappear; he might have been banished, but he had sons who were priests, and so the cycle of generations continued. Generations after Abiathar, we arrive at Jer 1:1, with a seeming non-descript and *non sequitur* genealogical orientation. This has

21. 1 Kgs 2:1–4.
22. 1 Kgs 2:26–27.

been a long time coming, but after 400 years, generations after Solomon, a descendant of Abiathar returns to Jerusalem and brings the painful message. The descendant of the banished one must now bring a message of exile to the inheritors of the Empire.

> [23] Thus says the LORD: Do not let the wise boast in their wisdom, do not let the mighty boast in their might, do not let the wealthy boast in their wealth; [24] but let those who boast, boast in this, that they understand and know me, that I am the LORD; I act with steadfast love, justice, and righteousness in the earth, for in these things I delight, says the LORD.[23]

About what the people should boast? The Hebrew word that is translated *boast* is *hallel* the common term for *praise*. In a way Jeremiah is saying, "do not sing your own praises about your wisdom"; "do not sing praises of your might"; "do not sing praises of your wealth." Instead, to know God is to sing praises to *steadfast love, justice, righteousness* in all the earth. This is what brings joy says the Lord. It is instructive that human wisdom, might and wealth are all objects. The people have tethered themselves to these "things." But the text ends on the unequivocal note as to who is the subject. "I am YHWH." It is *subject* versus *object*. In the midst of their anxieties, Jesus in essence told them, don't be like Solomon. So, Solomon has human *wisdom, military might,* and *wealth*, but really, Solomon had nothing compared to what I offer. Thus, we cannot lose track of who is central and the architect of our existence. YHWH is the subject of our existence and the object of our praise and lament, joy and grief.

> [4] The LORD your God you shall follow, *him* alone you shall fear, *his* commandments you shall keep, *his* voice you shall obey, *him* you shall serve, and to *him* you shall hold fast.[24]

One might note that this text is distinctly contrary to our far too common preoccupation with ourselves, expressed in the refrain, "me, me, me, me." It is often in the wilderness or exile of our lives that we are reborn, and nothing about a wilderness landscape suggests such a possibility. It casts remarkable doubt on the suggestion which implies otherwise but have never lived through times of wilderness and exile.

> [17] As he was setting out on a journey, a man ran up and knelt before him, and asked him, "Good Teacher, what must I do to inherit eternal life?" [18] Jesus said to him, "Why do you call me good?

23. Jer 9: 23–24.
24. Deut 13:4; my italics.

No one is good but God alone. [19] You know the commandments: 'You shall not murder; You shall not commit adultery;
You shall not steal; You shall not bear false witness; You shall
not defraud; Honor your father and mother.'" [20] He said to him,
"Teacher, I have kept all these since my youth." [21] Jesus, looking
at him, loved him and said, "You lack one thing; go, sell what
you own, and give the money to the poor, and you will have
treasure in heaven; then come, follow me." [22] When he heard
this, he was shocked and went away grieving, for he had many
possessions.[25]

Jesus shows a strong sense of empathy and compassion for the man,
and the text notes that he loved him. This is an aspect of the story that is
either frequently set aside or discarded, but it is indisputable that Jesus
is moved both by the questions, and the response of the man. Moreover,
it does not end as a matter of a rhetorical issue, but rather this love is
indelibly connected to truth and obedience. What is often emphasized is
the man's decision not to follow the mandate of love, that is, to disconnect
from that which binds him. One might say that he clings (*dbq*) to possession instead of "clinging to God." The last word in Deut 13:4 which is often
translated *hold fast* is the Hebrew *dbq*. There are two additional notes to
be made here, both of which reflect qualities as to who we are and how we
function in community.

First, in the midst of following the commandments, Jesus invites the
man to sell what he has and give the money to the poor; evidently this is
a burden too much for the man. According to the NRSV, he was "shocked
and went away grieving." But Jesus loved him. So, here is what is most often lost in this story. Jesus gives him a choice; he needs to choose. It would
have been the better choice to follow the invitation of Jesus, but he chose
not to, yet Jesus loved him.

Second, Jesus neither berates nor for that matter become angry at the
prospects of the man's decision. There is no coercion by Jesus, and herein
lies one of the most striking qualities of the encounters by Jesus where
there is choice without coercion. Perhaps the focus of the man's desires and
his allegiance will change in time, and, if and when he chooses the path
that Jesus invited him to travel, Jesus will meet him. What this reminds us
of is the reality that hope is neither a theoretical construct nor a narrowly
construed personal issue. One does not hope or *take heart* purely without
community or relationships.

25. Mark 10:17–22.

Conclusion

"Have patience with everything that remains unsolved in your heart. Try to love the questions themselves, like locked rooms and like books written in a foreign language." —Rainer Maria Rilke, *Letters to a Young Poet*, 35

"If a nation values anything more than freedom, it will lose its freedom; and the irony of it is that if it is comfort or money that it values more, it will lose that too." —W. Somerset Maugham, *Strictly Personal*

As I write this conclusion the presidency of Donald Trump ended ignominiously, as he incited sedition, insurrection, and violence against the nation within the sacred Capitol halls. This act of such devastating betrayal of the United States Constitution and his oath has led to an unprecedented second impeachment, a dubious distinction of infamy. Even so he has continued to perpetuate falsehoods about a stolen election and stokes a violence among his ardent supporters. Using the category of *cool*, Mendelson argues for the parallel with religious and political fanaticism.

> "Cool people, like cultists, fanatics and extremists, rely on contempt, disrespect, and name calling ... Fundamentalist religions and extremist politics share with the cool mentality the tendency to project a sense of unworthiness and degradation onto some despised other and thus to see all opposition as contemptible and degraded ... Both fanaticism and cool, therefore, lead logically to murderousness, always in spirit, but sometimes in fact as well. Cool's tendency to dehumanize is released and magnified by its amorality. The contemptible other is undeserving of fair play or respect or kindness; no humiliation or punishment inflicted on him is going too far ..." (Mendelson, 175–77)

The days, and months and years have become littered with broken promises, promises that have not be kept, and could not be kept. Promises became built-in casualties to be used and discarded for political purposes. These were the days that no one wanted to appear "weak." The list seems endless. There has been no sense of humility; no sense of vulnerability and little sense of needing to or wanting to listen to those who are ideologically different. In fact, ideological nationalistic bluster seems to be the default response to ensure that there is no indication of perceived weakness, shame or grief. Vulnerability or even the perception of grief would be viewed as a sign of weakness.

Trump administration's ban of seven predominantly Muslim countries, and the separation of families at the southern border and the caging of these refugees, coupled with the recognition of white Supremacy in its multiple manifestations as *fine people* only begins to underline the devastating nature of the Trump administration as he sought to recast the national identity. Suketu Mehta in a searing indictment notes: "So, the expelling of undocumented immigrants, the vast majority of whom are nonwhite; the severe limits on legal immigrants, and the types of migration that the Trump coalition wants to put an end to—the diversity lottery and family unification—have a clear end in mind: to keep whites in power."[1]

The invitation of foreign nations to interfere in the United States presidential election citing the reason being the investigation of the perceived investigation of a leading presidential opponent has led to the first impeachment of the President. Despite evidence that is indisputable, the President and his staunchest supporters, including the body of Republicans in Congress, have continued to insist on the propriety of his actions. One of the effects of the Muslim nations ban is not only the poorly veiled intended religious groups, namely Muslims, but once again, there is the systemic voice against the voice of dissent. Yet, what is being discovered is the fact that the voice of the people will be heard. Much of the voice of dissent is also grounded in hope against despair. Yet, the powerful voices of the system are seeking to silence the dissent either by disparaging or questioning their legitimacy.

The United States is painfully divided along racial, economic, ideological and religious lines. There have been conventional, well established ideological and political differences over time, but the Trump administration has intensified and magnified the despair. That this could and would happen at any point in our neighborhood, when every community is our neighborhood, in this day and age is utterly demoralizing. Such divisiveness is a stunning reflection of the long road of freedom to be seen as all equal members of God's creation. What is immediately apparent is the ongoing moments of massacre and violence that stain the fabric of our

1. Mehta, *This Land Is Our Land*, 139.

society. That which challenges the moral fortitude of many is the fact there are few condemnatory words, and even fewer by those in power who have aligned themselves with President Trump. Even so, the President seems so very reluctant to be forthright and specific in his condemnation of the hate groups. Why is that? Why is it that in these defining moments, when a word of *take heart* might make all the difference in the world, the message is diluted or even absent? Why is it so easy to speak *truth to power* when the context is safe and without the possibility of personal safety being at risk. These are the days when *truth to power* must take on notably concrete expressions and not only be driven by platitudes and clichés.

It seems almost impossible to write a conclusion at this point, as daily, there emerges violence based on race and ethnicity and religion and the President can only be coerced into making perfunctory statements that ring hollow, given his history.

Bibliography

Anderson, Gary A. *Charity: The Place of the Poor in Biblical Tradition*. New Haven: Yale University Press, 2013.

Arendt, Hannah. *On Revolution*. New York: Viking, 1963.

Armstrong, Karen. *Fields of Blood: Religion and the History of Violence*. New York: Knopf, 2014.

Backer, Eve-Marie, Jan Dochhorn, and Else Holt, eds. *Trauma and Traumatization in Individual and Collective Dimensions: Insights from Biblical Studies and Beyond*. SANT 2. Göttingen: Vandenhoeck and Ruprecht, 2014.

Beah, Ishmael. *A Long Way Gone: Memoirs of a Boy Soldier*. New York: Farrar, Straus & Giroux. 2007.

Beattie, Tina. "Fragments: Reflections in a Shattered Screen." *Political Theology* 12 (2011) 672–77.

Beck, Richard. *The Authenticity of Faith: The Varieties and Illusions of Religious Experience*. Abilene, TX: Abilene Christian University Press, 2012.

Benson, Sean. "Materialist Criticism and Cordelia's Quasi-Resurrection in King Lear." *Religion and the Arts* 11 (2007) 436–53.

Bering, Jesse. *The Belief Instinct: The Psychology of Souls, Destiny and the Meaning of Life*. London: Norton, 2011.

Bonhoeffer, Dietrich, "The Church and the Jewish Question." In *No Rusty Swords: Letters, Lectures and Notes 1928–1936*. New York: Harper & Row, 1965.

Bourdaloue, Louis. [1632–1704] Sermons.

Brooks, David. *The Second Mountain: The Quest for a Moral Life*. New York: Random House, 2019.

Brock, Rita Nakashima. *Journeys by Heart: A Christology of Erotic Power*. New York: Crossroad, 1988.

Brueggemann, Walter. *Genesis*. Interpretation. Atlanta: John Knox, 1982.

———. *Mandate to Difference: An Invitation to the Contemporary Church*. Louisville: Westminster John Knox, 2007.

———. "From Biblical Narrative to Economic Policy." *National Catholic Reporter* August 21, 2009, 1, 22–24.

———. *An Unsettling God: The Heart of the Hebrew Bible*. Minneapolis: Fortress, 2009.

———. *Money and Possessions*. Interpretation. Louisville: Westminster John Knox, 2016.

———. *Reality, Grief, Hope: Three Urgent Prophetic Tasks*. Grand Rapids: Eerdmans, 2014.

————. *God, Neighbor, Empire: The Excess of Divine Fidelity and the Command of Common Good*. Waco, TX: Baylor University Press, 2016.

————. "Conversations among Exiles." *Christian Century*, vol.114, #20, pp.1–6.

————. *Interrupting Silence: God's Command to Speak Out*. Louisville: Westminster John Knox, 2018.

————. *A Gospel of Hope*. Louisville: John Knox Westminster, 2018.

Bundang, Rachel A. R. "Home as Memory, Metaphor and Promise in Asian Pacific American Religious Experience." *Semeia* 90/91 (2002) 87–104.

Byron, John. "Cain's Rejected Offering: Interpretive Approaches to a Theological Problem." *Journal for the Study of the Pseudepigrapha* 18 (2008) 3–22.

Chaney, Marvin L. *Peasants, Prophets and Political Economy: The Hebrew Bible and Social Analysis*. Eugene, OR: Cascade Books, 2017.

Chung, Jae Hyun. "A Theological Reflection on Human Suffering: Beyond Causal Malediction and Teleological Imposition toward Correlational Solidarity." *Asia Journal of Theology* 20 (2006) 3–16.

Chung, Youjin. "Conflicting Readings in the Narrative of Cain and Abel: (Gen. 4:1–26)." *Asian Journal of Pentecostal Studies* 14 (2011) 241–52.

Claasens, Julianna M. "Resisting Dehumanization: Ruth, Tamar, and the Quest for Human Dignity." *Catholic Biblical Quarterly* 74 (2012) 659–74.

Coats, John R. *Original Sinners: A New Interpretation of Genesis*. New York: Free Press, 2009.

Cotter, David, W. *Genesis*. Berit Olam. Collegeville, MN: Liturgical, 2004.

Cover, R.M. "Violence and the Word." *Yale Law Journal* 95 (1986) 1601–29.

Craig, Kenneth, M., Jr. "Questions outside Eden (Genesis 4:1–16): Yahweh, Cain and Their Rhetorical Interchange." *Journal for the Study of the Old Testament* 86 (1999) 107–28.

Cuomo, Mario M. "Who Is God." *America*, November 16, 1991, 356–58.

Danner, Mark. "After September 11: Our State of Exception." *New York Review of Books*, October 13, 2011.

Dollimore, Jonathan. *Radical Tragedy: Religion, Ideology and Power in the Drama of Shakespeare and his Contemporaries*. 3rd ed. Durham: Duke University Press, 2004.

Duncan, Julie Ann. *Ecclesiastes*. Abingdon Old Testament Commentaries. Nashville: Abingdon, 2017.

Endo, Shusaku. *Silence*. Translated by William Johnston. New York: Taplinger, 1969.

Ericksen, Adam. "Truth, Lies and the NFL." Sojo.net. September 26, 2017.

Frechette, Christopher G. "The Old Testament as Controlled Substance: How Insights from Trauma Studies Reveal Healing Capacities in Potentially Harmful Texts." *Interpretation* 69 (2015) 20–34.

Gitlin, Todd, and Liel Liebovitz. *The Chosen Peoples: America, Israel and the Ordeals of the Divine Election*. New York: Simon & Schuster, 2010.

Goldberg, Carl. "Healing Madness and Despair through Meeting." *American Journal of Psychotherapy* 54 (2000) 560–73.

————. Concerning Madness and Human Suffering." *Pastoral Psychology* 50 (2001) 13–23.

Goldberg, Michelle. "First They Came for the Migrants." *New York Times*, June 11, 2018. www.nytimes.com/2018/06/11/opinion/trump-border-migrants-separation.html.

Goodman, Lenn Evan. *Love Thy Neighbor as Thyself.* Oxford: Oxford University Press, 2008.

Gossai, Hemchand, ed. *Postcolonial Commentary and the Old Testament.* London: T. & T. Clark. 2019.

———. "The Exile of Cain and the Destiny of Humankind: Punishment and Protection." In *T&T Clark Handbook to Asian American Biblical Hermeneutics.* London: T&T Clark, 2019.

———. "Reading Lamentations after the Shoah." In *Reading Lamentations Intertextually,* edited by Brittany Helton and Heath Thomas, 279–89. Library of Hebrew Bible/Old Testament Studies. London: Bloomsbury. Summer 2021.

Gruber, Mayer, I. "The Tragedy of Cain and Abel: A Case of Depression." *Jewish Quarterly Review* 69 (1978) 89–97.

Gutierrez, Gustavo. In *Seeds of the Spirit: Wisdom of the Twentieth Century.* Ed. Richard H. Bell and Barbara Battin. Louisville: Westminster, John Knox, 1995.

Harris, Beau and Carleen Mandolfo, "The Silent God in Lamentation." *Interpretation* 67 (2013) 133–43.

Heaney, Seamus. *The Cure at Troy: A Version of Sophocles' Philoctetes.* Farrar, Straus & Giroux, 1991.

Honig, Bonnie. "Ruth the Model Emigree: Mourning and the Symbolic Politics of Immigration." In *Ruth and Esther,* edited by Athalya Brenner, 50–74. Feminist Companion to the Bible, ser. 2, 3. London: Bloomsbury T. & T. Clark, 1999.

Humphreys, W. Lee. *The Character of God in the Book of Genesis.* Louisville: Westminster John Knox, 2001.

Jackson, Melissa. "Lot's Daughters and Tamar as Tricksters and the Patriarchal Narratives as Feminist Theology." *JSOT* 98 (2002) 29–46.

Joachinsen, Kristen, "Remembering and Forgetting in Isaiah 43, 44, and 46." In *New Perspectives on Old Testament Prophecy and History: Essays in Honour of Hans M. Barstad,* edited by Rannfrid I. Thelle et al., 42–56. Vetus Testamentum Supplements 168. Leiden: Brill, 2015.

Kaminsky, Joel S. "The Sins of the Father: A Theological Investigation of the Biblical Tension between Corporate and Individualized Retribution." *Judaism* 46 (1997) 319–32.

Kierkegaard, Søren. *Works of Love.* Translated by Howard V. Hong and Edna H. Hong. Kierkegaard's Writings 16. Princeton: Princeton University Press, 1995.

Kim, Angela, Y. "Cain and Abel in the Light of Envy: A Study in the History of the Interpretation of Envy in Genesis 4:1–16." *Journal for the Study of the Pseudepigrapha,* 12 (2001) 65–84.

King, Martin Luther, Jr. "Letter from Birmingham Jail." Africa Studies Center. University of Pennsylvania. http://www.africa.upen.edu/Articles-Gen/Letter-Birmingham.html.

Kraft, Houston. *Deep Kindness: A Revolutionary Guide for the Way We Think and Act in Kindness.* New York: Tiller, 2020.

Lasch, Christopher. *Culture of Narcissism: American Life in an Age of Diminishing Expectations.* New York: Norton, 1979.

LaCocque, André. *Onslaught against Innocence: Cain, Abel and the Yahwist.* Eugene, OR: Cascade Books, 2008.

———. "Justice for the Innocent Job!" *Biblical Interpretation* 19 (2011) 19–32

Leonardo, da Vinci. *Notebooks*. Selected by Irma A. Richter. Edited by Thereza Wells. New ed. Oxford World's Classics. Oxford: Oxford University Press, 2008.

Leonhardt, David. "All the President's Lies." *New York Times*, March, 20, 2017.

Levenson, Jon D. *The Death and Resurrection of the Beloved Son: The Transformation of Child Sacrifice in Judaism and Christianity*. New Haven: Yale University Press, 1993.

Levenson, Leila. "Cracking Open the Silence." *War, Literature and the Arts: An International Journal of the Humanities* 23 (2011) 295–305.

Levinas, Emmanuel. *Otherwise than Being or Beyond Essence*. Trans. A. Lingis. Pittsburgh: Duquesne University Press, 1998.

———. *Totality and Infinity: As Essay on Exteriority*. Translated by Alphonso Lingis. Pittsburgh: Duquesne University Press, 1969.

Levine, Ètan. "Justice in Judaism: The Case of Jonah." *Review of Rabbinic Judaism* 5.2 (2002) 17–19.

Lohr, Joel N. "Righteous Abel, Wicked Cain: Genesis 4:1–16 in the Masoretic Text, the Septuagint and the New Testament." *Catholic Biblical Quarterly* 71(2009) 485–96.

Magdalene, F. Rachel. "Job's Wife as Hero: A Feminist-Forensic Reading of the Book of Job." *Biblical Interpretation* 14 (2006) 209–57.

Marandiuc, Natalia. *The Goodness of Home: Human and Divine Love and the Making of the Self*. Oxford: Oxford University Press, 2018.

Mehta, Suketu. *This Land Is Our Land: An Immigrant's Manifesto*. New York: Farrar, Straus and Giroux, 2019.

Mendelson, Cheryl. *The Good Life: The Moral Individual in an Antimoral World*. London: Bloomsbury, 2012.

Middlemas, Jill. "The Violent Storm in Lamentations." *Journal for the Study of the Old Testament* 29 (2004) 81–97.

Mitchell, Beverly Eileen. *Plantations and Death Camps: Religion, Ideology, and Human Dignity*. Minneapolis: Fortress, 2009.

Moberly, Robert W. L. "The Mark of Cain: Revealed at Last?" *Harvard Theological Review* 106 (2007) 11–28.

Mohsene, Laura, "Letter to Evangelical Christians Who Support Trump: I'm Pretty Sure Jesus Wouldn't Do What You Guys Are Doing." *Medium.com*. October 26, 2018.

Murthy, Vivek. *Together: The Healing Power of Human Connection in a Sometimes Lonely World*. New York: HarperCollins, 2020.

Nauta, Rein. "Cain and Abel: Violence, Shame and Jealousy." *Pastoral Psychology* 58 (2009) 65–71.

Nielsen, Kirsten. *Ruth*. Translated by Edward Broadbridge. Old Testament Library. Louisville: Westminster John Knox, 1997.

Nussbaum, Martha. "Compassion: The Basic Social Emotion." *Social Philosophy and Policy Foundation* 13 (1996) 27–58.

———. *The Monarchy of Fear: A Philosopher Looks at Our Political Crisis*. New York: Simon & Schuster, 2018.

O'Kane, Martin. "Trauma and the Bible: The Artist's Response." *Interpretation* 69 (2015) 49–62.

Okrent, Daniel. *The Guarded Gate*. New York: Scribner, 2019.

Peels, H.G.L. *The Vengeance of God: The Meaning of the Root NQM and the Function of the NQM-Texts in the Context of Divine Revelation in the Old Testament*. Oudtestamentische Studiën 31. Leiden: Brill, 1995.

Petersen, David, L. "Genesis and Family Values." *Journal of Biblical Literature* 124 (2005) 5–23.

Portier-Young, Anathea. "Alleviation of Suffering in the Book of Tobit: Comedy, Community and Happy Endings." *Catholic Biblical Quarterly* 63 (2001) 35–54.

Putnam, Robert. D. *The Upswing: How America Came Together a Century Ago and How We Can Do It Again.* New York: Simon & Schuster, 2020.

Raphael, Melissa. *The Female Face of God in Auschwitz: A Jewish Feminist Theology of the Holocaust.* Religion and Gender. London: Routledge, 2003.

Reis, Pamela Tamarkin. "What Cain Said: A Note on Genesis 4:8." *Journal for the Study of the Old Testament* 27 (2002) 107–13.

Ricoeur, Paul. *Freud and Philosophy: An Essay on Interpretation.* New Haven: Yale University Press, 1970.

———. *Interpretation Theory: Discourse and the Surplus of Meaning.* Fort Worth: Texas Christian University Press, 1976.

———. *Oneself as Another.* Chicago: University of Chicago Press, 1992.

Rieman, Paul A. "Am I My Brother's Keeper?" *Interpretation* 24 (1970) 482–91.

Ro, Johannes Unsok. "The Theological Concept of YHWH's Punitive Justice in the Hebrew Bible: Historical Development in the Context of the Judean Community in the Persian Period." *Vetus Testamentum* 61 (2011) 406–25.

Roxberg, Åsa, David Brunt, Mikael Rask, and António Barbosa da Silva. "Where Can I Find Consolation as Experienced by Job in the 'Hebrew Bible.'" *Journal of Religion and Health* 52 (2013) 113–27.

Sacks, Jonathan. *Not in God's Name: Confronting Religious Violence.* New York: Schocken, 2015.

Sakenfeld, Katherine Doob. *Ruth.* Interpretation. Louisville: Westminster John Knox, 1999.

Sarna, Nahum. *Genesis.* JPS Torah Commentary. New York: Jewish Publication Society, 1989.

Schapera, I. "The Sin of Cain." *Journal of the Royal Anthropological Institute of Great Britain and Ireland* 85 (1955) 33–43.

Schellenberg, Ryan. "Suspense, Simultaneity, and Divine Providence in the Book of Tobit." *Journal of Biblical Literature* 130 (2011) 313–27.

Shulman, George. "The Myth of Cain: Fratricide, City Building and Politics." *Political Theory* 14 (1986) 215–38.

Wallis, Jim. *Christ in Crisis: Why We Need to Reclaim Jesus.* HarperCollins, 2019.

Wilkerson, Isabel. *Caste: The Origins of Our Discontent.* New York: Random House, 2020.

Wiesel, Elie. *Messengers of God: Biblical Portraits and Legends.* New York: Random House, 1986.

Author Index